RELIGION, POLITICS, MEDIA IN THE BROADBAND ERA

The Bible in the Modern World, 2

RELIGION, POLITICS, MEDIA
IN THE BROADBAND ERA

Alice Bach

SHEFFIELD PHOENIX PRESS

2005

First published in hardback in 2004
Reprinted in paperback in 2005

Copyright © 2004, 2005 Sheffield Phoenix Press

Published by Sheffield Phoenix Press
Department of Biblical Studies, University of Sheffield
Sheffield S10 2TN

www.sheffieldphoenix.com

A CIP catalogue record for this book
is available from the British Library

Typeset by Forthcoming Publications
Printed by Lightning Source

ISBN 1-905048-43-2

For Kassie Temple and for Robert Carroll

Words do not change their meaning so drastically in the course of centuries as, in our minds, names do in the course of a year or two.

—Marcel Proust

CONTENTS

Chapter 8

ACKNOWLEDGMENTS

By little and by little Elizabeth McAlister, Susan Crane, and the folks at Jonah House speak their impassioned indignation against the misuses of power and create peace in the middle of this world's chaos. Their example humbles me. For the peacemakers who witness by serving time in our prisons, I extend my gratitude and respect for their courage.

During the extended period of writing this book, Mary Fambrough, Nancy Dyer Babb, Nancy Johnson, Mary Barkley, and Suzanne Ferguson have been supportive friends beyond measure. They are my coaches, my mentors, and my safety net. Ellen Bach, Shirley Hawkinson, Lynn Singer, Judy Buck, Mim Rosenthal, Mary Callaway, Jane Schaberg, and Ti-Grace Atkinson have encouraged me in this project, even when they thought they were just having a meal or sending an email. Archetypal wise-women Mieke Bal and the Guerrilla Girls continually paint the world fresh and alert me to its fizz.

I am thankful for the generosity of the late Alice Powers and her late husband John Powers, for establishing the Archbishop Hallinan Chair of Catholic Studies at Case Western Reserve University. Their belief in the importance of sharing scholarly research with the wider community has provided me with the inspiration and the time to do the work that enlivens me. My colleagues in the Department of Religion, Peter Hass, Tim Beal, Deepak Sarma, and Bill Deal, continuously remind me of what it is to be a professional scholar. My fearless compatriots on the University Advisory Council on Women cannot be distracted from making our community a place of fairness, equity, and scholarly challenge. Serving with them is never like committee work.

Among many colleagues in the Guild I want to acknowledge Ed Greenstein, Doug Knight, Jack Sasson, Yvonne Sherwood, Elizabeth Castelli, Athalya Brenner, Francis Landy, David Gunn, Yairah Amit, Claudia Camp, Stephen Moore, Daniel Boyarin, and Elisabeth Shüssler Fiorenza for their creative insights and intellectual challenges, ever expanding the definition of biblical studies.

Rebecca Mason is a gold-medal research assistant, whose talents are not limited to polishing my prose and keeping me and my animals organized, filed, edited, watered, fed, and healthy. When she moves on to greener pastures, I shall miss her greatly, as will my students. During a long, hot summer, Catherine Newman Howe did careful research on evangelical Christianity and the politics of faith and was very generous with her time and astute with her observations.

My movie guru and consigliore, Peter Minichiello, has been a friend since the Loew's 86th first got air-conditioning. Even when the screen fades to black he keeps the dialogue sharp. Jennifer Glancy is a conversation partner par excellence. For a couple of decades she has accomplished most things before I have, encouraged me to write it plain, and conspired to tell it slant. I look forward to our continuing collaborations. Next year in East Jerusalem.

MacArthur reminds me of the joys of dailiness whenever he voices his opinions in a tone all his own. During the writing of this book, Inanna and Allegro have kept the desk tidy and Butter has deleted much prose. For their loyalty and persistent good will I salute the Fur family: Etienne, Tally, Star, Jake, Ashley, Pouf, Clarence and Petunia, Chloe, Iblis, Salem, Max, Mamu and Kiesta, Hannah, Lucy, Lucky, Marcel, and Albertine (*disparue*).

Finally, I am delighted to be on the first list to be published by the Sheffield Phoenix Press. In this era of cutting back and cutting corners, it is a joy to write under the protective wings of scholars committed to publishing serious work and keeping it in print, even without a movie deal. Duncan Burns is a gifted copy editor, for which I am grateful. Cheryl Exum and I have worked together for many years. It is an honor to have her as my editor.

1

CONNECTING TO THE RELIGION OF THE BROADBAND

A busy portrait of onrushing economic, technological, and ecological forces that demand integration and uniformity that mesmerize peoples everywhere with fast music, fast computers, and fast food—MTV, Macintosh, and McDonald's—pressing nations into one homogeneous global theme park.

—Benjamin R. Barber, *Jihad vs. McWorld* (1995)

A decade ago I probably would not have dared write about plush cucumber puppets named David and Goliath and First Ladies' wardrobes, far more precious than biblical rubies. I could not have had a bibliography studded with references to websites and newspaper citations from the Internet. What is considered scholarly fair game has changed. Broadband has added depth to the legitimate archive. I hope the reader will be willing to decipher broadband language, one whose alphabet is drawn with colors, shapes, and connections that religionists have earlier considered untranslatable. Part of my desire to challenge the concept that profundity comes in indigestible hunks of jargon is to make this book accessible to any reader who is as interested in the interrelatedness of politics, media, and the Bible as I am.

Popular religion is expressed within our culture in rock videos, televangelism, political rhetoric, children's books, films, and animations. Every sort of media from print to electronic to broadband is imbued with subtle and blatant religious imagery. The media is new; the message is not. The tightly woven pattern of religion, politics, and media has been part of the American fabric since the country was founded. When one examines this cultural cloth, varied colored threads are revealed, threads whose twists reflect both media coverage of religion and religious views of the media. The oft-quoted Alexis de Tocqueville, a French aristocrat who understood more about the United States in the early nineteenth century than most present-day Americans would want to admit about themselves, caught immediately the fusion between politics and religion.

> Upon my arrival in the United States it was the religious aspect of the
> country that first struck my eye. As I prolonged my stay, I perceived the
> great political consequences that flowed from these new facts. Among us,
> [the French republic] I had seen the spirit of religion and the spirit of
> freedom almost always move in contrary directions. Here I found them
> united intimately with one another; they reigned together on the same
> soil (de Tocqueville 2004: 282).

As I hope will become evident in this book, border crossing has become a
scholarly necessity. In analyzing popular culture, Martin Bernal waded
into Classics without the proper credentials; Cornel West raps with his
nonscholarly brothers; a biblical scholar can consider America's First
Ladies as modern-day examples of the tireless fantasy wife in whom the
author of Proverbs 31 so delights. In the three years since the horrors of
9/11, I confess to a powerful addiction, similar to the effects of nicotine—
tempting yet poisonous—from inhaling the religious smoke around the
events and interpretations of that day in September 2001.

Fragmented as MTV or a video game, American popular culture takes
bites of politics, swills down that rhetoric with a glass of piety, and digests
the whole. Bite after bite disappears so quickly that a carefully weighed
historical perspective is lost within the CNN syndrome of injecting
melodrama into the minutiae of each day. Starvation in Haiti holds us in
sway for a day or two and then dissolves into a basketball star's run-in
with the law, which dissolves into a Congressional scare about the stabil-
ity of Medicare. Such fragmentation is usually considered an appalling
result of video or techno-driven culture. I would argue that our world of
multi-windowed desktops permits us to shatter the borders that earlier
generations of scholars had erected between the true and the social,
between high art and low, between religion and public policy.

Current media rhythms designed to create interrelationships among
music, words, and visual images form an unbreakable connection between
the sacred and secular, soliciting multiple meanings from us, the audience, that resonate with or alter our experience. Thus, a study of religion,
politics, and media creates polyvalent interconnections in the arenas in
which modern culture is produced.

By this point, the reader is trying to determine where precisely this
book fits in the arcane academic complex of disciplines, centers, programs, and institutes. I shall state upfront that I am driven more by
exploring intellectual interests than by the constraints and models of
scholarly training and certification. I belong to more than one Guild,
dodging and twisting to avoid scholarly boundary markers, unwilling to
allow someone else to determine what counts and what is irrelevant. Like

most scholars, I am aware of how quickly ideas bubble up in the imagination. Graduate school taught me to choose one of those ideas and to cast it in the language and documentation of my discipline, the academic study of the Bible. A monograph or two down the road, the cognoscenti assured me, one is usually awarded a key to the kingdom. Fortunately, by the time broadband and high-speed Internet were widely available the old keys were corroded with rust. The doors were creaking open. Scholars of Bible and religion are now hard wired. Doors are dated.

I am part of the audience that hears undercurrents of piety (or is it politics?) in the President's Bible-laced speeches, watches the latest Jesus films, and applauds the poise and journalistically crafted goodness of the First Ladies. Unlike many of my colleagues, I confess to being a fool for media. Not just public radio and C-Span, alas, but the Food Network, NBA Pay-per-view channels, very local public access channels. Long before I realized that I was edging close to spending a couple of years writing about the mutual effects of religion and the media, I listened frequently to the moral warnings of Mother Angelica, Pat Robertson, Paulie Walnuts. I admit to having watched shimmering gospel singers, daily Mass, gender reassignment surgeries, emergency animal veterinarians, and Mexican soap operas with equal attention. After logging in untold hours of satellite-assisted TV, I can report with conviction that religion lives in the personae of preachers, pitchmen, and pundits.

Religion has gone public, and the much-discussed 'political pendulum' has been swinging widely to try to keep up with the eruptions of faith swelling the broadband. Private faith finds very public outlets through the media's appetite for voices and choices. Faith-based networks have become media savvy, urging their members to send barrages of emails, faxes, telephone calls, letters of praise or outrage to politicians. Those same politicians return the volley, using the broadcast media with great skill, wooing the faithful, convincing the cynical that God is on *our* side. It seems clear that only a deity could be on so many sides simultaneously. Month after month, as I write this book, the chapter on George W. Bush and 9/11 remains open on my desktop. Each day I add to the piles of articles, news accounts, and books around my desk, fearing that I am becoming an eagle building a nest that will eventually fall in of its own weight. As a biblical scholar, I have had to acquire different analytic skills to view the present paradigms of power and oceans of unredacted texts. Our Guild usually analyzes the relationship between ancient rulers and a heavily edited deity, with eons of years between each narrative action and its interpretations.

While the subjects I engage in this book are diverse, they all reflect a strong interactivity between subject and audience. In earlier scholarly discussions of religion and popular culture the two facets were considered as separate entities that could act independently of each other. This either/or strategy presents a static view, religion and media were each held in a different hand and occasionally brought together by the scholar studying them, similar to the intellectual 'contrary directions' de Tocqueville describes in the French antipathy to mixing religion and politics. Those of us who are currently studying popular media are challenging the tradition of studying biblical and other religious texts as privileged or apart from the larger body of cultural productions. Following the thread of my interests and reading, I finally determined the pattern. I am surrounded by a cultural ongoing religious revival, where the American flag has become entwined with the Cross, the Nightly News is reported by journalists in bed with the military, and twelve-step programs are as hip as a new dance craze. Evangelical churches in Ohio, a swing state in 2004, have been receiving demands or invitations (depending on ones political stance) to send to the Bush/Cheney Campaign Director copies of the church directory. One suspects that a tax-exempt organization (e.g. a church congregation) might run into trouble with the IRS for submitting such a document to a political campaign. A number of Catholic bishops have refused to serve the Eucharist to John Kerry (for his pro-choice stance) should he present himself to their altar rails. The White House official religiosity manifests itself in Bible study groups and prayer groups. As David Frum reported in *The Right Man*, Bible study was, if not compulsory, not quite uncompulsory, either.

Teaching Bible and culture in a secular university does not protect me from being peppered by questions from my students about Mel Gibson's theology and the Left Behind series. A stunningly successful mass-market dozen pulp fiction books, the Left Behind books seem to have stretched the biblical apocalypse into a never-ending twilight battle whose cliff-hanging plot points engage my students as the primary text rarely does. Christian rap songs and films like the *Omega Code* and *Dogma* engage my students as they do so many other people. The call of the glossy evangelical production number, be it a VeggieTale, a case against Hillary Clinton, or the Crescent Project has become the new Siren song. It clamors to join God, to be on the right side. Those who are on the Other Side are not mistaken, misguided, or even malevolent. They are evil, and the devil is whispering into the ear of each of them.

I am a scholar who disputes colleagues over the validity of Martin Bernal's scholarly conclusions, while trying not to engage in a disciplinary dogfight, snarling aggressively at anyone who would question multi-disciplinarity. My reasons for including an analysis of *Black Athena* in this book are twofold. I was initially drawn by the explosive nature of the discussion between those who defended Afrocentrism and the academics that longed for the continued recitation of classic humanities by specialists in a microdiscipline. Second, I envied Bernal his courage in writing a two-volume work that was bound to provoke and enrage the keepers of the Athenian flame. His erudite arguments span the time periods between the fourth millennium BCE and the present day. In reading Bernal's theories, I was convinced that pulling threads, classical or biblical, needed to be reflected in our contemporary world of scholars pulling each other's political chains. Tightly bound scholarship is never patterned without the colors of politics woven into the design.

Bernal was not the first academic who ventured into the 'civilian' or non-academic sphere and defended his work on television and on the college lecture circuit, but his appearances with his scholarly foes transformed a very intradisciplinary squabble into a well-publicized long-term business with articles, documentaries, and books as spinoffs from Bernal's original work. More than 70,000 copies of *Black Athena* were sold, although I am not willing to guess at how many copies were actually read. The bibliography alone is more than one hundred pages. There are more than 3000 footnotes. A combination of polemic and scholarly panache, Bernal's free-wheeling intellectual spirit infuriated a critical mass of vocal scholars. Thus tempted more by the *ad hominem* conflagration than by the scholarly flame, non-specialist readers and journalists were drawn to the book, or its author, in print or on TV, making *Black Athena* a truly successful media event.

Scholars entwined in the biblical hall of ivy share contempt for their colleagues, like Bernal, who receive attention from the popular press. Here the politics of academia are as full of animus as those fought about the City on the Hill. I remember one revered senior scholar whose hands trembled when Robert Funk or his Jesus Seminar were mentioned. Color coding the words of Jesus according to a *consensus* of scholars? Who would get credit for such a project? Who would take the intellectual fall for misreading Jesus? Red for the words that Jesus spoke (and your proof is?), and then pink, gray, and black for the likelihood of Jesus having said or having never said such words. Scholarship by committee! Even those of us who may not have considered the Jesus Seminar as striking a blow for or against the verifiable words of Jesus, it is clear to any careful reader that the Technicolor version of authenticating biblical texts gives the reader the false surety that one can determine a true text. What did Jesus say? What did Jesus do? No matter what shading or color one assigns to his words or deeds, the answers to such questions are interpretations. Funk claims fact. For all his colorful claims, he reads in black and white.

Of course Professor Funk knew exactly where he was leading his troops. In his opening address to the first Jesus Seminar, Funk set out to inspire his colleagues and appall his critics:

> We are about to embark on a momentous enterprise. We are going to inquire simply, In this process, we will be asking a question that borders the sacred, that even abuts rigorously after the voice of Jesus, after what he really said. In this process, we will be asking a question that even abuts blasphemy, for many in our society. As a consequence, the course we shall follow may prove hazardous. We may well provoke hostility. But we will set out, in spite of the dangers, because we are professionals and because the issue of Jesus is there to be faced, much as Mt. Everest confronts the team of climbers (March 1985).

The initial thirty scholars who formed the Jesus Seminar have grown into a group of more than two hundred 'professionally trained specialists' who can now debate, cast votes, and preach on the broadband.[1] One of the early Co-chairs with Funk of the Jesus Seminar, a rabble-rouser in the greatest scholarly tradition, is John Dominic Crossan. A longtime New Testament scholar at DePaul University, Crossan has written more than twenty books on the historical Jesus in the last thirty years, four of which have become national religious bestsellers.

Although it is tempting, one cannot give a quantitative measure of the degree to which Crossan's Irish background and Catholic training influenced his understanding of Jesus as a peasant resister to imperialism. Crossan's own words offer a qualitative sense of his candid perspective of traditional Christian theology; for him, it is 'a lethal deceit that sours its soul, hardens its heart, and savages its spirit'.[2]

With the reception of *The Historical Jesus: The Life of a Mediterranean Jewish Peasant* Professor Crossan became a commodity. Perhaps it was his undisputed command of sources, or his crackling unromanticized views of life in first-century Palestine, but scholars as well as non-specialists have acknowledged his unusual ability to charge through theological territory in plain-spoken sentences. Struggling with his bestseller status, the liberationist leprechaun has charmed more and more scholars in the Guild. Never meek or diffident, Crossan's scholarship is provocative and

---

1.   <http://www.westarinstitute.org/Jesus_Seminar/jesus_seminar.html>.
2.   <http://www.westarinstitute.org/Periodicals/4R_Articles/Crossan_bio/crossan_bio.html>.

his ability to laugh at his central position both in and out of the academy is endearing. 'Between myself and the publisher, HarperSanFrancisco, *The Historical Jesus* is known as "Big Jesus"'. Crossan has spoken of his success. 'This is to distinguish it from a reorganized, popularized, and updated version publicly, *Jesus: A Revolutionary Biography*, but privately, "Baby Jesus"' (oral communication).

Not all breakthrough scholars attack the tradition with the same sharp rhetoric. If Funk and his cohort threaten the scholarly sky with thunder and lightning, and Crossan speaks with the force of a great north wind, then Elaine Pagels would be the scholar whose voice is summer rain. A Princeton professor, Elaine Pagels is a recipient of the MacArthur Prize and has received the National Book Critics Circle Award and The National Book Award for *The Gnostic Gospels*. These awards gave Pagels the worldly credentials that were complemented by the scholarly credentials of awards from the Rockefeller Foundation, the Guggenheim Foundation, and the Institute for Advanced Studies at Princeton. Heavy credentials for a biblical scholar who has been accused by some Old School scholars of being a New Ager. At the time of terrible tragedies in her life no one spoke openly about them. More than a decade later, in her book on the *Gospel of Thomas*, she moves easily between the genres of spiritual autobiography and an erudite analysis of the *Gospel of Thomas*. Pagels talks openly about the death of her young son from pulmonary hypertension and the mountaineering accident that killed her first husband Heinz Pagels, a writer who could make the propositions of Quantum Mechanics clear even to the photon-phobic among us. While these events drove her away from creedal practices, her Christian spirituality has deepened. Her practice has a Gnostic pastiche, like her scholarship. Unlike the rather dogmatic Funk, Pagels promotes intellectual and spiritual diversity, understanding the Gospels to show how 'the impulse to seek God overflows the narrow banks of a single tradition'. She writes in *Beyond Belief*, 'What I have come to love in the wealth and diversity of our religious traditions—and the communities that sustain them—is that they offer the testimony of innumerable people to spiritual discovery, encouraging us, in Jesus' words, to "seek, and you shall find"' (2003: 54).

Conventional wisdom, or the politics of tenure decisions, as passed down to me by the aforementioned mentoring cognoscenti, was that no one in academia wants to be thought of as mass market. Well, maybe there is a savvier spin in the broadband era. The term public intellectual is a stroke, an appellation to be sought, while the term mass market is *déclassé*. One no longer discounts reviews in popular media; instead one counts the words and column inches and hopes for a clearly printed headshot. According to his website, Cornel West 'is a mainstay in the American media. So much so that he has virtually become a household word' (<www.Cornelwest.com>). The Princeton professor has a rap/hip-hop/spoken-word album and a Screen Actors Guild card to his credit. As the spin goes, West spent many hours deep in 'philosophical' discussions about reality and society with Larry and Andy Wachowski, the creators behind the *Matrix* movies. After tutoring the brothers, Professor West told the *Los Angeles Times* (20 May 2003) that the second movie, *Matrix Reloaded*, would present 'a devastating critique of all salvation stories'. One can imagine Cornel West leering with delight as he trotted these filmmakers through the philosopher's maze. The *Matrix* trilogy is pop prognostication, the kind of film teen viewers call 'deep'.

In a cameo appearance as a philosopher in the *Matrix* sequels, Professor West plays himself. As a rapper, he plays a version of himself, not unlike the version found in the classroom and in public lectures, where his quicksilver delivery ranges from the intonations of a Baptist preacher to the pronouncements of a pragmatist philosopher. There is very little media that Cornel West has not nourished or that has not nourished him. The liner notes to his rap album, *Sketches of My Culture* (Artemis Records, 2002), promise 'an invitation to take an educational journey through the traditional African-American medium—music. A nourishing, inspirational story that must be told to every generation for fear of being forgotten and replaced with a "safe" place of comfortable illusions. One that transcends legitimate bitterness and rage to arrive at an elevated place where the view is clearer and possibilities more attainable.' One individual who emphatically did not agree with West's self-evaluation was Lawrence Summers, President of Harvard University, the institution at which West was at that time a highly regarded professor. Summers was not happy about one of his University professors spending valuable research time participating in and producing a rap album. While some media reports claim that Summers is a scholarly hardliner who wants his University professors to produce work worthy of the Harvard brand, just as many claim that the President did not appreciate Professor West's unique contributions to postmodern theological scholarship, and racial discourse, as well as his forgettable and forgivable foray into rap.

My riff on Cornel West is meant to illustrate the complex connection between the scholarly approach to religion and popular culture. Cornel West has a media persona that Crossan and Pagels do not approach. Perhaps it is West's willingness to rap in public, to return the gaze? *Time* and *Newsweek* ran profiles of West that are of a length and style usually reserved for entertainment celebrities and big-name politicians. Articles centered on West have appeared in the *Boston Globe*, the *Los Angeles Times* and *USA Today*. Professor West has been variously described as our premier social critic, a fashion icon, a political pundit, a savant, and a social radical. A *Newsweek* critic sees not a radical but a dandy: an 'elegant prophet with attitude and a taste for fancy cars and flashy cuff links'. I suspect that Professor West make such great copy because he is at once all these things.

If any single occurrence has sealed the bridge from religion to popular culture it is Mel Gibson and his gang of soggy cinematographers. While writing this Introduction I have been distracted by the many biblical scholars dining out on Mel Gibson's film *The Passion of the Christ*, both in front of the camera and in print. Is there no one with a doctorate in religion without an opinion about the consequences of this film and the intentions of the filmmaker? Most biblical scholars who practice literary or cultural criticism when they are reading ancient work, piously acknowledge that texts have no intentionality and conviction; only readers or spectators bring polyvalent interpretations to texts. Alas, put these careful folk in front of Gibson's action flick and they act as though they have just finished breakfast with Mel Gibson. Ironically, the critics have cast Gibson in his own Jesus story: some accuse him as criminal but others proclaim him divine. They can report Mel's intentions, his spirituality, and his political positions with the same dexterity that an earlier generation of literary critics determined that the writer Flaubert *was* Emma Bovary. Academics cannot stop pontificating about this sacred snuff film.

While we all know that the word became flesh in the Gospel of John, what strikes me as oddest about the Gibson interpretation is that the flesh becomes flayed; in this crude version actions speak much louder than words. There are very few words spoken by Jim Caviezel's Jesus; he just bleeds from every inch of flagellated flesh, and staggers under the weight of the film. If a picture is worth a thousand words, the Gospel text dissolves under the snapping whips. My succinct film review can be writ very small: Jesus is a bloody mess.

In the broadband era academics, even the religionists, are eager to break into the magical mysterious world of trade books. Mel Gibson is not the only one making money from biblical images. Colleagues ask each other surreptitiously how do you get on the CNN Rolodex, who did those jacket closeups of you and your dog, who booked the readings at Borders in LA? Scholars want to be tagged with the monikers they used to fear: public intellectual, newsmaker. Writing a so-called trade book instead of a heavily footnoted monograph a decade ago would have elicited accusations of *popularizing*, an academic sin worse than spending ten hours researching designer shoes on eBay. 'Now university presses are turning away from cranking out piles of narrow monographs too expensive even for libraries and are actively looking for books that have at least an academic/trade market, books that will cross over to scholars in other disciplines or outside a narrow subfield', according to Rachel Toor, writing in the scholar's weekly rag, the *Chronicle of Higher Education* (19 March 2004). 'At the same time, commercial presses are hungry for serious, well-researched books that will appeal to people who want something more substantial than the next John Grisham.'

Cornel West has found a gray market for his intellectual products. And that fickle market has not yet deserted him. The public appears ready and eager for at least some form of philosophy in its daily diet. First, there is Tom Morris, a former Notre Dame professor, charging corporate IBM. and General Electric up to $30,000 an hour for his lecture on the '7 C's of Success', distilled from Cicero and Spinoza, Montaigne and Aeschylus. Former journalist, and self-described Johnny Appleseed of philosophy, Chris Phillips, the author of *Six Questions of Socrates* (2001) and *Socrates' Café* (2003), has one meta-goal: 'I left a lucrative career to wrest philosophy from academia, where the focus is on the microscopic study of the numbingly pedantic'. Third in my list of anyone-can-do-it philosophical inquiry models is 'Philosophy Talk', a San Francisco-based radio show modeled on NPR's 'Car Talk'. Two wisecracking Stanford philosophy professors, John Perry and Ken Taylor, shoot the intellectual breeze with call-in guests, tackling topics that often draw religionists into the radio-based conclave: Does belief in evolution undermine morality or belief in God? Has science replaced religion?[3]

So I stand at a confluence of biblical narratives, politics, and popular culture, in the middle of 2004, resisting the temptation to wish for one smooth meta-interpretation. There is no bottom line, no linear argument that can enclose each item of popular culture within a religious frame. Of

---

3. The desire to democratize scholarship and erudition is engaging the public. Professors are committed to raising the level of talk, not erudition, in the contemporary marketplace. Journalist Daniel Duane (*New York Times Magazine*, 20 March 2004) describes the new philosopher as a 'life coach/bodhisattva'. Duane reports that the desire for the examined life is growing as itinerant philosophers wander in Europe, Israel, South Africa, India and especially the UK, where Alain de Botton's best seller *The Consolations of Philosophy* (2000) became a six-part TV series. Taylor and Perry's radio talk show carries the tag line 'The program that questions everything—except your intelligence' (<http://www.philosophytalk.org/>). See also *Philosophy Now*, a general 'philosophy can be hip' glossy-stock journal published since 1991 in the UK and distributed also in the US and Canada.

course I am not the first scholar who recognizes this paradox. In his reconstructions of the historical Jesus, Crossan points out that even in the first century some people executed Jesus while others worshipped the Christ. Even before the Mel Gibson chatter! Finally, I must acknowledge that there is no objective, neutral presentation of political events. How could there be when a baby girl in my neighborhood was recently baptized Jihad Ayishah, friends are serving time for protesting US policy on preemptive military strikes, and 40 per cent of Palestinians living on the wrong side of the Israeli-built wall are not expected to have more than one meal a day.

2

WHITEWASHING ATHENA: GAINING PERSPECTIVE ON BERNAL AND THE BIBLE

> Donald Kagan, Mary Lefkowitz, Allan Bloom, and William Bennett also mine classical antiquity for lessons concerning out political system and the need to protect it from immigrants of the wrong sort, from sloppy Afrocentric thought, and from a lack of virtue, defined in part as obedience to leaders like Kagan's Pericles and his analogue in the present, Henry Kissinger.
>
> —Page duBois, *Trojan Horses* (2001)

Scarcely a stone's throw across the Mediterranean from Classics, the field of biblical studies has been uninterested in the so-called Bernal debate—at least so far as I can tell. This silence reflects more of a disciplinary myopia than a disinclination to deal with the subject of race within biblical literature. Bernal is Classics' problem; we in the discipline of Bible have enough problems in struggling with the Jesus Seminar's obsession with the actual words Jesus spoke. It is too facile to grumble that the compartmentalism of knowledge exhibits the need for a blending of approaches. One needs to examine the powerful human force behind the fear of interdisciplinary perspectives and to acknowledge that tearing through borders is not the magic solution. The first tentative steps in this direction have been taken by scholars proposing interdisciplinary programs such as Mediterranean studies. But the disciplinary power base, both in Classics and in Bible, stands stolid, takes no steps away from its protected, familiar center—the canon. By using Bernal's interaction with his voluble critics as a case study, I intend to examine the situation that is lurking just beyond the reach of disciplinary security—the bias against new types of interdisciplinary interpretation. When the bias turns vituperative, as it does in the case of the Bernal uproar, we have a case of what Marjorie Garber calls Discipline Envy. Scholars bristle with righteousness as they defend their turf, hiding their own self-doubt under claims of keeping the discipline 'pure'.

In spite of the special affinity between the Greek tradition and the biblical one, the fear of mutual disciplinary border crossings is not new. For any biblicist tempted to try such peri-Mediterranean comparisons, the contempt sprayed upon the efforts of anthropologists W. Robertson Smith and Sir James Frazer to compare biblical and classical texts functioned as a scholarly slap in the face.[1] Each discipline had its own canon, and they were not to be commingled. Lest anyone slip underneath the canonical barrier, each discipline remained behind the barricades of classical philology. Because professional scholars in any discipline can get bogged down within their own rhetoric and ritual, it often takes a so-called outsider to challenge the rhythms of one's familiar routine. Martin Bernal is certainly such a figure.

One of my own scholarly concerns is to trace the intellectual and theological route taken by the God of ancient Afro-Asiatic Israel on the way to becoming the God of European civilization. Phrased another way, how did an Oriental God become the center of Western civilization? Many of Bernal's insights have helped me place some markers on my travel route. First, I must note that I am starting in the West and working my way eastward. My directional route has been predetermined by my cultural background. Of course I acknowledge that the 'West' is a fictional construct embroidered with myths and fantasies like its orientalizing counterpart, the 'East'.[2] But somewhere along the route taken by the majority of biblical scholars, East became West in the present day, Israel is seen as a Western country, while Turkey (much of which lies to the west of Israel), Egypt, Libya, and Morocco are all 'Eastern'. My point here is not to get caught in political binaries, but rather to call attention to

1. The devaluing of scholarship that goes against the agenda of those scholars who control a discipline is not unusual. See my comments later in this study about the Lefkowitz series of essays excoriating the project of Martin Bernal—this is certainly a clear-cut example. Mary R. Lefkowitz and Guy MacLean Rogers, *Black Athena Revisited* (1996), hereafter referred to as *BAR*.

See also Lefkowitz 1996. When Elaine Pagels first published her popular edition of some Nag Hammadi texts, *The Gnostic Gospels* (1979), the scholarly buzz among those in control of New Testament scholarship was that Pagels's Coptic was weak. Moreover, her translations were inaccurate. The comparison is not an idle one. Like Bernal, Pagels was threatening a canon.

2. In a geographic sense, the concept is relative too. What the West calls the Middle East is from a Chinese perspective Western Asia. Situated in California, one refers to the Far East, which lies a few thousand watery miles to the west. In Arabic, the word for west (*Magreb*) refers to North Africa, the westernmost part of the Arab world, in contrast the *Mashreq*, the eastern part. For a history of the way the term 'West' becomes overlaid, see R. Williams 1976.

the arbitrariness of the standard cartographies of identity because they influence designations of readings of literary pantheons and theological texts.[3]

Concurrent with the move from East to West, Yhwh became God, and the gods from the surrounding Near Eastern cultures lost their divinity.[4] There is a Christocentric line or argument that reflects this development but does not explain it. Since 'God' is the only deity in the canon, 'God' has provided the model of what the category of God should look like. This category of one is supported and reflected in the first commandment: You shall have no other god before me. The flaw in this argument is that it is made from within the intellectual world encircled by the category of one. In ancient cultures, other gods did exist, only a few miles away. Thus, believers had a real choice to make.

Revisiting Black Athena

Martin Bernal, a professor of political science at Cornell University who came to ancient Middle Eastern studies from Chinese studies, published the first volume of a projected four-volume work, *Black Athena: The Afro-asiatic Roots of Classical Civilization* in 1987. (The title 'Black Athena' alludes to Bernal's suggestion that the Greek goddess of wisdom, Athena, originated in Egypt.) In that first volume, he focused on what he considers to be the racist character of nineteenth-century classical studies. Like Edward Said, who argued in *Orientalism* (1978) that European scholarship focusing on the 'Orient' served colonialist aims, Bernal condemns Westerners for misunderstanding the role of imperial conquests in shaping their culture—a culture they continue to regard as superior to all others. *Black Athena* aroused great interest and sparked several symposiums and volumes of discussion among scholars primarily from the discipline of Classics. These scholars have fought valiantly to whitewash

3.   There is of course a north/south axis, which the Victorians adhere to, contrasting their own cold and pragmatic north with the bright erotic Mediterranean, where the Greeks disported. Dickens uses two schools to show the contrast: Gradgrind's school is characteristic of northern England—scientific, utilitarian, factual—while down in Sussex Dr Blimber offers a wholly classical training to the children of the upper middle class. 'Mrs. Gaskell's contrast of south and north is a contrast between gentry and bourgeoisie, between leisure and industry; but it also marks the opposition between past and present, between ancient Greece and Victorian England' (Jenkyns 1991: 48).

4.   For an extended discussion of the loss of potency of the Greek gods, see my article 'Whatever Happened to Dionysus?' (Bach 1995).

Athena, that is, to protect themselves from the charges Bernal makes against them. Not surprisingly, the work appealed to readers with an animus against Western culture, many of whom took up the mantle of *Black Athena* without ever reading the book. The second volume of *Black Athena*, entitled *The Archaeological and Documentary Evidence*, reviews archeological sites and artifacts, ancient Egyptian inscriptions and Greek legends to support Bernal's thesis that Egypt and the Middle East influenced the civilization of ancient Greece from the Bronze Age to classical times. Bernal continued in his second volume to castigate the Europeans, and the scholars who consider their culture superior to all others for the sin of cultural arrogance. While upon a surface reading the split seems irrevocable, Richard Jenkyns has suggested that Bernal's Athena may be neither black nor white. A careful reader, Jenkyns suspects that Bernal may be tempted to rescue Europeans from their cultural arrogance 'because he fears that they have all too much to tempt them' (*BAR*: 420).

Orientalism pointed to the Eurocentric construction of the East within Western writing. In a newer book, *Culture and Imperialism* (1993), Said developed his view of the scholarly connections between the histories of Western imperialist powers and the places they colonized and dominated. Through understanding a shared history, Said argues, one can counteract the divisive and destructive forces of contemporary movements to rediscover 'essential' cultural values, be they American, British, Arab, Muslim, Christian. Said criticizes both imperialists and those they dominated. And he condemns dictatorial leaders of successful national liberation movements for putting national security above the goals of human liberation and democratic participation. Said's criticism of essentialist thinking is as important to the scholarly study of the biblical culture as it is to Bernal's purview of the classical/Afro-Asiatic axis. Narrative histories that ignore the imperialist context in which they developed and histories of dominated peoples that stress their preservation, rather than their innovative uses, of tradition both fuel dangerous stereotypes—the canonical as dynamic and the Afro-Asiatic or the Canaanite or the Egyptian as conservative or backward.

While scholars in departments of modern literatures and cultures were tracing the lines of imperialism through the constructions of nationalisms, often through inflated discourse such as the aesthetics of otherness, the poetics of imperialism, many classicists and biblicists still were not prepared for Martin Bernal to offer a parallel model of scholarship focused upon the complementary Eurocentric construction of the West via the obliterating or 'writing out' of the East (and Africa). Bernal (1987: I, 241) describes the process in relation to Africa in *Black Athena*:

> If it had been scientifically proved that Blacks were biologically incapable
> of civilization, how could one explain Ancient Egypt—which was incon-
> veniently placed on the African continent? There were two, or rather
> three solutions. The first was to deny that the ancient Egyptians were
> black'; the second was to deny that the ancient Egyptians had created a
> civilization; the third was to make doubly sure by denying both. The last
> has been preferred by most 19th and 20th century historians.

Bernal distinguishes between the 'Ancient model' which simply assumed
classical Greek civilization's deep indebtedness to both African (Egyptian
and Ethiopian) and Semitic civilizations, and the 'Aryan model' which
developed in the wake of slavery and colonialism. Evidence for the
Ancient model appears in 'a mass of literary and artistic circumstantial
evidence' suggesting that the Ancient model existed in Archaic (776–
550 BCE) and possibly Geometric times (950–776 BCE) (Bernal 1987:
II, 4). The early dating for this model allows Bernal to argue for the
advantage of the Ancient model having existed nearer the period it
concerned than the Aryan model.

Another aspect of Bernal's project to undermine the originality of
Greek culture is to focus upon Hermetic practice, once again insisting
upon an early dating to give the Hermetic material chronological priority
over the other contemporary syncretic religious movements, Neo-Platon-
ism and Gnosticism. This move allows Bernal to argue Egyptian influence and primacy over the Greek, emphasizing the heavily Egyptian
nature of Hermetism over the more Hellenistic qualities of Neo-Platon-
ism and Gnosticism. This dating squabble involves the Hermetic texts
that developed from the blend between the Egyptian deity Thoth and
the Greek Hermes. Most scholars agree that the manifestation of this
commingling—the god Hermes Trimegistus—was worshipped in rituals
that drew upon both Greek and Egyptian practice. As Fowden points out,
'the Olympians seemed out of place on the banks of the Nile. Even in
areas that had a large Greek population, the immigrants were often
happy to attach themselves to the dominant local gods' (1987: I, 19-20).
The conflict arises from Bernal's habit of taking a position of scholarly
agreement (the syncretistic nature of the Egyptian–Greek rituals particularly in Alexandria) and pushing the argument too far, often into the
land of the incredulous. In the argument concerning late antique Her-
meticism, Bernal eagerly, and quite possibly naively, follows Flinders
Petrie's dating parts of the Hermetic literature to a period as early as the
sixth century BCE. By traveling back in time, back to the work of Petrie,
who seems to have been discounted by Eurocentric scholars, Bernal is
able to continue his push toward an Egyptocentric and often explicitly
Hermetic view of early modern European thought.

The Aryan model, established in the Victorian era, had to perform ingenious acrobatics to 'purify' classical Greece of all African and Asian contaminations. It had to explain away Greek homages to Afro-Asiatic cultures, such as Homer's descriptions of the 'blameless Ethiopians' and the frequent references to the *kalos kagathos* (handsome and good) Africans.[5] Not surprisingly, the scholars structuring the Aryan model sought to justify European and American imperialism and colonialism, which was at its highest tide from 1880–1940. Since this was also a period in which humanist scholars—and I include here archeologists, classicists, and biblicists—wished to appear scientific, they did not indulge in speculative theories, but were rather more comfortable with the pointillism of arguing small details. Since sweeping theories can result in charges of speculation or irresponsibility, scholars took the safer route and juggled theories of dating and provenance for ancient activities. While few cultural scholars would dispute the Victorian predilection for romanticizing the ancient Mediterranean world, Bernal seems extreme in his polemic against the 'fierce racism' of the imperialist British in their erasure of the Egyptian influence upon the Greco-Roman culture. What Bernal ignores is that each critic and interpreter, ancient or modern, is influenced by social, political, and cultural values.

Bernal proposed to replace the Aryan model with the Revised Ancient model, which would accept that Egyptians and Phoenicians settled in and had a massive influence upon ancient Greece, while considering the fact that Greek is fundamentally an Indo-European language. Bernal (1987: II, 2) writes that the

> conception in sin or ever error [of the Aryan Model] does not necessarily invalidate it. Darwinism, which was created at very much the same time and for many of the same 'disreputable' motives, has remained a very useful heuristic scheme. One could perfectly well argue that Niebuhr, Muller, Curtius, and others were 'sleep-walking' in the sense that Arthur Koestler used the term—to describe useful 'scientific' discoveries made for extraneous reasons and purposes which are not accepted in later times. All that I claim for this volume is that it has provided a case to be answered. That is, if the dubious origin of the Aryan Model does not

---

5. Another cultural blur occurs in the representation of Africa as sub-Saharan area of the continent, sustaining the artificial gap between European civilization and the strange Other. The American film factory turned out the Tarzan films in the Thirties, in which the colonial clash between the European and the African was evaded, Eurocentric view of the African–Europe relationship was presented as normative. Later action films such as *Stanley and Livingstone* (1939), *Mogambo* (1953), and *Hatari* (1962) continued the double-edged process of mythification and defamation that had operated in relation to African cultures and the African continent.

> make it false, it does call into question its inherent superiority over the
> Ancient Model.

One flaw in Bernal's system enters with the suggestion that the Ancient model is innocent. He indicates this position by interpreting the ancient texts at face value, avoiding a critical analysis of traditions, conferring on myths the value of true history.[6] This concept of a serene core of cultural values at the center of Western civilization is, of course, false. Part of this construction has been generated by his misreading of ancient literary and historical texts as a bias-free mirror of what happened. Bernal adds more motives to the mix in claiming that the Victorians who established the Aryan model were racists and anti-Semites. While Bernal claims to promote Africa, he remains Eurocentric in approach and method. He neither attempts to show that the values or achievements of African societies are independent of the West or superior to it. Rather, his argument is temporal, concerned with establishing that African achievements were anterior to those of classical and later Western civilization and that these achievements were subsequently diffused to much of the world.

Those scholars who argue for a linear production of *Wissenschaft* seem to think that our job as scholars is singular: to transmit knowledge, not to create it. If, however, one of our tasks is to understand what we ourselves are about when we create history, the mirror is cracked. In fending off an attack on his own 'ideologic readings of biblical history', Thomas Thompson has drawn a line in the sand with which I am comfortable. While defining what he understands as his role as a historian of ancient history, he writes

> In no way would I restrict the kinds of questions to be asked of the past. Rather I address the code of our discipline in answering questions in a disciplined and critical way, beginning from within the grounds of what we, in fact, know about the past and addressing that much greater world of the unknown and the not yet known (Thompson 1995: 683).

While Thompson presents a sharp critique of the politics of present-day Euro-American academia, it must be said that he is just to the west of disingenuous when he ignores the politics of his own Hellenistic dating of the Hebrew Scriptures. While he and his colleagues Philip Davies and

---

6.   In the view of Liverani, 'hardly a single chapter (or even page) of *Black Athena* escapes the blame of ignoring correct methodology, adopting old-fashioned explanations, and omitting relevant data and literature' (BAR: 425). I cite Liverani, rather than some of the other contributors to this volume, because I believe his article to be calmer and freer of the classical frisson that many of his colleagues exhibit in this collection.

Niels Peter Lemche have suggested to biblicists the importance of looking at ancient Israelite history as it is inscribed in the Bible as a national-
ist literary fiction (my term, not theirs), they omit the parallel notion of
what Mikhail Bakhtin has defined as 'chronotypes', mediating between
the historical and the discursive, providing fictional environments where
historically specific constellations of power are made visible. Like Bernal,
Thompson and Lemche have been pilloried by members of the academy,
although it seems to me that there is nothing inherently sinister in their
project—except that it may be deployed asymmetrically, to the advantage of some national and ethno/racial imaginaries and to the detriment
of others. They have not to my knowledge tried to close off or write out
the work of other scholars, to put an intellectual lock on conflicting
discourses.

A major difference between Thompson's method and Bernal's is their
response to the ancient texts. Bernal aims to revise current understanding of ancient Middle Eastern history by taking seriously the ancient
Greeks' legends that portrayed much in their civilization as originating in
the Middle East, and especially in Egypt. For instance, Bernal takes liter-
ally Herodotus' statement that there was a black population in Colchis at
the eastern end of the Black Sea. Bernal sees considerable historical
value in Plato's treatment of the Atlantis myth. By contrast, Thompson
interprets epic texts as legends, products of the times when they arose,
not as accurate reflections of earlier periods.

Blackening Bernal

It seems clear from the attacks upon Afrocentrism in general and the passionate depths of the hostility toward Bernal's *Black Athena*,[7] by Mary
Lefkowitz (and some of the other classicists she has gathered together in
BAR), that these scholars assume that the classical world has already
revealed its secrets. Secure in their learned towers, they need not inhabit
a position that considers 'addressing that much greater world of the
unknown and the not yet known'. As a feminist, accustomed to the
denigrating reactions of masculinist scholars, I could teach Bernal a thing

---

7. In the Preface to the second volume of *Black Athena*, Bernal writes of 'one
Indo-European linguist who compares my work—in private conversation—to that of
the "revisionists" who deny that the Holocaust ever took place' (p. xix). Another
example, in my opinion, of scholars attempting to create a battle where none should
exist. Many of the blustery attacks on Bernal have the antique flavor of accusing him
of scandalous behavior and threatening to horsewhip the swine on the steps of his
London club.

or two about surviving the slings and arrows of disciplinary reactionists. In her terse essay on the battle of the classicists, Page duBois reminds those of us observing the game, if not her scholarly colleagues, who are so entrenched that they no longer have the flexibility to alter their opinions, about the importance of not sentimentalizing the Greek myths for the sake of contemporary political views: '...refuse the heterosexualization of the ancient Athenians, the celebration or denunciation of ancient democracy, and read Sappho and Herodotus as well as Plato' (2001: 137).

In *Not Out of Africa* (1996) Lefkowitz argues (p. 162) for a clear-eyed view of ancient Mediterranean history—her own:

> It is another question whether or not diversity should be applied to the truth. Are there, can there be, multiple, diverse 'truths'? If there are, which 'truth' should win? That one that is most loudly argued, or most persuasively phrased? Diverse 'truths' are possible only if 'truth' is understood to mean something like 'point of view'... The notion of diversity does not extend to truth.

Throughout her polemic, exactly the perspective that duBois is warning against, Lefkowitz assumes for herself the power to define: to define the role of the academy, scholarship, and the ideological stance of *other* scholars.[8] She does not accept that setting critical standards for scholarly competence is a value-laden process. Lefkowitz critiques the scholars whose 'motivation and identity have been taken as the equivalent of professional credentials' (1996: 166). She is referring to Afrocentrists, attaching motives to their scholarship that she does not attribute to her own. That her agenda is to protect and promote the Classics as prime Eurocentric currency is apparent to this reader if not to her. The effect of her bristling diatribe is to proclaim that the properly trained academician is the keeper of the keys of knowledge.[9] Through their interpretations

---

8.   An additional power is illustrated by Lefkowitz's book, the power to publish with a mainstream press. Her book is published by Basic Books, a division of the megalith HarperCollins, owned by Rupert Murdoch. Many of the Afrocentrist books she critiques are available through such publishers as Africa World Press in Trenton, NJ; Alkebu-lan Books in New York City; and Black Classic Press in Baltimore, MD. The power of the press brings along with it the money for media-savvy advertising and promotion campaigns, an extensive sales force for wide distribution, the capital and warehouse space to keep the book in print. For positive versions of Afrocentrism, see Onyewuenyi 1993 and Tsehloane 1995. For Afrocentric interpretations of Christianity, see Usry and Keener 1996, and Sanders (ed.) 1995.

9.   In a 1984 *New York Times Book Review* treatment of German novelist Christa Wolf's work, *Cassandra: A Novel and Four Essays* (1984), Lefkowitz seems not to

such scholars resist the winds of change and offer a timeless ideal, guaranteeing that the Eurocurrency will not be devalued. This allergy toward new interpretive perspectives is all too familiar to me as a feminist scholar. There seems to be a striking similarity between the devaluing and dismissal of Bernal's intellectual abilities, and finally the attack upon his work from the security of the academy, and the 'orientalizing' of feminist scholarship.

What Bernal shares with most of his critics is the lack of an examination of the constructedness of the basic concept of race. Acknowledging the slipperiness of defining race, Bernal reminds his scholarly audience that for the past 7000 years the population of Egypt has been a mix of African, South-West Asian, and Mediterranean types, but the civilization was fundamentally African (1987: I, 242). It is with his use of the word *African* that one runs into difficulty, since the term seems as constructed and as full of myth as either *European* or the binary *white/black*.[10]

---

understand the workings of the creative mind and its appropriation of ancient myth. In her negative review Lefkowitz seems hopelessly lost in a fictive or mythic realm. 'To the East German novelist Christa Wolf, Cassandra is the symbolic representative of women in the Western world, whose talents and intelligence have been suppressed in order to serve the interests of men, power and destruction', writes Lefkowitz. 'Mrs. Wolf arrives at this ambitious equation by a series of imaginative leaps. She sets the familiar and unfamiliar characters of Trojan legend in a world she reconstructs not from ancient myth but from the speculations of archeologists and historians—and even more, from her own perceptions of the modern world, especially the capitalist West.' I cite this text in order to show Lefkowitz's predilection for outrage at the possibility of a writer or scholar tinkering with ancient texts.

10. For detailed whitewashing of the issue of who was black in the ancient Mediterranean world, see Snowden 1970. In this work, Snowden claims that 'in spite of the association of blackness with ill omens, demons, the devil, and sin, there is in the extant records no stereotyped image of Ethiopians as the personification of demons or the devil' (p. 107). It seems to be a thin argument, since connecting blackness with ill omens, demons, the devil, and sin appears to me to clearly be the kind of negative stereotype that Snowden wants to deny.

A decade later, in BAR, Snowden has become one of the boys, arguing, 'Many Afrocentrists, however, continue to reject valid criticism of their inaccuracies and denounce their critics as Eurocentric racists if they are white, and as dupes of white scholarship and traitors to their race if they are black. It is neither racist nor traitorous, however, to insist upon truth, scholarly rigor, and objectivity in the treatment of the history of blacks' (p. 117). Note that in his recent work Snowden introduces a political and ideological argument on the part of Afrocentrists and then allies himself with the objective, non-ideologic classicists who deal in fact and truth rather than ideology. Yet in his earlier work his examples show the color prejudice his argument tries to hide.

Often he uses the terms 'black', 'Egyptian', and 'African' interchangably. Thus, Bernal shoots himself in the foot, generalizing about Eurocentric cultural politics, maintaining a monolithic focus upon European imperialistic agendas. Therefore, his focus, like a monolithic focus upon any class or ethno-racial group, approaches a racist position—at the same time it tries to decry Eurocentric racial supremacy.

In the first volume of *Black Athena*, Bernal traces the historiographic scholarship that resulted in the creation of the discipline of Classics as we know it today. He dates the finished product of Classics with precision: 1815–30, the period of the Greek War of Independence, when Christian Europe united against the traditional Islamic enemies from Asia and Africa (1987: I, 440-41). First, it is ironic that Bernal, questioning the bias of cultural nationalism, goes back to the canon to establish historic credentials. Second, as he freely admits, he is more interested in exploring a 'sociology of knowledge' than in *proving* distant linguistic connections. In his claim that such proof is impossible, he clearly provokes those linguists who interpret their research as exactly that. A third irony, at least for me, is that neither Bernal nor his critics question the absence of African history, of any historical period, within the Western culture of academia.

I do not want to leave the reader with the idea of a totally polarized scholarly discussion between a singular Bernal on one side and all classicists on the other. Each side occupies a sharply angled subject position. Acknowledging the importance of Bernal's work for his insights about 'the biased approaches of former (and present) classical scholars' (BAR: 417), Italian classical historian Mario Liverani agrees with his colleagues in the field of Classics that Bernal's major difficulty lies in his lack of historical methodology and control of primary sources. Liverani is more even-handed, acknowledging the messiness of Bernal's work (his dismissing as biased the racist approaches of European scholars of past centuries, without understanding the rules these same scholars established in the areas of philology, etymology and comparative linguistics, and religiohistorical method investigating the nature of myths and legends), but at the same time recognizing the importance of the larger questions that Bernal has raised, the questions that have become such irritants within the academy. Thus, Liverani does not try to blind the reader to the fact that Bernal, like most of us, is both salt and wound.

What I find most interesting about this Bernal vs. classicists argument, which has taken on a life of its own, is simply that. Ordinarily, a book as riddled with errors involving basic philology and reading of myth as history would not have caused more than a ripple on the literary and scholarly landscape. But *Black Athena*, first published in England and then in the US by Rutgers University Press, a small publisher by any standards, has generated an industry: several major colloquia at national scholarly meetings, special issues of scholarly journals, more than fifty articles, cited frequently in discussions of the priority of Western culture within American college curricula, as well as Mary Lefkowitz's protestations about the arguments and expertise of Bernal in *Not Out of Africa*, and *BAR*.

From Athena to Europa

Those of us who teach Bible are caught in a similar dilemma as those who teach Classics. We see the world through a 'cradle of Western civilization' lens. We have the technical expertise in ancient languages to patrol the disciplinary boundaries against any outsider. Our own training and much of the research we produce are based on the assumptions and models that Bernal is trying to topple. Rather than acknowledge that the ancient texts are not the exclusive property of classicists or biblicists, and welcome analyses from those scholars who may have different training and thus different perspectives, we too often diminish the work of a Bernal by claiming that he doesn't have the expertise to read the texts 'properly'. This tautological argument defends the borders, but more pernicious, it keeps the discipline safe from external development and change. An added irritation is the cavalier attitude of much biblical scholarship toward the gods of the ancient Near East and Greece and Rome. These long-ago pagans belong to nobody's pantheon. They are literary artifacts stripped of respect. In analyzing these other Mediterranean texts, no one need proceed with caution. It is the insistence of a monotheistic culture that can not fathom the religions of the ancient Mediterranean, except as literary productions.

'Zeus is just a story now', writes Salman Rushdie in the *New York Times*, reflecting the same perspective as my students. 'He is powerless, but Europa is alive' (1997). Simultaneously with demoting Zeus from divinity to protagonist, he recalls the myth that brought mythic Europe into being. As the Italian novelist Roberto Calasso put it, 'Europe began with a bull and a rape' (1993). Traveling back through time along mythic roads, back to the archaic world, we encounter the Asian maiden Europa, who became the beloved of Zeus. Europa was abducted by Zeus (who changed himself into a white bull for the occasion) and was held captive in a new land that came, in time, to bear her name. The prisoner of Zeus's unending desire for mortal flesh, Europa has been avenged by history, enshrined in the canon. But the stop-time of the literary canon is enlivened by the movement of history. Rushdie wants history to be more powerful than the canon, envisioning history as human and the canon as the discarded divine. At the very dawn of the idea of Europe is an unequal struggle between human beings and gods and, for Rushdie, an encouraging lesson: 'While the bull-god (Zeus) may win the first skirmish, it is the maiden-Continent (Europa) that triumphs in time'. The object of a *fatwa* proclaimed by the Ayatollah Ruhollah Khomeini, Rushdie claims that we live in the time when the tyranny of the gods should be vanquished. 'The loss of the divine places us at the center of the stage', Rushdie insists.

The 'us' provides a clue to Rushdie's angst. It is little wonder that when people sought to wrest control of their persons and lands from imperialists and colonizers, they should begin by claiming the right to represent themselves. But, like Bernal, Rushdie is caught between the worlds of black and white. His 'us' is a hybrid. As a colonized person, he is seemingly outside the traditional European story, yet it is within that Western world that he found his own place in the sun as a writer and public intellectual. Reading Rushdie's 'Indian-Anglian' work made clear to me the fragility of identity. As he observes rather tartly about criticism of his own work from the Indian subcontinent,

> the ironic proposition that India's best writing since independence may have been done in the language of the departed imperialists is simply too much for some folks to bear. It ought not to be true, and so must not be permitted to be true (*The New Yorker*, 23 and 30 June 1997).

Initially I found it curious that Rushdie could write with such surety of the death of a god while writing of the necessity of his own dodging of Khomeini's divinely launched thunderbolts. What sort of bravado had lulled him into thinking that history had indeed subsumed the theological canon? Then I thought of his personal history. There is a missing piece in Rushdie's proclamation. He does not acknowledge the dislocation that stems from his own bifurcated world. As a colonized youth, he had a great success and took on the demeanor of a successful British writer, a member of the London intelligentsia. What Rushdie has been experiencing is the outrage of one who has observed the overturning of the natural order of things: Eastern thunderbolts permeating the privileged protected Western landscape. Not unlike the thunderous attack of Bernal upon the cozy construction of the discipline of Classics, Rushdie may be a Janus figure, looking back to his Indian culture while suspecting that the British world truly is superior. With whose god should he look to find his supposedly authentic traditions? I suspect his rage comes from understanding that Western history has enshrined one god within the canon and expelled all others. And he has been tempted to do the same.

In writing this chapter, I faced a problem similar to what I critique in the work of Bernal: how to write about historical transformations in ancient cultures without invoking, however unwillingly, an evolutionary meta-narrative implying that changes toward contemporary Western models are progressive. I am reminded of Henry James' reflections in *The American Scene*: 'I draw courage from the remembrance that history is never, in any rich sense, the immediate crudity of what happens, but the much finer complexity of what we read into it, and think of in connection with it' (1946: 136-37). While seeming to be the doyen of European centrality, James is clearly aware of the false claims of historicity. He knows that he is looking at some oblique connection between narrative and event.

Bernal's main intent, to lessen European cultural arrogance (1987: I, 73), ignores the seeming disinterest of the nineteenth-century European world in the blackness of Athena. Like many scholars, Bernal rises and falls on his own rhetoric, making his own narrative central. In discussing the supposed racism of the European cultural elite, he acknowledges that 'at the end of the eighteenth century the predominant view was that of Mozart and his librettist Emanuel Schikaneder in *The Magic Flute*: that the Egyptians were neither Negro nor essentially African' (1987: I, 244). Yet he paints a picture of a hegemonic Greek civilization that is a purely European phenomenon. And in the final analysis, I fear, he is as Eurocentric as his critics, imposing their own cultural standards upon the East. Why, after all, should African or Egyptian culture be made to squeeze into a paradigm of European design? European imperialists and their colonialist African and Asian states have been interacting over the past two centuries. Cultural flow is not only upstream. In this conclusion, however, I fear I need to caution myself as well. I am also rooted in Western soil. Unable to shed this strong perspective without great difficulty, if at all, I can do little but lay my cards on the table. Establishing one defined cultural perspective from which to read a text is as much a problem for most writers and critics as it is for Rushdie. Perhaps all one can hope for are moments of identity in a very mutable world. What strings the moments together is a loosely constructed narrative, usually linear, that indicates movement *toward*.

The appearance and desire for evolutionary progress is not coincidental. Western imperial powers had, and continue to have, control over communication technologies and the military might to define our culture, our legal, economic, and political system as the goal of human development. Even writing in the English language awards work, both creative and critical, an international power. Situating the modern critic, like Bernal and his critics, within this political tug of war is one thing. But can this recent whitewashing of Athena make claims for ancient cultural imperialism? And what of judging African cultures within their own spheres, instead of comparing them with European advances from the same time period? These are the questions that Bernal's work raises for me, while challenging the reader not to overlook the temptation to deracinate the ancient texts from even the vestiges of antiquity. Post-colonial criticism has its element of parochialism. While biblicists may have tried for too long to read from the perspective of an ancient Israel-ite, that stance seems similar to a reading strategy in which postcolonial scholars turn the tables and impose the East upon the West. Alas, that provides scholars no advance from reading from the perspective of the Western imperialist. Neither reader is eager to hold a conversation with the other, but prefers the release of shouting down the wind.

3

CRACKING THE PRODUCTION CODE:
WATCHING RELIGIONISTS READ FILMS

Cue the Sun.

—Ed Harris as Christof, *The Truman Show* (1998)

Coming out of the movie theater one night in the late Nineties, I felt as
though I was surrounded by religious studies professors. But it was a balmy
summer in northern California, and this was no esoteric foreign film: Jim
Carrey, starring in *The Truman Show* (1998). Walking through the park-
ing lot, the voices persisted. 'It's an allegory for the Garden of Eden… It's
a lesson on predestination… It's crammed with verses right out of the
Bible… No, it's a Buddhist example of the illusions that bind us… It's
definitely a sermon… Yes, it is a sermon against complacency.' 'Aren't all
sermons about complacency?' I wondered aloud. Feeling somewhat harsh,
I turned to my companion, who had not even heard me. 'This guy is
clearly the strongest Christ figure since Cool Hand Luke', he assured me.
Well, maybe.

The movie's storyline is that Truman Burbank's life has been the subject of a television show since his birth. (Yes, this is the sort of subtle
allegory that calls its main character True Man from Burbank, the sitcom
mecca. Warning: there is an unpleasant demiurge named Christof.) Surrounded by actors, Truman is the only character unaware that his life is a
staged production. The jolly face that Truman/Carrey presents to the
world each day belies his inner pain. Television viewers and the actors
around Truman see through his pretense. They have witnessed the sad
dreams that he practices before the bathroom mirror each morning. And
they know that he is trapped in his own false reality. Who isn't? The
film's heavy-handed humor is often built around the ad game, for example, Truman's Stepford-type wife showing off some chocolate drink mix.
To Truman, to the audience, to us. To cut to the chase (and there is no

chase in this film in spite of its summer release date): one woman breaks through all restraint and tells our hero the truth. Amid all those who pretend to love Truman, she is the only one. Yada yada. In order to find her, he must go outside the complacent sitcom set, into the unknown. Like Porgy leaving Catfish Row to find his Bess.

My companion was still talking as we turned into the driveway. 'So we must break free of these wrong-headed ideas about God', he said with accompanying hand movements. 'It's "Gnostic", it's moving into the spiritual.' Of course I know that people's interpretations of *The Truman Show* tell as much about their religious leanings as they do about the screenwriter's cosmology. But I worry when people go to a multiplex and come out spouting theological codes. It reminds me of how close to the surface those codes rest in our minds.

*   *   *   *   *

It was a dark and stormy night in Mel Gibson's Gethsemane and in my Cleveland suburb. I had reluctantly decided to see Gibson's *The Passion of the Christ* for the same reason I had read Dan Brown's popular page-turner, *The DaVinci Code*. Too many people have been asking me at the mall, in the classroom, at dinner parties, even at the airport, those searching questions, 'Is it real? Did it really happen that way?'

As people streamed out of a mall multiplex (*The Passion* showing on three screens four times a day), I was struck by the number of teenagers weeping. I stopped next to a girl wearing a red satin heart on her jacket with a crucifix pinned at its center. She was weeping and holding onto the shoulder of a woman, who turned out to be her mother. That woman had both hands clasped with another family member. The three women formed a knot of grief, clearly overcome by the film. 'I don't like violence. But this was Jesus. It did not seem like a movie. The suffering was real. Those nails went through his hands. He was bleeding. I saw Jesus on the Cross.' A fresh wave of tears flowed as they stumbled out of the theater. I thought of the women at the Cross, and moved away from the women at the mall.

Jesus Christ, Celluloid Superstar

Talk about a slippery slope. Jesus films are fraught with theology, ideology, sentimentality, pageantry, and sophistry. I am certain that it is a losing battle to talk about favorite or most effective Jesus films, sometimes called biopics, especially with scholars who are still wrestling with images of the historical Jesus. So much has been written about *The Passion of the Christ*, from the US Catholic Bishops to the American Defamation League, from biblical scholars to irate film critics, that I have chosen not to write about the film here. At the end of Chapter 4, I will examine the marketing of the film, as the selling of the greatest story ever told is central to the mutual influence of Bible and popular culture.

Not surprisingly, one's favorite Jesus film often tells us a great deal more about the spectator than the film itself. One person's faith in another person's fantasy. For instance, I have a colleague who thinks Monty Python's *Life of Brian* is brilliant, another who hums along with *The Greatest Story Ever Told*. Full of self-revelation, I am willing to admit my own strong connection to Martin Scorsese's *Last Temptation of Christ*. Lest you think you have me typed, dear reader, I also love some of the great pious films such as *The Diary of a Country Priest* (1954), Henry Koster's *The Robe* (1953), Henry King's *The Song of Bernadette* (1943), and a film that defies category, Franco Zefferelli's *Brother Sun, Sister Moon* (1972). Often showing these films to students without secondary analysis can result in meatier discussions than offering other critics' analyses, which tend to intimidate students. What? No *Ben-Hur*?

The greatest example of how film can illuminate and extend the Gospels is surely *Vangelo secondo Matteo* [*The Gospel according to St Matthew*] directed by Pier Paolo Pasolini (1964). Clearly my own biased view, but fortunately shared by Lloyd Baugh, whose chapter 'The Masterpiece: The Gospel According to Saint Matthew' (Baugh 1997: 94-108) provides both excellent background on Pasolini as a creative artist and a crisp analysis of the Italian filmmaker's portrait of Jesus. Baugh focuses on Pasolini's representation of the Matthean Jesus as a human rather than a divine hero, but one who is much more distant from the people and his disciples than the Matthean figure. Cutting to the bone, Baugh argues that Pasolini sees an irritable Jesus, one not well integrated into human society. 'Solitary, aloof, he is a kind of biblical intellectual, who despite an intense desire to be organically linked to the people, cannot breach the immeasurable gap between them' (p. 104). Baugh argues, and I think rightly, that Pasolini's Jesus is an extreme figure who discomforts many interpreters of the film, but that the severity of the film's interpretation is in keeping with the radical nature of the Gospel. Pasolini's broken-faced peasants are much closer to a Gospel peasantry, I suspect, than the bland Hollywood peasants or even the Bronx-voiced disciples of Scorsese. Baugh also notes (p. 103) the nuances of Pasolini's Jesus:

> When Jesus heals the leper, there is a marvelous warm exchange of smiles between him and the man; and when Jesus cures the cripple, he smiles at him and later he even speaks gently and reasonably to the Pharisees.

> During his triumphal entrance into Jerusalem, Jesus is anything but
> solemn. He is clearly enjoying himself and participating in his popular
> manifestation.

There is something so fitting in Pasolini's hollow-cheeked slight Mediterranean Jesus, a rough-edged man who adds precision to my own internal
portrait. After seeing one of these Jesus films, particularly the Pasolini or
the Scorsese film, one never reads the Gospels in quite the same way
again. One proof of the power of the spectator in interpreting film is that
the so-called New York accents found in the Scorsese film sounded
normal to me (a native New Yorker) and the tough guy Judas played by
Harvey Keitel finally gave me a 'henchman/betrayer' figure who was
simultaneously intimate and inimical, one who brought depth and complexity to Judas that I had never understood. And the scoring of the
Congolese Missa Luba at the final scene of Pasolini's film is a triumph. The
pounding drums and joyful cries of the women pick up the ultimate
triumph as they approach the tomb. As the drumbeat picks up urgency,
so does the message of the Gospel, as death is silenced by the fierce and
harsh music of the victory of the risen Christ. And what better visual
interpretation of the triumph of the embattled Matthean community
than Italian peasants, sure-footed on rocky terrain, in a fight against
hostile forces.

While 2004 may be the year of Mel Gibson's martyrdom or villainy,
depending on your cultural politics, there is another recent Jesus film that
has gone almost unremarked. Overshadowed by The Passion is British
director Philip Saville's The Gospel of John (2003), a film whose text is
the Gospel of John, word for word from The Good News Bible translation by the American Bible Society. That is where the similarity to the
grittier Pasolini work ends. Jesus is played by the Shakespearean actor
Henry Ian Cusick, whose edgy performance gives great depth to the
Johannine scenes in which Jesus tells the crowds that the way to eternal
life is to follow him. Under Saville's direction, the shock and disbelief of
the Romans and the traditional Jewish leaders seems justified when they
hear such extraordinary claims. Perhaps it is the skill of the actors in this
interpretation of the Gospel, but Jesus' words to his followers present
more challenges and nuances to the audience of the film than the same
words spoken by earlier actors proclaiming to be the son of God. When
Daniel Kash's Peter denies Jesus three times, the spectator can feel how
difficult belief is for even the most ardent of Jesus' followers. The film is
narrated by Christopher Plummer, whose authoritative voice makes the
text seem like gospel. I suspect that the film has not ignited the passions
of critics because its emphasis is upon the teachings and ministry of Jesus,

rather than the intense violence and suffering that is the focus of Mel Gibson's Passion play. The stentorian tones of Plummer's narration add to the cinematic quality and help to distance the audience from the characters. Thus, one is always a spectator of the Saville *Gospel of John* since the film does not cut into ones passions in the way that the Gibson film threatens one's emotions as it flays the flesh of Jesus.

Once Upon a Time in Hollywood

There are so many aspects of film and its relation to religious studies that is impossible to cover all areas of film in this chapter. Particularly important are the ethnic interpretations found in analyses of Jewish filmmakers and the powerful influence of Jewish humor and thought both in front of and behind the camera. African-American film shares some of the characteristics: if Jewish films often show Jews as Gentile audiences expect to see them, then black films often play to a white audience. Both these subgenres reflect a benign interest in the Other. In the pre-Sixties world of Hollywood studio films they fed a sanitized interest in the hyphenated American way of life to a large section of the movie-going population. Blaxploitation films (gangsta films in the pre-hood era) were more exotic than the Jewish films, thick with desire to have whatever the Gentiles enjoyed in suburbia.

A Jewish daughter of Hollywood through her father Dore Shary, the one-time head of MGM and writer/director/producer of Broadway hits, Jill Robinson characterizes Hollywood in her novel *Bed/Time/Story*:

> Russian Jewish immigrants came from the *shtetls* and ghettos out to Holly-wood… In this magical place that had no relationship to any reality they had ever seen before in their lives, or that anyone else had ever seen, they decided to create their idea of an eastern aristocracy… The American Dream is a Jewish invention (Robinson 1975: 35).

While Robinson's view may be a slight exaggeration, it is certainly true that the American film industry was operated by Eastern European Jews who themselves seemed to be anything but the quintessence of America. Neal Gabler argues along with Robinson that the Jewish filmmakers, such as Harry Cohn, the Warner brothers, Adolph Cukor and Louis B. Mayer were visible targets for wave after wave of anti-Semitism. The Jewish moguls envisioned behind the barricades of Gentile gentility the respectability and status that they envied. The movies were to become the bridge into the American dream, for the dream makers as well as the other European minorities who shared their dream and aspirations. For the white immigrant working-class, the picture palace was a view into American royalty.

There are a couple of classic Jewish films that emphasize the folk tradition of religious belief. The ethnic emphasis on the naïve faith of simple *shtetl* inhabitants is most clearly portrayed (caricatured?) in *Fiddler on the Roof*, an interpretation of the folk stories of Sholem Aleichem. In this 1964 musical, the characters speak a Yiddishized English that emphasizes the pure hearts and minds of the folk characters. According to literary critic David Roskies, Yiddish writers had been striving to reinvigorate the rabbinic tradition by interweaving old (rabbinic) and new traditions. They did such a good job that later generations accepted the Yiddish tapestry as the genuine article.

Both *Fiddler* and Streisand's quasi-feminist New Yorky *Yentl*, an adaptation of a story by Isaac Bashevis Singer, are more rooted in the filmmaker's imagination than in any historical accuracy. Depending on one's point of view, *Fiddler* and *Yentl* are either blatant and corny, or serious and profound plays on the challenge and end to the *shtetl* world. The two films have major differences: the impoverished milkman's appeal is centered upon his archetypal identity. Tevye is a descendant of Abraham, the patriarch of his family, the one who talks to God, in the familiar tone of a borscht-belt comic. So why have Jewish audiences embraced *Fiddler* on the stage and as a film? In a much-quoted essay from *Commentary* in 1964, written soon after the musical opened on Broadway, Irving Howe suggested that New York Jews were delighted with any positive representations of their faith within the popular media:

> American Jews suffer these days from a feeling of guilt because they have lost touch with the past from which they derive, and often they compound this guilt by indulging themselves in an unearned nostalgia. The less, for example, they know about East European Jewish life or even the immigrant experience in America, the more inclined they are to embrace it.

Streisand never transcends her starry draw. Even playing a teenage boy with earlock curls, she is reassuringly Barbra. One never truly believes in the subterfuge. The film is clearly a star vehicle in which Barbra will surely get her man. A new film made in Afghanistan, *Osama* (2003), begins in much the same way as *Yentl*. A young Afghani girl, Osama, passes as a boy in order to support her family. Free of her burqa and fundamentalist prohibitions against women appearing in public and earning money, she works in the marketplace. When the Muslim authorities find out that she is a girl, she is abused, thrown in jail, and finally married off to an octogenarian. A painful film, *Osama* is probably closer to reality than *Yentl*. The harshness of the European experience has been glamorized in *Yentl*, made for an American audience willing to accept old customs in an old country, so long as there is the celebration and triumph of a happy ending. The violence and hardship that were clearly part of real *shtetl* life were given a fresh coat of paint and tricked into romantic nostalgia by the Hollywood studios. One possible justification for the popularity of these fairy-tale versions of European Jewish life is that they predate the Holocaust and the innocence that was blown away by World War II. In spite of poverty and hard physical days, the world of the *shtetl* was a happier time for American Jews to contemplate. To be enveloped in the world of Tevye or Yentl was for the Jewish audience to remember how far they had come since the prelapsarian *shtetl*.

Old Country Jewish roots and history were treated very differently by the subsequent group of Jewish filmmakers, who used humor grounded in the common occurrences of daily Jewish life in America, events through which tragedy and suffering are drained of a pretentious Eastern European backdrop. The lived experience of middle-class American Jews has been minutely documented and examined by the major films of Woody Allen, Sidney Lumet, and Paul Mazursky. The motifs in these films play on images of outsiderdom, and created an American Jewish identity that reflected the new country, not the rural *shtetl*. For these filmmakers, their very Jewishness, differently understood by each of the three, played a dominant role in how they were perceived by the dominant society. Whether as a small man, inept, ambivalent, neurotic, a success in business, a failure in business, the Jewishness of the character colors and directs his worldview. For most of the Jewish films from the Sixties, the American Jewish experience was a triumph, and the immigrant community became a curiosity, a memory of an earlier generation.

There was one minority group that was kept out of the business by all the others. And that of course was the African-American community, so long portrayed as the happy servant class. The early films were bathed in the soft focus of sentimentality, much like the Jewish films analyzed above. The study of African-American film will bear tempting fruit, especially since there are religious matrices and metaphors in so many of these films. The films of the Thirties and Forties, upon which I am focusing, did not portray or examine the realities of black poverty, illiteracy, and hunger. Rather, they emphasized the temptations of the toys of the devil: whisky, sex, and slippery dice.

One of the most familiar films of this period is the spectacle *The Green Pastures* (1936), written by Marc Connelly, produced by a white establishment (Warner Brothers) with black actors. Who is the audience for a film featuring a jittery trumpet-toting archangel Gabriel who punctuates the film's dialogue with 'Gangway, gangway, for da' Lawd God Jehovah'. Eager to enact his role as the trumpeter who ends the troublesome earth drama, Gabriel (Oscar Polk) punctuates the Lord's heavy-hearted observations about his children with a hopeful shake of his instrument: 'Now, Lawd?' The dialect is matched by the sweet women angels who clean the Lord's quarters in Heaven. Wearing gingham-covered wings, they are nurturing mammies even in the idealized world of heaven. 'Bein' da Lawd aint no bed of roses', one of the women says to another while feather-dusting the Lord's study. The Lord is played by Rex Ingram, a physically impressive, mellow-voiced actor, who was the first black man to earn Phi Beta Kappa at Northwestern University, and then was graduated from Northwestern in 1919 with a medical degree. He had been seen in *King Kong* (1933) and *The Emperor Jones* (1933) before playing God in *The Green Pastures*.

A very popular play on Broadway, clearly the story was intended for white audiences who were charmed by the naïve folk spin to traditional biblical tales. One is reminded of the *Fiddler on the Roof* scenario, even though *The Green Pastures* predated the Zero Mostel vehicle by several decades. There seems to be a box-office comfort level in the Jewish peddler and the Negro crap shooter who are looking for God and their faith to get them through tough times that pleased 'American' audiences.

When the film version of *The Green Pastures* opened it got the star treatment: the film opened at Radio City Music Hall, the great Art Deco palace of popular culture in New York City. And the film became a major hit for the studio, although many of the cast members returned to their not-so-green pastures as porters, maids, and short-order cooks. Today's film critics are rightly appalled by the Good Book's world according to Hollywood, Connelly, and others:

> It is now evident that *The Green Pastures* rested on a cruel assumption: that nothing could be more ludicrous than transporting the lowly language and folkways of the early twentieth-century Negro back to the high stately world before the Flood (Bogle 2001: 68).

Most of the black films with a religious theme emphasized the great theological antimonies interpreted folklorically; right and wrong are played out in all their standard heart-wrenching forms: sin and redemption, seduction and salvation. Spencer Williams was one of the most prolific filmmakers of the Forties, making nine black-subject films in the decade. His early films were based on religious themes and pious sentiments:

Brother Martin: Servant of Jesus (1942), *Marchin' On* (1943), *Go Down Death* (1944), *Of One Blood* (1945). There were a variety of similar Thirties films made expressly for a black market, most of which have disappeared from archives (a few are available in the African-American film heritage video series), such as *Moon over Harlem* (1939), *Lying Lips* (1939), *The Girl from Chicago* (1932), and *The Scar of Shame* (1927). These films were distributed to African-American 'ghetto theaters', but never succeeded in general release. According to film historian Donald Bogle, these early examples of black films may seem naïve or dated today, but were very important to the black audiences for whom they were a source of great pride (2000: 109).

Of particular interest to biblical scholars will be *Blood of Jesus*, written and directed by Spencer Williams in 1941. This fantasy is rooted in the soil of the African-American south, filled with the sounds of gospel singing and baptisms in the river. Briefly, it relates the story of a wicked crap-shooting fellow who accidentally shoots his newly baptized wife with his hunting rifle. Just after their marriage, Martha asks her husband Raz, 'Why don't you pray and try to get religion? We could be so much happier if you did.' This wish of the young pious woman becomes the soul of the movie. After being shot, lying inert on the bed, Martha is escorted by an angel away from the cabin, away from reality into a somewhat clumsily photographed out-of-body experience. However, dark reality follows Martha; slick Satan in the person of zoot-suited, fancy-talking Judas Green, tempts Martha with fancy clothes and hot 'city life'. Predictably, bad turns to worse, water to whisky, and things look very dire for Martha. The redemption scene is glittering with goodness.

The scene at the foot of the Cross is particularly memorable. After being chased out of the juke joint by a bunch of rowdy, wicked, drink-soaked men, Martha is about to be killed by them on the dusty road between town and cabin. Standing under a crude road sign that points the way to Hell or Zion, Martha and the men hear God's voice: 'He who is without sin, cast the first stone at her!' The crossroads sign dissolves into the Cross of Jesus. Frightened by the spectacle, and presumably by the presence of God, the men run away. Drops of the Precious Blood fall onto Martha, and miraculously she is returned alive and awake to her bed in the small cabin... Was Martha truly dead? Did prayer actually bring her back to life? The cast includes Cathryn Caviness, Spencer Williams, and Juanita Riley—and has enough sin and redemption for all.

A higher budget film given the cash and marketing of the white Hollywood establishment has an all-black cast and parallels the plot of *Blood of Jesus*. In *Cabin in the Sky* (1943), the African-American folk-tradition is

examined with a rich dose of sentimentality. The film, produced by Hollywood mogul Arthur Freed and directed by Vincent Minnelli, was a black-
cast musical, adapted from the stage, by white filmmakers, photographers,
costumers, and marketers. Another naïve, country, good, Christian black
woman is involved with a boy who wants to be good, but keeps goin' bad.
This film cast with star entertainers, featured Eddie 'Rochester' Anderson
as Little Joe Jackson, and the classic temptress Lena Horne as the devil
woman who snares him away from true believer Ethel Waters. Like *Blood
of Jesus*, Minnelli's *Cabin* is replete with stereotyped characters: holy
rollers, happy plantation workers, juke-joint weaklings, and the Bible-
carrying good women whose eyes are full of sorrow. The caricature of
happy god-fearing Negroes persisted in the moviegoers' psyches, as well
as in the thoughts of film critics. The *New York Times* reviewed *Cabin* as
a 'beautiful entertainment, sparkling and completely satisfying...by turn
an inspiring expression of a simple people's faith in the hereafter and a
spicy slice of their zest for earthly pleasures'.

Selling the Celluloid Bible

That scholars of Bible and religion have been incorporating film study
into their work is not a sudden move. There were a few considerations of
the connection between the two as early as the moralizing concerns of
Forman (1933) and Moley (1938). But in the past handful of years, a
scholarly interest in Bible and film has grown steadily, parallel to the
development of both cultural studies and the elevation of popular culture
to academic heights. There are many 'usual' films that will not be not
covered in this chapter, and many articles by Bible scholars and film
critics that were not reviewed. My intention is rather to examine the
reciprocal and heuristic relation of the spectator to the work. The uses
of history, whether it be biblical history or American pioneer history,
are not fixed but become the pre-text to a fashioning of a new narrative,
that create an intertext between the religious and the cinematic interpretation.

There are basically two categories of books in this subdiscipline: the
one in which the scholar 'reads' a film about a biblical character or event
(the Exodus, the Crucifixion, the fall of Sodom are popular themes), and
the other ties contemporary films with basic biblical tropes and themes,
woman as harlot, heroic good guy combating the forces of evil, and recently, in honor of the millennium I suppose, the Apocalypse. In the first
group, it seems as though those scholars who are gifted at reading texts
have also produced interesting work in the area of reading cinema. David

Gunn, Cheryl Exum, Jane Schaberg, and Jennifer Glancy come to mind. Their articles in *Semeia* 74, a volume I edited in 1996, are, in my (biased) opinion, representative of the best work being done by religionists reading film as narrative. More recently the work of Adele Reinhartz and Brent Plate have offered valuable contributions to viewing films through religionist eyes.

Both Schaberg and Glancy have remained within the topics of their current research interests (Mary Magdalene for Schaberg and first-century Mediterranean slavery for Glancy) and explored how those subjects have been addressed in Hollywood films with New Testament narratorial background. Glancy makes a particularly telling point in her connection between the romanticized version of first-century slavery and the filmmaker's 'slavery' as seen through the American experience of slavery. Conscious analysis of this cultural schism is a vital element to successful film critique, and Glancy deftly peels away the layers of interpretations of slavery for the culture in which the story is placed and the culture in which the filmmaker and the spectator live. According to Glancy, Hollywood's films indicate what it is like to be a free man, rather than a slave. In *Demetrius and the Gladiators* (1954), the Christian freedman Demetrius, played by Victor Mature, is forced back into slavery as a gladiator. Given the odds, he is most likely to die in combat. For some reason that I do not fully comprehend, the lions in the gladiator films, as well as the one who wrestles with Samson (also played by Victor Mature), are somewhat woebegone and weary, threadbare of mane, and ragged of tail. Glancy argues that Hollywood's version of slavery owes more to the American Cold War—what it means to be free rather than enslaved, American rather than Soviet, and to the cinematic pageantry of masculinity than to any historical examination of first-century Roman slavery (Glancy 1996: 133-38).

Schaberg's feminist focus and her scholarly work on the position of Mary Magdalene and other women in the Gospel accounts reflects her intimacy with the character of the Magdalene. Such a view could be evinced only from a scholar as thoughtful and focused upon the role of women in the New Testament narrative as Schaberg. Whether in visual narratives like film or in verbal narratives, Schaberg argues, the Magdalene is a focalizer for the experience of early Christian women. Schaberg rightly observes that in the traditional characterization of the Magdalene and in the films that reflect the tradition the Magdalene is not even a follower of Jesus. She is an outsider to the male world of Jesus and his disciples, and is described as a prostitute in the Scorsese film, as well as the Zefferelli *Jesus* (1973), and the Webber and Rice *Jesus Christ Superstar*.

The words of Barbara Hershey, the Magdalene in Scorsese's *Last Tempta-tion of Christ* (1988), give added depth to the character she portrays:

> My most important scene, as a prostitute in Magdala, was also the most
> difficult because I was going to show Magdalene with a series of men.
> Even though Marty's films have a lot of sexuality, there hadn't been any
> nudity in them—so he asked me if I wanted a double, so at first I said sure.
> Every atom of me wanted a double. But I didn't feel that a double would
> be Magdalene. I knew that if I did the scene, I'd really feel like a whore
> (Scorsese 1989: 225).

Clearly, Hershey has bought into the written and cinematic tradition of
the Magdalene the portrayal of a multi-layered prostitute, which of
course makes for a much juicier dramatic portrayal than if she had been a
compliant silent woman, rumored to have a past, following the male
disciples at a respectful distance.

Gunn and Exum have each compared the biblical David and Bathsheba narratives with their visual interpretations. Gunn's cultural study
encompasses medieval *Books of Hours*, and the Fifties Hollywood film
David and Bathsheba (1951), starring Gregory Peck and Susan Hayward,
and the popular ephemera that accompanied it. Exum analyzes both still
visual images, particularly the paintings of the naked Bathsheba in her
bath by Rembrandt, van Haarlem, Maratti, and van Aachen; and also
the Hayward/Peck film and Bruce Beresford's *King David* (1985), with
Richard Gere as a thoroughly modern king. While both these excellent
critics use recent feminist theories of the gaze in analyzing interpretations
of Bathsheba, both as King David sees her and as the camera and the
spectator see her, they seem to be spectatorial captives of the power of
the gaze. That is, they dare not look away, nor do they question that the
gaze is universal, through the sight lines of a heterosexual woman or man.
Such an acceptance of an ideal spectator leaves the analysis essentialistic.

My own interest in the connection between biblical narrative and
American filmmaking started before I knew there was more to film than a
story. First along my journey of analysis were the sword and sandal films,
when my gaze rested upon the eye candy of Cecil B. deMille. He recognized before many of us were born that there was gold in the Bible, that
consumers would gaze time after time, ticket after ticket, at biblical
figures projected large as dreams on the big screen. DeMille was a canny
marketer too. He understood that, hiding beneath the supposed authenticity of the biblical world, he could have his cake and his sentiment too.
The female characters were able to wear the gossamer revealing costumes
that the Hayes Commission disallowed in storylines that costumed ordinary women. But even the Hayes Commission was not willing to argue

with the portrayal of biblical women as seducers and temptresses of the men who would follow God. Thus Bathsheba and Salomé had to be rehabilitated in the final pious reel.

In working with the theories of the gaze, it is necessary but tortuous to switch the gaze, to turn the head, to refuse to look where the camera is coaxing you, the spectator-interpreter. Perhaps comparing Raymond Massey's grumpy prophet Nathan, whose irritation with God's favorite Gregory Peck, turns to vitriol after the nasty business with Susan Hayward, would be instructive. The tension between the two actors reveals a very different male gaze from each one: David's is the intimate lover's gaze; Nathan's the forbidding moralistic 'Production Code' gaze.

In that same *Semeia* volume I was guilty also of allowing myself to be transfixed by the gaze, instead of fixing my own spectatorial limits, as I gazed at Salomé. While writing 'Calling the Shots: Directing Salomé's Dance of Death', I thought about a homosexual gaze, I thought about a disinterested gaze, but I blinked while I was juggling them, thus dropping the alternate gaze, and followed a linear argument, one that traced one sort of gaze from the biblical period, through the medieval, encompassing the Victorian/Wildean Salomé, and ending with the Rita Hayworth film portrayal. Naturally, I found Wilde's verbal portrait far more erotic than Hayworth's good-girl Salomé cheerleader of the Fifties. But while I acknowledged Wilde's homosexual gaze, I did not carry a homoerotic possibility over to the Cold-War cinematic version.

There are a number of research volumes that will prove helpful to the scholar wanting to get background on film; among them is Campbell and Pitts's, *The Bible on Film* (1981). This book gives brief descriptions of films from Hebrew Bible and New Testament narratives. The book ends with films made in 1980. One caveat is that a number of the early films described here are no longer in existence, so don't get your hopes up about tracking down the 1909 Vitagraph *Saul and David*. The book does provide interest, however, in seeing the number of early films devoted to Samson and Salomé. Clearly, these are characters whose narratives caught the imagination of the earliest filmmakers.

Shadows of the Bible in Film

The second current has been formed by a wave of biblicists and scholars of that broader epithet, 'religious studies', using biblical tropes as heuristic tools in analyzing films. While I understand Owens' claim that allegory in a postmodern sense exists 'in the gap between a present and a past' (Owens 1983: 68), I have trouble reconciling my own readerly location in this gap between sign and meaning with the biblical texts, where sign and meaning overlap. Too often the comparisons between contemporary films and biblical tropes in recent collections attempt such a false unity, one that bridges an unbridgeable gap. I find McLemore's attempt to trace this connection between filmic and social representation in David Lynch's surrealistic film *Blue Velvet* (1986) compelling on a theoretical level, that is, where she presents the various contemporary concepts of allegory, as well as the reactions to Lynch's complex and elusive work. However, I do not think she presents as sophisticated an understanding of the codes in the biblical narratives in her discussion of the possible allegorical interpretation of *Blue Velvet* as 'Christian typology, replete with Jeffrey as the angelic choirboy, Adam in the garden, and Sandy as his Eve' (McLemore 1995: 136). Nowhere does she admit to the 'over the top' quality of such an interpretation.

Biblicist Bernard Scott's *Hollywood Dreams and Biblical Stories* is a parade example of tropic hermeneutics. Scott's Table of Contents provides a clue to the matrix of his vision, especially titles such as 'From Graven Image to Dream Factory', 'The Poor You Always Have with You', and 'Loss of Innocence'. My biggest difficulty with Scott's argument is that I got bogged down in the vast unexplored territory that separates the biblical world from which he draws his trope and the film in which he finds the trope. All of Western culture and knowledge is situated in that world. Try as I might, I could not find the road that Scott had used to lead from Jerusalem to Hollywood, from graven image to dream factory. It seems fair to suggest that Hollywood is particularly a world of graven images, of icons, of gods erupting from celluloid, and that the Bible is certainly a dream factory, one that may have been in business longer than any other in the Western world.

Scott's most successful chapter is 'From the Destruction of the Temple to *Mad Max*', a discussion of biblical apocalypticism, particularly in Matthew and Mark, and science-fiction imagery. While I think some of his film analyses are cursory at best, especially his treatment of *Metropolis* (1926), with its tempting Eve/Eden motifs, and *Blade Runner* (1982), the chapter illustrates the real plus to a cinematic reading by a biblical scholar. Scott gives a credible reading to *Mad Max Beyond Thunderdome* (1985), connecting it as a part of the sci/fi genre dedication to global destruction, doom, and dewy-damp rebirth. Then he gives a marvelous thumbnail of recent New Testament criticism focusing upon the dark warnings from the Gospels. I may well be missing Scott's intentions, but I long for a genuine connection, of character, of plot, something more than proclamations of doom two thousand years apart.

Now Scott is certainly not the only biblical scholar to hitch his Bible to the Hollywood sign. When one is teaching a Bible and Film course, any of the following volumes will give students the requisite background to spark discussion. The books of Holloway (1977), Kreitzer (1993, 1994), and Miles (1996) all climb similar scaffolding, that is, either biblical echoes in contemporary films, or a reading of the appropriation of a biblical narrative into a biblical epic film. Kreitzer's two books are the weakest, mere retelling of the filmic plots, pointing out where they differ from the written biblical narratives. Miles gives a strong theoretical grounding, with a focus on the desirability of cultural readings, but most of her readings seem vague to me, putting the films in service to some meta-topic of 'religious thought'. I would recommend her book for students to get a sense of how one might think about film in a religious-studies context. I personally found the tone annoying, as though the author had already tried to explain things to me several times. But that artificial simplicity may work well with some undergraduates.

Babington takes this genre, called sword and sandal films in the industry, a bit further, and his work is thus instructive, for he connects the culture and the politics of the Fifties with the genre he is examining. As Babington points out many times over, the use of the biblical narrative by the Fifties dream-spinners had much more to do with the end of World War II and the pre-eminence of the USA and the Soviet Union in the Cold War. The American Fifties of homemaking and prosperity was yoked to the fear of Communism that pervades both domestic politics and foreign policy. The vast majority of religious studies readers/spectators of film feel obliged to find fragments of Jesus or biblical morality behind every camera lens. They would do better, in my opinion, to move away from such New Critical analysis, and find the cultural engine that spits out Bible movies, so certain about right and honor and God on our side. In spite of or perhaps because of the Production Code that had maintained stringent control over Hollywood productions since 1934, a group of religious Protestants and Catholics censored films to make sure that they were 'clean family entertainment'. For more than three decades these men tried to incorporate their theological values into the very marrow of movie making. And what could reflect righteous purity more than the Bible itself? And what could be more protective for the assimilationist Jews of Hollywood who produced much of Hollywood's American myth than the Christianized biblical epics, where the theology was more America as God's chosen people in God's chosen land than any biblical version of chosenness? Delighted with celluloid Scripture, the Hays Commission overlooked the half-naked stars, suggestive dancing, and frequent passionate embraces in the sword and sandal films—after all, that was how people, especially pagans, behaved in those days.

Most of these films were produced for the Fifties American culture by Hollywood power-brokers who created other America first and best myths too. Hollywood was under siege by the anti-Communist madness, a time when accusations without proof were immediately granted the status of truth, when guilt was assumed, and innocence had to be documented. Of all cultural scholars looking at the biblical epics of the Fifties, surely the power of the right-wing politicians to give or withhold 'clearance [of accused actors, directors, writers] required repudiating all liberal opinions and associations, former Communist, were required to perform a humiliating public ritual of expiation by naming names of other Hollywood Communists' (Sklar 1994: 266). In a time when any ideas outside the picket-fence norm were being challenged, what could be safer than the certainty of the Bible? The iconoclasm of the class comedies of the Thirties, the violence and shabby good guys of *film noir* were abandoned. The Forties feminist working girls and Jezebels played by Joan Crawford, Bette Davis, and Katharine Hepburn were replaced by the soda fountains and pony tails of Annette Funicello, Doris Day, and Debbie Reynolds. No one in Hollywood was willing to take the slightest chance on anybody or anything. Safety, caution, and respectability were the watchwords of the studio chiefs, and controversial or even serious subject matter was avoided at all costs. The Bible itself was prettified: Salomé became a devout Christian after trying to save the Baptist; Bathsheba married her David in an extravagant wedding with an overwrought choir singing Psalms. As Sklar argues so well (1994: 268), in describing the fear-ridden days in Hollywood, the filmmakers

> dared not make a movie that might arouse the ire of anyone… As a result they lost touch both with their own past styles and with the changes and movements in the dominant culture at large. Let it not be said that television killed the movie industry: the movie industry must take that responsibility itself.[1]

Charles Ketcham's (1992) piece, '*One Flew Over the Cuckoo's Nest*: A Salvific Drama of Liberation' had its ups and downs for me. At the outset

---

1. Navasky's history of the McCarthy era, *Naming Names* (1980), gives an excellent, clearly partisan, analysis of this terror-ridden time. See also Carmen (1966) and Randall (1968). Sklar (1994) has helpful notes on sources in his cultural history of American filmmaking; Baugh's (1997) general bibliography on religion and film is excellent; his bibliography on Jesus films is very helpful, especially for French and Italian critical sources.

I should say that aside from his religiosity, Ketcham's work in general is some of the best in finding the religious patterns in film. His work on Ingmar Bergman and Frederico Fellini is illuminating and opens up new avenues for discussion for religionists. In his analysis of Milos Forman's *One Flew Over the Cuckoo's Nest* (1975) I certainly agreed with Ketcham's characterization of the American audience's appetite for explorations of freedom and human dignity often obtained through violence, and with his observation that the Forman film is more nuanced than the Kesey novel from which it is drawn. However, treating the Jack Nicholson character McMurphy as the Suffering Servant is too romantic for me. Ketcham argues that McMurphy has been crucified by lobotomy:

> Chief Bromden, seeing the stigmata, holds McMurphy in a position reminiscent of the Pieta. Saying 'You're coming with me', the chief suffocates the persecuted body, pulls the great marble stone water dispenser out of the floor releasing fountains of 'living water', hurls it through a window and escapes. The jubilation in the ward has all the ringing affirmation of the shouts 'He is Risen!' (1992: 148).

Silenced by those in power, the Nicholson character is a martyr, but hardly Christ, whose death and resurrection overturned the powers and principalities forever. That is quite a leap from the victim McMurphy, whose cinematic death is anticlimactic after the lobotomy. Further, Ketcham suggests other Christocentric imagery that seems extreme—for instance, that the patients ingest their daily meds as though they were receiving the Eucharist. In spite of the temptation to draw straight lines from the Christ story to the *Cuckoo's Nest*, that is just too hard for me to swallow.

Which Way is West?

Tramping through the tropes related to Bible in film, I found myself surprised only twice: that the rich genres of American Western and *film noir* have been ignored, or at best underused. With the exception of Baugh's superb analysis of *Shane* (1953), I have not encountered many trenchant analyses of Westerns, in spite of their tantalizing, one might say Manichean, outlook on human nature. Probably the best study of the Western from a theoretical perspective is Tompkins' *West of Everything* (1992). I particularly recommend her understanding of the finitude of the landscape in the Western—as opposed to the mythic shift to infinite space in the hero-action films that followed, where the hero rode a rocket ship instead of a Palomino. The desert location, she argues, is like the world before Eden—dry, dusty, no people, no trees, brutal. I would push the analogy further to say that the desert landscape sounds like YHWH's punishment to Adam: rife with thistles, unyielding, sweated ground. The location for Everyman seeking to live a moral life resists him; the horizon recedes forever beneath the sky:

> The desert pushes the consciousness of the hero and the reader/viewer beyond itself and into another realm... It is not only the body that is tested here; the desert is a spiritual proving ground as well. The landscape, which on the one hand drives Christianity away, ends by forcing men to see something godlike there (Tompkins 1992: 85).

I tend to read with Tompkins over Baugh in the Western hero as Christ figure argument. He tends toward an honorable hero, who looks to do the right thing for the world, to protect women and children. Tompkins sees the hero as loner, isolated from other human beings, not part of the social structure. While that notion might leave the impression that Tompkins and Baugh are splitting hairs, there is a further, crucial bifurcation. Baugh understands the hero to be the suffering servant of the badlands, sacrificing himself for humankind, while Tompkins situates the hero in this life, only concerned with keeping the peace on the range, in the saloon, at the garrison. He is not looking toward an afterlife, but only a well-ordered roundup and a patient wife in bonnet and gingham, so different from the rustling silks of the saloon gal. The Western hero assured us of harmony between human beings and even an unforgiving stretch of nature. The male hero suppresses feeling, kills when he must, and seems to walk through the mythic landscape without relating to woman, to Indians, or even to his horse. Similar to biblical story-telling, the focus on the hero, his code of conduct, and his standard of judgment, the story is expected to influence the audience's moral beliefs.

A topic that needs further exploration in the Western is the minor role that women play, not unlike the helper/facilitator female character found in many biblical narratives. The hero's aspirations in the Western have little to do with the domestic life overseen by women. For the hero to admit to feelings and frailties would be to admit parity with other characters, particularly women, and to jeopardize his status as potent being. Silence functions in much the same way as in the biblical narrative; it preserves the mystery of the ineffable self, it protects the silent one from inspection and possible criticism by offering nothing for the audience to grab hold of. Silence in the Bible is often interpreted as obedience, as in the case of Noah listening to God. Imagine the difference if Adam had not proclaimed to God, 'She did it, the woman whom you gave to me' (Gen. 3.12). His dialogue diminishes him. In the Western it is usually the woman who is seen to crumble through a mixture of dialogue and tears:

> Even Marian, Joe Starett's wife in *Shane*, one of the few women in Western films who, we are made to feel, is also substantial as a person, dissolves into an ineffectual harangue at the end, unsuccessfully pleading with her man not to go into town to get shot. When the crunch comes, women shatter into words (Tompkins 1992: 63).

Rushing's trenchant analysis in 'Evolution of "The New Frontier" in *Alien and Aliens*' (1995), traces the development of the rich imagery of the feminine presence in the background of the Western as helpmate, mother, captive of the Indians, and schoolmarm to the powerful feminine archetype, as portrayed by Sigourney Weaver as Ripley in *Alien/s*. This article has been particularly useful to me because of Rushing's understanding that the surface feminist appearance of the film is not the whole story:

> The dominant text of *Alien/s* subverts patriarchal consciousness (as represented by the military, the bureaucracy, and frontier exploitation), introduces the feminine descent and revenge motif into the New Frontier, and provides an appealing heroine; thus, it appears to reaffirm the feminine principle. A close examination of the subtext, however, discloses that the story mixes the feminine descent and revenge motifs with the more familiar ego-hero myth (1995: 104-105).

Another product of the Fifties postwar mindset, the science-fiction genre has provided great interest to religionists. I have found that several articles which consider myth and morality in film to have a direct connection with religion. My main concern with this sort of link is that it presents a false sense of unity of thought, as though there is a direct line that connects all dualistic presentations of good and evil, beginning with biblical representations. Andrew Gordon's article on *Star Wars* does not look into the morality of victory through violence, which is the backbone of Lucas's trilogy. It is the hawkish morality of the Western with lasers/phasers instead of six-shooters. However, Gordon's work is a fine example of reading the popular Fifties cultural world with the film and Lucas's connections with the comic-book heroes of his own childhood: Flash Gordon, Terry and the Pirates, Buck Rogers, and all those *pow-wham-zam* Marvel comic heroes (Gordon 1995: 76-77).

More than reflecting a relationship between good and evil, *Star Wars* shares with the rest of the genre a mythic vision of the relationship between humanity and technology at a time when that relationship had crucial bearing on the future of American society and the entire Western world. A more precise example of the genre than *Star Wars* as an American epic film is Kubrick's *2001: A Space Odyssey* (1968). In the interest of fairness, I should award equal time to George Lucas, who has acknowledged:

> I didn't want to make *2001*. I wanted to make a fantasy that was more in the genre of Edgar Rice Burroughs, that whole other end of space fantasy that was there before science took it over in the fifties. Once the atomic bomb came…they forgot the fairy tales and the dragons and Tolkien and all the real heroes (1977: 43).

Former *Christian Century* editor James Wall's article gives a first-rate background on the reception of *2001* and has some excellent analysis. His characterization of Stanley Kubrick as a modern-day Henry Adams is a literary *coup*, and illuminates the existential quest of both artists: 'Like Henry Adams, who found meaning in the concrete achievements of the building of magnificent church structures, Kubrick celebrates the tangible' (Wall 1992: 43). Moreover, Wall is comfortable amid the complexity of a film like *2001* and shows well the conflict in a man who wants to believe in the ultimate and yet is trapped in the mindset of modernism.

Both *2001* and another classic Kubrick film, *Dr. Stangelove or How I Learned to Stop Worrying and Love the Bomb* (1964), focus upon human predilection for designing machinery that functions with perfect logic to bring about a disastrous outcome. The US nuclear deterrent and the Russian doomsday machine function exactly as they are intended, and destroy life on earth. The computer HAL 9000 in *2001* serves the space mission by attacking the astronauts.

Sadly, Kubrick's *Dr. Strangelove* does not seem dated or irrelevant forty years after its release. Peter Sellers in one of his bravura three-for-one performances plays the multiple roles of Dr Strangelove, Captain Mandrake, and President Merkin Muffley. My favorite scene features George C. Scott, whose character, General Buck Turgidson, is informing the President that it is quite likely a B-52 bomber will be able to fly under Russian radar and deliver its payload even though the entire Soviet air force knows where the plane is headed. 'He can barrel in that baby so low!' Scott says, with his arms spread wide like wings, and his head shaking in admiration at how good his pilots are. While such performances parading the staggering US military might are now found on the evening news and all day long on cable, military and civilian player alike too often reflect the lunatic performances of Sellars and Scott.

When the black comedy was released, according to Terry Southern, who was hired by Kubrick to rewrite the script of *Dr. Strangelove*:

> Columbia was embarrassed by the picture and tried to get people to see Carl Foreman's *The Victors* instead. They would steer ticket buyers away from *Strangelove* and try to get them to see *The Victors*. At the time we thought we were going to be totally wiped out. People would call up the box office and be told there were no seats for *Strangelove* and asked if they would like to see *The Victors* instead. Gradually, the buzz along the rialto built word of mouth in our favor.[2]

One can understand the executives at Columbia Pictures being nervous about portraying mad, over-the-top Pentagon types with glazed grins and shining eyes, trembling with excitement about world destruction and apocalypse. The end of the film trembles with the uncertainty of the Cold War: after the first nuclear blast, Kubrick cuts back to the War Room, where Strangelove muses that deep mines could be used to shelter survivors, whose descendants could return to the surface in 90 years. The film abruptly ends in a too familiar montage of mushroom clouds, while Vera Lynn sings, 'We'll Meet Again'. These sugary lyrics underscore the death-dealing, ironic vision of Kubrick:

> We'll meet again, don't know where, don't know when,
> But I'm sure we'll meet again some sunny day.
> Keep smiling through, just the way you used to do,
> Till the blue skies chase the dark clouds far away.[3]

Another Kubrick political film was made when the director was only thirty-one years old. Using blacklisted screenwriters, Kubrick openly defied the Hollywood studio heads. With an intelligent screenplay by then-blacklisted writer Dalton Trumbo (from a novel by semi-blacklisted writer Howard Fast), its message of moral integrity and courageous conviction is still quite powerful. The all-star cast (including Charles Laughton in plus-size toga) is full of entertaining surprises. Fully restored in 1991 to include scenes deleted from the original 1960 release, the full-length *Spartacus* is a grand-scale cinematic marvel, offering some of the most stunningly choreographed battles ever filmed and a central

2. <http://www.altx.com/interviews/terry.southern.html>. *The Victors* (1963) is Foreman's weighty, but ultimately unsatisfying study of the Second World War. He gathered a formidable cast for the story, which follows a US infantry unit through the latter part of the war. Although Albert Finney, George Hamilton, Melina Mercouri, and Jeanne Moreau were in the cast, the film collapsed under its own weight.
3. 'Til We Meet Again', written by Ross Parker and Hughie Charles, was a big-band hit of the era of World War II, making the musical reference even more pointed.

performance by Kirk Douglas that's as sensitively emotional as it is intensely heroic. Jean Simmons plays the slave woman who becomes Spartacus's wife, and Peter Ustinov steals the show with his frequently hilarious, Oscar-winning performance as a slave trader who shamelessly curries favor with his Roman superiors. Not incidentally the restored version (1991) includes a formerly deleted bathhouse scene in which Laurence Olivier plays a bisexual Roman senator (with restored dialogue dubbed by Anthony Hopkins) who gets very sweaty over a muscle-beach slave, played by Tony Curtis.

The Wrap

In the light of videos, broadband, and all matter of creation, delivery, and distribution of visual media, many of the films that I have considered here reflect a politics and propaganda of an earlier era. In the time of broadband one can create a 30-second political film and distribute it across the world in a matter of hours. One need no longer plead for underwriters, try to seduce stars and co-stars to join the project, and finally spend millions on pre-distribution marketing. If filmmaking apparatus functioned as a prosthetic equivalent for the human eye, representing a type of cyborgism that stands for the spectator's own vision, then the broadband world allows every spectator to mediate the sort of spectatorial reciprocity that one had in a minimal fashion between the characters on the screen and in film or TV. As the 2004 Presidential campaigns have shown us, everyone can twist their ideology into a Woody Woodpecker cartoon or tape from a Presidential news conference. Any familiar image can be co-opted in the service of political or religious ideology.

More critical study needs to be done in order to analyze the directors and studios for their political ideologies reflected in American films before the broadband era. In this chapter I have formulated an argument about the relationships between biblical narratives and popular culture. The films I have analyzed represent ways in which the culture has influenced religious traditions and values in order to present a view of a particular population. The broadband suggests a kaleidoscopic set of infinite opportunities for the spectatorial eye to open even wider.

4

THE POLITICS OF THE BIBLICALLY CORRECT: BOOKS, FILMS, AND VIDEOS

How do you sell any product, company, or idea? In marketing media, you search for a buyer, a target, who loves your book, your film, your video. When your book is the Bible and your product is Jesus, your targets are people who are already wired for success. As recently as the 'turbulent Sixties', a familiar cliché to those who collect media mantras, it seemed clear that secularism was going to drown out the voices of religiosity in Europe and the US. However, before one could say 1976 and Jimmy Carter, the world of evangelical Christianity was center stage. A militant piety had erupted in every major faith, dragging God and religion back to center stage from the sidelines to which they had been relegated. It was the militant and Orthodox version of Islam as understood by the Ayatollah Khoumeni that removed Carter from office and replaced him with the great salesman of the Evangelicals Ronald Reagan. Despite the arguments of politicians and intellectuals, people all over the world have demonstrated that they want to see more religion in public life. The various fundamentalist ideologies show a worrying disenchantment with modernity and globalization.

Popular media has become the place where the politics of the biblically correct have fought their battles. In *Glorious Appearing*, the final volume of the Left Behind series, millions of Jews call the authorities frantically at the last minute, trying to convert. Author Tim LaHaye, one of the founders of Jerry Falwell's Moral Majority, describes himself as an 'unashamed conservative'.[1] 'The world doesn't have the answers', he says, 'Jesus does. There is reason to believe Christ could come in this genera-

1. The former co-chairman of Jack Kemp's presidential campaign, LaHaye was a member of the original board of directors of the Moral Majority and an organizer of the Council for National Policy, which ABCNews.com has called 'the most powerful conservative organization in America you've never heard of ', and whose membership has included John Ashcroft, Tommy Thompson, and Oliver North. George W. Bush is still refusing to release a tape of a speech he gave to the group in 1999.

tion more than any other.' While they wait, LaHaye and his co-author Jerry B. Jenkins are planning a prologue to the series and a sequel in which Christ does battle with Satan one last time. Seeing through a glass darkly never looked so profitable.[2]

The top books on the *New York Times* bestsellers list since 2002 are consistently spiritually based. As a plot line the Christian Right's expansion on the New Testament Apocalypse has replaced spy and cold-war dramas.

Not all entries, however, are as blatantly Christian as the exhausting Left Behind series. The 2003 book, *The Five People You Meet in Heaven*, according to its author Mitch Albom, was not written as a *religious* book. Both publisher and author are overtly nervous that appealing to one group might cut sales to another. Removing the brand name of religion from their product has resulted in great success: in less than a year the book has sold almost four million copies and has been widely adopted by churches and synagogues because they find within it 'something that relates'.[3] There are subtly faith-oriented messages that can be pulled from TV shows like *Touched by an Angel* or *Joan of Arcadia*, and yet none of those products mention Jesus, Allah, or any other religious figure else. Like *Five People*, these new media battles with the powers of darkness are denominationally vague, promoting the idea that heaven is more than a place, it is an answer. Rather than talking of God's grace, Albom seeks to explain the unexpected connections of our lives as well as Heaven and other possible mysteries, all washed clean of specific religious definition.[4]

Popular herself as the intellectual's link to God is Karen Armstrong, who has a dispassionate way of guiding one through the spirals of Christianity, Judaism, and Islam. A former nun who now claims only an inner spirituality, Armstrong makes religion safe for discussion. Note how she maneuvers among incendiary issues:

2. Within hours of its release, the *Glorious Appearing* shot to number 1 on Amazon. com's bestseller list. Tyndale House, publisher of the series, has already shipped 2 million copies—not overly optimistic, considering that the other 11 books have sold more than 40 million copies, and that's not counting the audio books, the young adult series or the comic books.

3. Mitch Albom, quoted in *Entertainment Weekly* (16 April 2004). Besides *The Five People You Meet in Heaven* (2003), Albom wrote *Tuesdays with Morrie* (2002). He is an award-winning sports reporter for ESPN and *The Detroit Free Press*.

4. For those people who have not or may never read this book, I shall provide a clue to Albom's concept of heaven: heaven is not a lush Garden of Eden, but a place where your earthly life is explained to you by five people who were in it. These people may have been loved ones or distant strangers, yet each of them changed your path forever.

Even in the United States, where secularism has been very good for religion, many in rural areas feel belittled and colonized by the ethos of the academic and political elite. Indeed, arguably the first modern fundamentalist movement was developed among US Protestants in the newly industrialized northeastern cities during World War I, when it became apparent that science could be applied with lethal effect to modern weaponry. The terror and alienation of fundamentalist Protestantism is shown in its apocalyptic vision, which sees the world as so wicked and perverted that God has to smash it in a final, fearful cataclysm. Even the benign institutions of modernity—international organizations like the League of Nations and more modern groups like the United Nations, the European Union, and the World Council of Churches—are seen as infected by the Devil or the Antichrist. More generally, fundamentalists are haunted by a fear of anything approaching world government. The global village is a threat to their identity, and without this singularity they are nothing (2004: 13).

I would add to Armstrong's pithy analysis that the biblically correct phenomenon is fueled by a feeling that there has to be more to life than materialism—and by people who are simply scared and miserable. The books' fans have a simpler explanation. They uniformly praise the books' blend of action and a fundamentalist interpretation of the prophecies in the book of Revelation. 'They're entertaining. They deal with good versus evil', says Steve Smith, a forklift operator at a San Diego Costco. 'These books are nothing less than the fulfillment of biblical prophecy. Jesus is absolutely coming back to earth.'[5]

Unhealthy VeggieTales: Freeze-Dried Faith for Children

Before attending graduate school I wrote a series of books for young children about twin bears. These books had no connection with religion, Bible, God, or aspects of faith, although my books wrestled with many of the problems that continue to confront those who construct religious media for children: how to depict gender, race, ethnicity, how to break down social and sexual stereotyping. Publishers and packagers show little desire to test stereotypes for the benefit of world harmony—rather they want to market their universal product to every demographic group. One size fits all.

One of the timeless ways to avoid gender identification has been to use animal characters, since as we all know storybook animals from Peter Rabbit to the Cat in the Hat or Barney have no sexual organs. Many the

5.   <http://www.leftbehind.com/channelbooks.asp?pageid=171&channelID=46>.

times my editor, illustrator, and I would have fervent discussions about
the propriety of showing Mother and Father Bear without clothes. *Bare*.
The deal we cut was that the little bears could bound around in the buff,
but Mother Bear would wear a frilly apron and Father Bear would wear
overalls. Aunt Bear, a gender-defying bear, wears a huge hat with edible
fruit on it although she lives outdoors and catches salmon in her bare
paws. The little bears are without sex but loaded with gender. Both
nominally possessing Y-chromosomes, one wants to be the smartest bear
in the world, his brother likes to cook and eat and sleep. Although not
visibly marked with sexuality, the brother bears' characters contrast with
markers usually connected to gender: one is s smart, decisive, active. The
other is passive, nurturing, and cuddly. The twins are the same and different, too.

Twenty years later, those who package culture and religion for children have solved the problem of bears being a bit too bare. A best-selling
Bible video series for young children is cast with computer-animated raw
vegetables. That's right, we have thrown out the bears with the bath
water. Now we have tomatoes, cucumbers, a couple of mouthy asparagus,
with boys' names, a girly carrot named Laura, and the nefarious enemy
Veggies, which look like plump peas and sound like Maurice Chevalier
with butter sauce, in an uncanny preview of the current rash of Franco-
phobia.

Oddly enough, there are many F words that come to mind to describe
religious material culture for children: fluffy, fruffy, fancy, frumpy, flippant, funky, frustrating, frivolous. Let us review some of the market stars.
Fully posable action figures abound: everybody from Daniel, two resin
lions, and Nebuchadnezzar upon a royal throne (in a pack with Michael
the Archangel); David and Goliath; Jesus; Moses with the Command-
ments; Samson (with, again, a lion); there are no action figures that I
have been able to find of the prophets or the Gospel writers. There are so
many varieties of Noah's Ark, from plush to resin to leather, that one
could start life with a Noah's Ark mobile over the crib, and enter kinder-
garten wearing a Noah backpack, with the giraffe's head peeking over
your shoulder. There are plush Easter bears, bar mitzvah bears, baptism
bears. Catholic-opoly is a religious board game. According to the game
instructions pack, the goal of the game is not to accumulate wealth, but
to build as many churches and cathedrals as possible in order to spread
the Word of the Lord. Apparently players will also learn Scriptures and
Church history. In addition, the game addresses financial management as
well as charity and tithing. Game tokens include an angel, ark, chalice,
donkey, dove, and fish. The drawing cards are 'Faith' and 'Community

Service'. My favorite entry is a Catholic version of the children's card game Go Fish, renamed 'Go to the Grotto'. This game features full-color images of Mary from many cultures and time periods, ranging from the classic Pieta and Our Lady of Guadalupe to a seven-year-old Mary visiting Elizabeth.

In my opinion the mega-popular, mega-pious VeggieTales should be coded with another F word: foolish. The Veggietarian creators combine rock, jazz, and funk music with plenty of treacly dialogue, resulting in stew that evokes a naughty F word from me. These biblical crudités for kids attempt to present moral questions in a snappy cartoon format, familiar to children, who are meant to absorb the morals painlessly. In our present media ambience, where books, movies, videos, and spin-off merchandise circulate concurrently, the Veggies have outgrown their small patch of evangelical Christian ground, where they were first seeded, and seem to be harvested in every secular outlet from eBay to Wal-mart. These generic vegetable rep players are not nourishing anybody's religious life: rather they are emblematic of a culture desirous of avoiding troublesome moral obligation.

The most confounding question for me involves the *why* of Veggies as super-successful books, films, videos, songs, plus toys, tee-shirts, keychains, and a host of other merchandise. These mass-produced, heavily marketed, biblically based products seem antithetical to the 'live simply' dicta of traditional Christianity. Perhaps it is a question of giddy spirituality rather than a concern with meanings and interpretations within biblical narratives.

Veggie versions of Curly and Moe, Bob the Tomato and Larry the Cucumber, narrate most of these Christian-lite lessons. Bob's omniscient voice is that of his creator: Phil Vischer, whose confessional bio is enough to make one believe in holy capitalism. Take a headed-for-trouble guy who was kicked out of a Minnesota Bible college for missing too many chapel services, give him some cash borrowed from friends and family, and let's call his company Big Idea Productions. In a spare bedroom of his parents' house, working on one computer, Vischer and his college roommate and partner Mike Nawrocki (who gives voice to Larry the Cucumber) 'dreamed up a collection of vegetable personalities because it would be technologically easier—and cheaper—to animate characters who didn't have arms, legs, or clothing'.[6] Tossed out of the same college at the

6. Gilbreath's article provides some background on Vischer: 'His unique pedigree supports that conviction. His mother is a professor of child development and Christian education at Wheaton College; his dad was an advertising executive and

same time as Vischer, Nawrocki is every bit as confident as his partner. 'We wanted to create characters that were sort of reflections of our own personalities', Nawrocki says. 'Phil and Bob are both very driven, while Larry and myself are a bit more laid back. They are sort of extreme versions of who we are in real life' (Gilbreath 2002).

Like their creators, the Veggies act like stereotypical little boys as well. At first blush, it would seem that vegetables simply erase the gender questions. But aside from the carrot-girl, all the main characters are male down to their roots; since the stories focus upon Joshua, David, Daniel, the usual boy-centered biblical figures, the putatively non-gendered Veggies are as markedly male—active, assertive, brave—as their earlier biblical counterparts, and as their creators. *Tie him up and beat him up and throw him out of Babylon!*

Vischer prophesied that 2002 would be the year his company 'exploded into the marketplace'. With the release of new video titles, a live stage show, and the full-length animated feature film *Jonah: A VeggieTales Movie* (a $14 million production that opened in 1200 theaters in October 2002), it's hard to doubt him. Big Idea has never been secretive about its ultimate aim: 'To markedly enhance the moral and spiritual fabric of our society through creative media' and ultimately to become 'the most trusted of the top four family media brands', the others being Disney, Nickelodeon and Dreamworks. When speaking to Christian audiences, Phil Vischer sounds even more ambitious: 'We want to change the world' (Gilbreath 2002).

Jim Hill, a columnist for the online publication *Digital Media FX*, has gushed about the sophistication and humor of Big Idea's productions: 'So what is it that makes the programs that Big Idea puts out so entertaining to right-minded religious folks as well as heathens like myself?', he wrote. 'It's simple, really. Not since the late Charles Schulz was working at the top of his game while drawing his acclaimed "Peanuts" comic strip has there been something that was this silly but profound' (<http://www. digitalmediafx. com>).

Caution: Profound is a stretch. Let me give a quick run-through of a few of these stories, each of which focuses upon a child's formless fears. A child who feels too small to be effective or special (that would be David, or Shadrack, Meshack, Abedneggo, the salad bowl trio); a child who is

"an amazing storyteller". His mothers's grandfather was the Rev. R.R. Brown, a legendary radio preacher from Omaha whom Billy Graham once claimed as a major inspiration. His father's father was a "world-traveling industrialist" who helped build what was once the world's largest tire retreading business.'

afraid of the unknown (that would be Daniel), and a pious bean who is obedient to God in spite of the jokes made at his expense (that would be Joshua).

One egregious nutritional video, *Rack Shack & Benny: A Lesson in Handling Peer Pressure*, a Daniel redux, focuses upon one of the most powerful F phrases, *following the fellas*. (I use the masculine pronoun for visually, vegetally genderless Larry because his voice sounds boyish [and squeaky as a mouse] and he 'acts like a boy'. Did I really say that?) There's trouble brewing at the Nezzer Chocolate Factory! (Any resemblance to the renowned children's novelist Roald Dahl stops right there.) To celebrate the sale of their two millionth chocolate bunny, company president Nebby K. Nezzer, a capitalist to warm the hearts of any good entrepreneur, announces that his workers can eat as many bunnies as they like! Three boys named Rack, Shack, and Benny (played by Bob, Larry, and Junior Asparagus) remember that their parents taught them not to eat too much candy. Can the boys do what's right even when all their friends are doing something else? And why is Mr Nezzer building a 90-foot tall chocolate bunny? Rack, Shack, and Benny are about to find out just how risky it can be to stand up for what you believe. Despite the fairly witty transformation of Nebuchadnezzar's *treyf* food into sweets, the image of the chocolate bunny reduces the awesome biblical golden statue to something trivial, in a word, foolish. What are children to do with this 'retelling' of the story? From a vivid, compelling image of faith, Vischer and Nawrocki breed a garden of verse in which very little is at stake, and the message has become totally blurred and even secularized.

In *Josh and the Big Wall*, Larry the Cucumber has overslept, affording us the opportunity of meeting the plucky Junior Asparagus, who narrates the story of the wall of Jericho with the help of our usual MC, Bob the Tomato. We follow Josh, who has taken over for Moses, another of those plump gourdish prophets. Josh leads the Israelite gourds and squashes to the Promised Land. In their way is the city of Jericho, full of nasty French peas armed with purple slushies to soak the Veggies. Focusing on being obedient to God's wishes, as all these videos do, our Veggies endure the purple slush and eventually cook the ethnic peas. The Joshua retelling underscores the importance of obedience, a concept with which most kids are all too familiar. Marching in circles instead of hurling goop at the peas, the Israelites win and take over Jericho. Again, the trivialization of a story full of pith and majesty renders it ludicrous, I believe. When the child who has seen this version of the fall of Jericho finally does come upon the original, will she immediately flash back to Israelite gourds and Philistine peas, as we flash to Charlton Heston and Yul

Brenner? Could any viewer, child or adult, take seriously a bunch of power-washed gourds representing the chosen of God?

Particularly unpleasant in my opinion is *Dave and the Giant Pickle*, which pits a very small greenish yellow sprouty Veggie, more squash than gourd, complete with starched kaffiyah, against a warty green aged cucumber Goliath. Again *très* French, especially odd, since he represents a Philistine. Little David is twitted for his smallness by his squash and gourd brothers. He is good for nothing except to be a shepherd to some Mr Whippy-looking sheep. Even the drawing and animation skills are low-budget, beneath the sophistication of twenty-first-century children acquainted with the pixar fantasies of Industrial Light and Magic and Dreamworks.[7] After Goliath spends forty days looking for an Israelite brave enough to fight, little David with his five smooth stones, steps forward—pops the pickle with one blow. Proving that 'With God all things are possible'. What is Matthew doing in this Old Testament tale? Well, in a VeggieTale all references are possible, including the information that the Philistines want to take over the Israelites' land and make them slaves. Slaves who 'will have to scratch our backs, clean our rooms, and cook our food'—slaves who have all the sassiness of younger brothers. Hmmm. Slavery can be fun?

Besides the relentless focus on 'boy' Veggie heroes, there is a prevalent disparagement of female Veggies. The story in which Madame Blueberry stars is about an acquisitive blueberry (one critic actually compared the story to Madame Bovary) that just wants *more stuff*. Why so blue? Well, Madame Blueberry is turning green. Some of her friends have more than she does. Sure, she has everything a piece of fruit could hope for—good friends, plenty of food, a nice tree house to live in. Fortunately after spending 18 minutes with the DVD or VHS of Madame Blueberry, kid

---

7.   Located north of San Francisco in San Rafael, California, ILM was founded in 1975 to produce the visual effects for *Star Wars*. Although owned by George Lucas, ILM produces visual effects for more than Lucasfilm productions, e.g., the *Star Wars* and *Indiana Jones* films. Many other studios seeking that bit of something extra on the cutting edge of special effects use ILM. ILM has received fourteen Academy Awards, including ones for its work on *Forrest Gump*, *Jurassic Park*, *Terminator 2*, *Who Framed Roger Rabbit?* and *E.T.*

Stephen Spielberg, David Katenberg, and David Geffen launched Dreamworks SKG in October 1994. Dreamworks is now a leading producer of live-action motion pictures and animated feature films, such as *Shrek*, *Prince of Egypt*, *Chicken Run*, and *Catch Me If You Can*. The Dreamworks 'campus' is located in Glendale, California, between Hollywood and the San Gabriel mountains. Another major Dreamworks resort-like facility is in Redwood, California, about fifty miles from ILM.

viewers discover that 'being greedy makes you grumpy, but a thankful heart is a happy heart!' David, Josh, and Lil' Joe are all dealing with real problems, familiar—however trivialized—from biblical narratives. But Laura Carrot and Madame Blueberry get to exemplify only 'girl' problems. This gender split reflects the old stereotype of women as consumers and men as producers.

I can find no justifiable reason for transforming the biblical characters into Veggies, other than the peculiarity that stimulates sales. An experienced children's book writer, I could probably write dialogue for talking granite chips or computer chips or chocolate chips, any object a publisher threw at me. Currently the hot kid toy is a rebirth of the Mexican jumping bean, shaped like a capsule with a ball-bearing inside. Limbless as the Veggies, these capsules are characters, such as a hard-hatted worker bean, a nurse, a fairy princess, an evil queen bean. Limbless but comfortably stereotyped. At the time of writing the Beanz have been given no storyline, secular or biblical. While inherently Veggies have few gender markings, the VeggieTales characters have all the gendered markings of the boys who play with action figures of Samson, David, and Daniel. Goliath cast as a pickle is just as violent as he was as a Philistine. And Bob the Tomato is just as annoying as any Nabob. Anyone who feels that these limbless Veggies bouncing around highlight any sort of fantasy to stretch the imagination of children needs to take a closer look. These Veggies have no charm, small wit, and no creative interpretation of the biblical stories on which they are based. What is here to encourage children to think about biblical stories as anything other than fast-food moralizing good vs. evil, us vs. them, winners vs. losers?

Lest I seem to be pushing one point of view, there is another hermeneutic. According to the creators of the Veggie supermarket, Big Idea's game plan is not really about marketing: 'A content carrier is any product that carries a message—mainly videos, books and music. All content carriers serve Big Idea's mission.' And how are they making the world a better place? The spin goes like this: the Veggies are healthy role models, unlike those angry human action figures of secular mass culture. The central question in this pro-Veggietarian argument is the invisibility of the human figure. Animated animals have facial features similar to the human, and of course limbs, easing the child into the fantasy of blurring the boundaries between human and animal. But vegetables have no faces, no limbs, they have no power of locomotion or of speech. The voice of Bob the Tomato, as a narrator and interpreter of God's word, and as invisible as the biblical narrator. God remains invisible, but the other characters, being vegetables, are as invisible as the deity. If humans in the *Ur*-text are created in the image of God, in the world of the Veggies, is God a plump tomato? By moving into the realm of vegetables, the authors have demanded a level of audience creativity that almost demands ignorance of the biblical narrative in order not to be completely confused. Phil Vischer has said, 'I promised my mother I would never depict Jesus as a vegetable'. Perhaps that is why we have as yet not been force-fed a Cauliflower Jesus with celery disciples.

So where is the F word, *fantasy*, alive and healthy and thriving for children? In the cartoon world there is no imaginary creature more memorable than Oscar the Grouch. And Tickle-me Elmo, is unmatched in the category of silly. I have survived Pet rocks, Mood rings, Cabbage Patch dolls (who were more hydrocephalic than vegetable-based), Tamagotchis, Beanie Babies, Power Rangers, Powerpuff Girls, all sorts of kid merchandise that flashed for a moment on the consumer horizon, and then fell into the abyss of garage sales. So why am I bothered by all this low-carb biblical buffoonery?

One possibility is my discomfort with the F word, *faith*, explored in a non-challenging and less than memorable fashion. If there is faith connected to the Veggie empire, it is to be found in the faith in merchandizing. eBay routinely has servings of more than 750 Veggie items online for the highest bidder; my personal favorite is the plastic Esther purse.[8] A Vegetable Queen (a slim slice of generic green, possibly a wild onion, with very Jennifer Aniston hair) carrying a bag of gold is a rich image, although we know that the human Queen of England carries no money in *her* handbag. Tall and lissome, Esther is a dish, but a dish of what I cannot discern. It has been suggested to me that Esther is a wild onion, and King Xerxes is a green onion. But nowhere is the audience given a chance to reflect. All answers are provided in catchy slogans that dumb down the narrative facets of the Bible as they supply a buzzing high of self-righteousness—without having to sit through an hour-long religious service, or worse, to puzzle through a biblical narrative. For a toy with a wholesome lesson and the requisite Veggie splash, there are five different

---

8. Esther is the star of the fourteenth VeggieTale adventure, a direct home VHS release of *Esther: The Girl who Became Queen*. Following the basic biblical plan, Esther is a girl living in small-town Persia. Esther must learn how to be courageous when King Xerxes' right-hand man Haman gets Esther's cousin Mordecai in big trouble. Will she confront the king, or let Mordecai and their whole family be arrested and sent away forever? No, Esther has courage; she teaches the audience that you never need to be afraid to do what's right. The king is a round green veggie with skin identical to Esther. I owe the observation that Esther may be a wild onion, and her king a green onion, to a VeggieTales chatroom reader.

four-color, glossy, durable, inspirational cards with messages such as 'Compassion and Mercy! We all need to give 'em, because we all need to get 'em!'

With scenes from VeggieTales stories, and corresponding familiar phrases, these durable and attractive cards are sure to become staple in the back pocket of your burgeoning VeggieTales collection. And what if you are torn between the Veggie pack and some baseball cards? There is of course a Veggie answer: 'If you regularly spend money on character merchandise or apparel, try to spend it with a company you think will use the profits to make the world a better place'. Apparently these words have been taken to heart by the faithful. Big Idea Productions has grown from a staff of three people to nearly 200, adding the infrastructure to produce books, apparel, and other licensed products, as well as expanding the animation studio to take on larger, more elaborate projects: feature-length films, new secularly based properties, beginning with 3-2-1 Penguins, another limbless group of personalities, more nattily dressed.

Inspirational Sales

Like most market-based commercial produce, Veggie sales depend on booksellers, advertisers, and consumers. Every year thousands of bookstore owners and buyers, literary agents, and the media gather at the annual Christian Booksellers Association (CBA) convention. This is a once-a-year opportunity for Evangelicals to discover new authors and artists, to sample products, and to learn new ways to grow their businesses and ministries. There are daily devotions, evening concerts, and fellowship events to enhance relationships among Christian publishers, authors, and bookstores, ranging from Accordia Books and Arsenal Christian Publishers to Zondervan Books. In 2003, Xulun Books became the largest of the fast-growing arm of Christian self-publishing books. (Prices start at $499!) Most Christian book companies started as small family affairs or as publishing arms of Bible colleges. Many CBA stores started as mom-and-pop operations. General-market bookstores have long realized their most worrisome competitor is not the independent bookstore across town but the large bookstore chains and big-box retailers such as Wal-Mart, Costco and Sam's Club. 'The Christian industry is so focused on the next big bestseller, both publishers and stores alike, that we're causing a feeding frenzy', Heath Hill, director of sales/marketing for Appalachian Distributors, told *Publisher's Weekly.* 'We're causing the bestseller wars with Sam's Club because we're focusing on the bestseller too, rather than supporting the broad spectrum of materials and showing customers that, yes, we have Max Lucado's[9] latest book, but we have all his other titles, too. If we didn't focus so much on advertising *Left Behind*, Wal-Mart and Sam's Club wouldn't have such easy targets'.

While no Christian chain yet rivals Barnes & Noble, Family Christian Bookstores has several hundred outlets across the US. In the summer of 2003, the online site for Family Christian Enterprises, assured the potential consumer: 'At Family Christian Stores we're mindful of the tough economic times and your desire to be a good steward of the resources God has entrusted you. That's why we're offering a summer blowout: hundreds of specially priced books to choose from and low prices on best-selling books, Bibles, music, gift items and kids products.'

At a particularly difficult time in America's history, the 'God Shed His Grace on America' tee-shirt has been reduced to $4.97 in all adult sizes. From all sources, it seems clear that the profits are multiplying faster than loaves and fishes. It's difficult to fix the dollar figures with any kind of precision, but sales through CBA member stores and distributors—a large segment but by no means all of the industry—came to $4 billion in 2001.

Licensing activity in this market is growing rapidly. Thomas Nelson has sold more than 10 million Precious Moments[10] Bibles since 1984; the property's licensing agent, United Media, estimates publishers collectively have sold more than 25 million Precious Moments books in North America. Nelson also publishes Thomas Kinkade Bibles, mostly in the New King James Version. Nowhere has Christian-sector licensing risen more than in children's titles. Tommy Nelson, the children's division of Thomas Nelson, publishes The *Prayer of Jabez* and *Secrets of the Vine* children's books. 'It's cooled off, but for a while it was hotter than hot', said Dan Lynch, Tommy Nelson's senior Vice-President and publisher, noting that customers purchased more than one million *Prayer of Jabez* children's books in less than a year.

But it is the merchandise, what Madame Blueberry would call *the stuff*, that is helping Christian publishers, booksellers, and licensees move into

9. Max Lucado, minister for the Oak Hills Church of Christ in San Antonio, Texas, is the author of multiple bestsellers including *Traveling Light: Releasing the Burdens You Were Never Intended to Bear* (W Publishing Group, 2001), which was listed for several weeks on the *New York Times* bestseller list. Lucado's books have sold more than 28 million copies.

10. Precious Moments dolls, toys, figurines, and other inspirational collectibles are the creation of Sam Butcher, who has a ministry in evangelizing children, through books, 'chalk talks' in schools and churches, and of course through the heavily marketed sentimentilized little tear-drop eyed figures, who are intended to comfort and encourage those who collect them. See <http:www.pmcdolls.com>.

greener pastures. VeggieTales is credited with raising the visibility and desirability of Christian merch. Books and merchandise based on properties such as *The Beginner's Bible, Precious Moments, The Prayer of Jabez*, as well as VeggieTales have been successful on mass merchants' shelves as well as in the CBA chains, although they tend to cycle in and out of the former. *Publisher's Weekly* reports a significant percentage of ZonderKidz' VeggieTales spinoff books are sold through mainstream channels, ranging from grocery stores to Barnes & Noble outlets. More than a quarter of some titles' print runs end up in knee-high book piles at low-end chains such as Meijer, Sam's Club and Target through the independent distributor Chas Levy. Tommy Nelson holds Christian-market rights for Porchlight Entertainment's Jay the Jet Plane, a public television series for preschoolers. The company's top license is artist Thomas Kinkade: juvenile Bibles, journals and other titles tied to the 'Painter of Light' have sold more than 2.5 million copies.

My particular favorites from a recent trip to a Family Christian Store in Elyria, Ohio, are Scripture mints shaped like little fish ('reaching the world one piece at a time'); hand puppets of a wooly Samson and a black-bearded David; action figures of Moses (available in a choice of black or white skin); tee-shirts and summer beach towels with brightly printed biblical verses; Praying Puppy, brown plush with small Velcro patches that hold his praying-paws together; and a toddler-size cuddly Larry the Cucumber. The Cross of Thorns lapel pins sold out while I was at the cash register. The Internet has revealed Bible bobbleheads, resin figures of Moses, Samson, and Noah. Sensitive to the accusation that the toys might be examples of scurrilous sacrilege from an increasingly heathen society, the creators assure their customers: 'in no way do we want to leave the false impression that we are making fun of these great heroes of faith. In fact, our intent is to create an even greater hunger and desire to go to God's Word and learn more about these imperfect people used by a perfect God.'[11]

What is the difference between Scripture mints and an Isis table lamp or an Aphrodite soap dispenser? The Isis lamp sheds no Christian light but is loaded with cultural allusions. Clearly the spiritual value of a Scripture mint is limited, but people are gobbling them up both online and in brick and mortar stores. The market for Christian merchandise has more than doubled in the past decade, which indicates that someone is feeling good about Christian-lite. Perhaps Dana Long, inspirational

---

11. Nord quotes the creators of the Bobbleheads as being inspired by Veggie-Tales' success.

products brand manager for Thomas Nelson, has the right idea: 'It's just a really sweet and simple and nonoffensive way for [customers] to share their faith with people who may not have a relationship with Christ'.[12]

How to Make a Tomato Taste Like a Twinkie

Perhaps the one F word I have overlooked is food. Reminiscent of the supersaturated colors of Betty Crocker ads in Fifties women's magazines, Bob the Tomato and his Veggie companions are photographer's vegetables. Eye candy with allusions to vitamins. Supersaturated, maraschino cherries for a new millennium. The pleasure of the eye compensates for the loss of reality vegetables. Garish, bright, relentlessly cheerful, the Veggies are like animated Jello molds. Thus, a cartoon becomes a comestible at the same time as the tomato becomes a Twinkie.

Leaving aside the ethical, nutritional, and aesthetic questions of whether we want to transform a tomato into a Twinkie, because clearly some people do, let us look at the process of conducting this transformation. First, we position the tomato as a naturally occurring beneficial item, and we define the Twinkie as an almost limitlessly produced product that must be disposed of in order to make room for more Twinkie product. Now the Veggietarians have made Bob the tomato into a product. As French theorist Jean Baudrillard has noted, the goal of capitalism is to get rid of the product in order to make more product. Baudrillard is expanding upon the major economic shift in American consumerism, a time Galbraith and others have identified as the moment when marketing cars became more difficult than making them.

Unloading the product gets more difficult with time. Even Bob the Tomato has a shelf life. Marketing and moving the product has always been more difficult than actually making the limbless jokesters. The Big Idea folks have extended the line of Veggie offerings, since their new 2004 line of toys, games, plushies, and songs are more secularly based. As most of us who teach Bible have learned a while ago, the Bible wears thin with students. So too there are a finite number of biblical narratives that lend themselves to vegetable interpretation. In time for the Christmas surge of 2003, Big Idea moved the product into a more generic ethical realm. Its newest offerings inculcate morals in small children, of course with the assistance of Bob, Larry, and Junior Asparagus. Perhaps its most reassuring title is *God is Bigger than the Boogie Man*. Another secular but ethical

12. Personal communication.

topic is *Peas and Thank You!* What happens when a village of well-mannered peas meet a bunch of rude beans!

One final step in the transformation of tomato to Twinkie. Accept the alchemy that transmutes Bob and his kind into synthetic Twinkies. Junior Asparagus and Larry the Cucumber are to a discourse of faith what Twinkies are to diabetes. In sum, the Veggies choke me because they are predigested. No fiber, no roughage, none of the vitamin-rich attributes that make a tomato proud to be a tomato. Rather, these Veggies spare us the effort of thought, of chewing on the complexities of biblical narratives. The greatest danger of the Veggie world is their greatest selling point: they provide their audience with shortcuts to the pleasure of sorting through moral questions. As of the summer of 2004, VeggieTales have sold 35 million videos. Twinkies all around!

Selling The Passion of the Christ

I was not going to get suckered into a discussion of Mel Gibson's *The Passion of the Christ.* I was going to be one of the few biblical scholars not trying to make a buck off Gibson's bloodbath. What may be a lesson for our time is the Gibson version of that wonderful old children's story The Little Red Hen. No studio or independent producer would make the Gibson film in Hollywood, no one would distribute his film once he had shot it, so he had to put up the 30 million himself, and eventually his production company Icon Films partnered with Newmarket Films as distributor. After the first week in general release, the film ranked about fifth in all-time one week sales. For the next three weeks, *The Passion* was the top-grossing film in the US, taking in $31.7 million and pushing its total beyond a quarter of a billion dollars. With solid receipts through Pentecost 2004, and with the film in worldwide distribution, *The Passion* has grossed more than half a billion dollars, which puts it in the top three all-time grossing films. What has driven that public response is not clear. Are people streaming into theaters for a religious experience, for a big gulp of bloody violence, because everyone is talking about it?

But in writing about Christian marketing I would be remiss not to mention a few numbers connected to this greatest marketing epic ever sold. By including this discussion in a chapter on ludicrous vegetables turned biblical, or Bible transformed into vegetation, I can justify my musings on *The Passion.* I am not including the film in the chapter on religious films. Suffice it to say flesh is flayed in grotesque detail. Body fluids spurt in exquisite patterns. Slow motion captures any action or glance Gibson deems significant. For Catholics it is the Sorrowful

Mysteries writ way too large; it is the Stations of the Cross with no meditation on redemption. What the even deeper mystery is for me, however, is how this bloody mess became the marketing and money story that dwarves scholarly questions of morality or historicity.

The film opened on 25 February 2004, in more than three thousand US theaters, on at least four thousand screens, and that's not counting the private showings and pirated tapes. By the end of the third day the film had risen to new heights: more than $50 million grossed. Bigger than *Ben-Hur*, greater than *The Ten Commandments*. The actual numbers are impressive by any standards: 'The opening box office gross for Newmarket Films' *The Passion of the Christ* exceeded even the most optimistic early projections, grossing a stunning $26.6 million in North America through Wednesday [opening day]'. The opening figures included an estimated $3 million from private group screenings Monday and Tuesday, and marks the fifth-biggest Wednesday debut in history. The films that earned more than *The Passion* opened during the summer 'blockbuster' season, not on Ash Wednesday, typically a slow time at the box office. By the end of the first weekend, *The Passion* had generated more than $117 million in North American box office sales. Officially licensed fan packs were disseminated online, and included posters, door hangers, buttons, and dollar-bill sized buck slips, which could be slipped into church bulletins, used as bookmarks, sent home with school children. One could order 500 door hangers or buck slips for the cost of shipping and handling.

Before the movie opened, Christian bookstores began racing to keep up with the demand for merchandise related to *The Passion*. Pins, pocket crosses, tee-shirts, mugs, soundtracks, books and jewelry are among the items licensed by Gibson's Icon Productions to be sold in conjunction with the movie. Tara Powers, a spokeswoman for Family Christian Stores, said the company has sold 3000 copies of a coffee-table book with pictures from the movie's production in the first week alone. 'It's certainly been our fastest-selling coffee-table book ever', Powers said. 'We weren't expecting this big of a response (so soon). People have been coming for the past couple of weeks looking for these items, and we're still trying to ship them.'

Probably the most excitement generated in the press has been a pendant fashioned from a single nail made of pewter and attached to a leather strap. Bob Siemon Designs has been licensed by Gibson's Icon Productions to produce lapel pins, necklaces and various regalia tied to the film. The pendants represent the nails used in the film to fasten Christ to the cross. 'This thing has turned into this kind of overnight phenomenon that we can't believe', Siemon said, referring to the pendant.[13] For months his staff worked 10- to 14-hour shifts six days a week to keep Christian bookstores supplied with the pendants, crucifixes and other items. The company has shipped about 75,000 cross pendants and about the same amount of nail pendants, said Dwight Robinson, the company's marketing manager.

Less than a week into the film's release, the soundtrack for *The Passion* and the 'official companion volume' to the film were the third biggest sellers on Amazon.com's online list. The book about the fim, *The Passion*, with commentary by Mel Gibson and photos by Ken Duncan (Tyndale Books, 2004), is glitzy, full-colored, reminiscent of one of those books one buys at the circus. Gibson provides a foreword in which he briefly describes the inspiration for making the film and explains his decision to draw on Scripture and 'accepted visions' of the Passion as the sole texts for the screenplay. In the book, relevant Scripture passages (from the New Living Translation, alongside Latin and Aramaic) are juxtaposed against stunning full-color photographs of the film's depiction of Jesus' final 12 hours. Startling stills show Jesus kneeling in Gethsemane, Jesus bloodied by soldiers, Jesus dragged before Pontius Pilate, mocked by Herod and nailed to the cross. Some images are simply unforgettable— Judas hanging himself from a tree; Mary recalling a poignant moment from Jesus' childhood; a spike being driven through Jesus' palm. Several pages of photos at the end of the book chronicle some behind-the-scenes moments in the making of the film. The book opened at number 5 on the *New York Times*' bestseller list, as non-fiction, and rose to number 2 within a week.

As I write this in the late spring of 2004, I feel the caprice of the media writing the ending for Gibson's marketing miracle. Does anyone even think about the *Sturm und Drang* over Mel Gibson and his bloody film? While the VeggieTales survive audience ennui with fresh entries into the marketplace, a few years ago I would have thought that *The Passion* had a limited storyline. But I have understood from watching the continuing success of the multi-volume Apocalypse that the battle is not yet won. In book 12, finally we have the *Glorious Awakening*, with as much gore as Mel Gibson could wish for. When hapless non-believers are executed by Christ, their 'innards and entrails gush to the desert floor… their blood pooling and rising in the unforgiving brightness of God.' Will Gibson find a violent enough backstory?

13. <http://www.amarillonet.com/stories/022604/new_sellsquickly.shtml>.

5

BUYING GOD: AMERICAN MYTHS
AND MAINSTREAM MEDIA

Our Fathers wrung their bread from stocks and stones
And fenced their gardens with the Redman's bones.
                            —Robert Lowell, *Children of Light* (1946)

And the Devil took him up to a high place, and showed him all the
kingdoms of the world in a moment of time, and said to him, 'To you I
will give all this authority and their glory; for it has been delivered to me'
(Mt. 4.8-9).

Dates, chronology, signifiers that stop time. Some dates are chiseled in
stone, some fade away. 25 December is an internationally recognized
date; 22 February (Washington's birthday) and 4 July (US Independence
from the oppressive British state) are American dates; 5 November (Guy
Fawkes Day) is purely British, a date that memorializes the terrorist act of
attempting to blow up the Houses of Parliament in 1605. There are personal dates revealing family significance; such dates are important only to
an intimate few. There are dates in which the year identifies and tele-
scopes a collection of events into one massive occurrence: 1066, 1492,
1865, 1968. Does anyone remember the precise date in March 2003 when
the United States began precision-bombing Baghdad? We remember the
night-vision, grainy-green of the TV version, but when did it happen?
How does a date stop time? How did 9/11 get chiseled in stone?

I have been writing and researching the connections among George
W. Bush, 9/11, and evangelical Christianity for more than two years.
After much frustration I realize that I cannot use either a chisel or a
stone to follow this story. I have not learned the magician's secret of
stopping time. That dream has given way to the CNN rolling tape. If the
dialogue is more than a week old, it is 'historic'. Just when I think I have
a scholarly argument in place, the President will say or do something that
overrides or outdates now, transforming it into then. The now in which I
write will never be the now in which the reader reads this chapter.
Perhaps publishing in print in this nanosecond age renders prose un-
timely and thus compels an author to begin 'Once upon a time'.

Being submerged under an Internet's worth of URLs and piles of print documents about 9/11 makes clear how different the scholarly approach to ancient texts is from reading contemporary popular culture. Scholars of antiquity have layers of interpretations and compare the cultural differences and similarities usually with other ancient societies. What I am trying to do is find the whispers of biblical antiquity that run through the political and cultural dialogue in our present day.

From the earliest days of European immigrants' mission to the Promised Land of New England, their errand in the wilderness, there has been a mythic sense of American chosen-ness by God, that the American colonies were the New Israel. From those first tentative wilderness treks through New England through the claiming of land from sea to shining sea, Americans have followed the biblical model of Moses leading God's people into a land of milk and honey, with native Americans, French trappers, Mexicans, and any others who blocked the way playing the role of the Canaanites. Our coinage proclaims our trust in God; our most popular anthem begins 'God bless America'. For a nation founded by people fleeing state-supported religions, a nation built on the separation of church and state, we seem to demonstrate a great deal of separation anxiety. There are few countries that exhibit in both domestic and foreign policy such self-consciously pious symbols and rhetoric in their public discourse as the US. Robert Jewett and John Shelton Lawrence consider this rhetorical style a pungent form of civil messianism, 'a form of American civil religion that fuses biblical texts with the imagery of superheroic battles against supervillains' (Jewett and Lawrence 2003).

In leading us into divinely sanctioned battle, our exhortative super prophets take a lesson from the prophet Joel, who reversed Isaiah's call for a kingdom of peace in suggesting that one beat plowshares into swords and pruning hooks into spears (Joel 3.10). Walter Wink, in *The Powers that Be*, exhorts in prophetic terms against this seizing of God's pruning hook, the silencing of the peacemakers:

> The myth of redemptive violence speaks for God; it does not listen for God to speak. It invokes the sovereignty of God as its own. It misappropriates the language, symbols, and scriptures of Christianity. It does not seek God in order to change; it embraces God in order to prevent change. Its God is the tribal god worshiped as an idol. Its metaphor is not the journey but the fortress. Its offer is not forgiveness but victory. Its good news is not the unconditional love of enemies but their final elimination. Its salvation is not a new heart but a successful foreign policy. It usurps the revelation of God's purposes for humanity in Jesus. It is blasphemous. It is idolatrous. And it is immensely popular (1998: 86).

Turning the Sermon on the Mount on its head, following the prophet Joel and ignoring the peaceable visions of Isaiah (2.4) and Micah (4.3), our profiteers preach a winner-take-all, high-octane manifest destiny as the divine mission given to the United States. A powerful charge indeed, one that conflates politics, profits, and propaganda, and calls the result God's pruning hook. The tool of propaganda is simple to wield: first, lay out the bare bones of an incident or event, such as the connection between Saddam Hussein and Osama bin Ladin or the assurance of Iraqi weapons of mass destruction. To this base, add a steady flow of repetition (called 'staying on message') and within a few media-soaked days or weeks the individual finds it difficult to stand back and form an independent judgment. This strategy is often referred to as 'unifying the country'.

Since the Puritan days of Jonathan Edwards and Cotton Mather, our public discourse has been studded with messianic proclamations of civil religion. The myth of redemptive violence that values victory over forgiveness has now become the spirituality of our national security state. Following the Puritan fathers, a staple of American moral life has been to stand ruthless in inflicting an inflexible will upon dissenters and those whom we judge as sinners. The keynote of this religious view of American life is overriding confidence in the correctness and importance of the Calvinist cause in the service of God. The Puritan conviction that they had created in *New* England a visible kingdom of God, a sanctuary for true believers, reflects the elitism of Puritan salvation. The covenantal agreement between the Puritans and God emphasized the chosen quality of the Puritans, and God's blessing of their ventures. Whatever had to be done to establish and maintain God's kingdom on earth was right. The covenant may have changed its wording, but the sense of privilege has remained central.

On 21 November 1899 President William McKinley explained to a delegation of the Methodist Church why he colonized the Philippines:

> The truth is I didn't want the Philippines, and when they came to us, as a gift from the gods, I did not know what to do with them…and I am not ashamed to tell you, gentlemen, that I went down on my knees and prayed to Almighty God for light and guidance for more than one night. And one late night it came to me this way…1) that we could not give them back to Spain—that would be cowardly and dishonorable; 2) that we could not turn them over to France and Germany—our commercial rivals in the Orient—that would be bad business and discreditable; 3) that we could not leave them to themselves—they were unfit for self-government—and they would soon have anarchy and misrule over there worse than Spain's was; and 4) that there was nothing left for us to do but to take them all, and to educate the Filipinos, and uplift and civilize and

Christianize them…and the next morning I sent for the chief engineer of the War Department and told him to put the Philippines on the map of the United States.

Expressing the position of President McKinley in his first speech in the US Senate in January 1900, Albert J. Beveridge, Senator of Indiana, addressed the Senate with these words:

Mr. President, the times call for candor. The Philippines are ours forever … We will not renounce our part in the mission of our race, trustee under God, of the civilization of the world… And we will move forward to our work… with gratitude for a task worthy of our strength, and thanksgiving to Almighty God that He has marked us as His chosen people, henceforth to lead in the regeneration of the world. We are the trustees of the world's progress, guardians of the righteous peace.

This Christian messianic franchise has been taken over by the current occupants of 1600 Pennsylvania Avenue.

Not that Americans consciously connect their religious traditions with nationalistic pride. There has been a historical reluctance to accept the religious roots of nationalism. Nathaniel Hawthorne, in *The Scarlet Letter* refers to the New England Puritans as 'black-browed witch hunters'. In a public letter to President Lyndon B. Johnson turning down an invitation to speak at the White House at the heightening of the Vietnam War, poet Robert Lowell wrote:

What we will do and what we ought to do as a sovereign nation facing other sovereign nations seem now to hang in the balance between the better and the worse possibilities. We are in danger of imperceptibly becoming an explosive and suddenly chauvinistic nation, and may even be drifting on out way to the last nuclear ruin. I know it is hard for the responsible man to act; it is also painful for the private and irresolute man to dare criticism.

Almost forty years later, the choices remain the same. To this day the majority of Americans are torn between their individualism and their mission to be the worldwide model to be copied. Salvation is more dependent on a strong foreign policy than on the biblical model of a people united under God. Evangelicals invoke not what the Bible determines is the sovereignty of God but rather the sovereignty and priority of our 'city on the hill' state. James Morone argues in his superb book *Hell-fire Nation*, which recasts American history as a moral epic, that from its earliest Puritan days America has been driven by its covenant with God 'to meddle in the behavior of its neighbors' (2003: 36). If this perception is accurate, then religious intolerance may be the 'original sin' of nationalism, whether it is American Puritanism or Islamic fundamentalism.

When President Bush used the term 'crusade' to describe the war on terrorism, was he inadvertently or deliberately claiming Christian roots in
American patriotism? Or was this seeming 'mistake' part of the product
launch that would permit the Bushes to flaunt military muscle in the
name of peace.

Whipping up a strong sense of nationalism often begins with demonizing the Other and separating us from them. In 1492, one of *those* Ameri-
canized dates, King Ferdinand and Queen Isabella, who united Castille
and Aragon to form the new kingdom of Spain, ousted the Moors from
Southern Spain and decided to expel the Jews from their territory. The
Spanish Inquisition was a central mechanism in consolidating royal
power and conferring legitimacy on the new Spanish state. In recent
media rhetoric Americans have declared 'them' as the axis of evil, and
Fox Broadcasting has slyly offered an anti-Gallic term, the axis of weasel.
By linking all Americans with a spiritually rooted collective responsibility, the holier than all the rest of the world rhetoric has been indelibly
superimposed upon a war of self-defense against terrorists. To be anti-war
is to be anti-American, as though there is only one describable American,
and that is the familiar mythic one, stretching back to the Puritan days,
when personal salvation was simultaneously collective salvation. The
Puritans had a covenantal relationship with God, summed up by John
Winthrop:

> Thus stands the cause between God and us. We are entered into a cove-
> nant with Him for this work... That which most churches maintain as a
> truth in profession only, we must bring into familiar and constant practice.
> If the Lord shall be pleased, he shall make us a praise and glory. For we
> must consider that we shall be as a city upon a hill, the eyes of all people
> are upon us.[1]

This heady idea of America talking to God while the whole world
watches and waits on the outcome has been one of the founding myths
of our society. Doing the work of the Lord was open to every man, the
cobbler, the cartwright, and the cooper. Heralding the work of the hands,
no matter how servile, over spiritual employment set the Puritans and
their followers on the path to founding capitalism as a society's glory to
God. In the choice of vocation, or calling, one was expected to perform,
not for ones individual good, but for the public or communal good. How
holy capitalism became vengeful nationalism forms a subtext of American

---

1.   Winthrop's well-known model has been requested, recited, and retaped during
a recent American spectacle, the funeral of former President Ronald Reagan, produced and directed by Nancy Reagan (see Chapter 6).

public policy. Rather than striving to follow Jesus' dictum to love our enemies, clearly a central New Testament teaching, we eliminate them.

Certainly we have encouraged publicly pious men in their ambition, or better, their vocation, to become President of the United States. We prefer to think of ourselves as the redeemer nation rather than an imperialist power. Since 1960, the blue-chip connection between High-church Protestants and politics has faded. The so-called elite traditional Protestant faithful leaders have given way to representatives of faiths that had never held sway at the national level: we have supported John Kennedy, the Catholic President; Jimmy Carter, a Southern Baptist who taught adult Sunday-school; Ronald Reagan who helped create the powerful connection between the evangelical Christian media and the White House. By 1976, when Jimmy Carter ran for the White House, personal religiosity had become an unusual phenomenon to some political and cultural observers. During the presidential campaign, NBC News anchorman John Chancellor showed a clip of Carter talking about the fact that he was 'born again,' and then felt obligated to inform the audience: 'By the way, we've checked this out. Being "born again" is not a bizarre, mountaintop experience. It's something common to many millions of Americans—particularly if you're Baptist.' Twenty-five years later, it seems unthinkable that any commentator would make such an aside. In the 2000 presidential election, professing a 'born-again' faith or sensibility was close to a requirement for candidates for the Republican nomination. Even Presidential candidate Al Gore commented on what the catchphrase 'WWJD—What Would Jesus Do?' meant for his personal faith.

Perhaps none has been so noisily pious as our current President, George Bush 43,[2] who has cast himself as the American action figure of Moses, chipper in his born-again connection to the prophetic call from God. As he revealed in 1999 to James Robison, a Fort Worth televangelist, and his TV audience, 'I've heard the call. I believe God wants me to run for President.' In the summer of 2000 (Carnes 2000: 64) Governor Bush continued his exuberant witness while on the stump, unconsciously imitating the fundamentalist preacher Billy Sunday, who had often proclaimed, 'When the word of God says one thing and scholarship say another, scholarship can go to hell'. Ignoring any knowledge he might have been exposed to at Yale, Bush played to his anti-intellectual base:

2.   For the sake of clarity, I am adopting the Bush family system of reference to father and son Presidents: George 41 and George 43, indicating their numerical designations as Presidents of the US.

'Christ [is my favorite political philosopher] because he changed my heart... When you turn your heart and your life over to Christ, when you accept Christ as the Savior, it changes your heart and your life.' When he found God, Bush found a future.[3]

The public biography of Bush gives extensive information about the faith–alcohol connection, touting the key to giving up alcohol as the new spirituality he had embraced. The perfect standard-bearer for pious politics, a sinner who was redeemed through Christ, Bush drank in the accolades from his supporters. Using the confessional mode became the center of his appeal to the Evangelical Right. Bush is not a particularly introspective man, but whatever soul-searching he did, occurred in the summer of 1985, after a conversation at the family summer retreat in Kennebunkport. In search of spiritual direction, Bush 43 consulted the man Bush 41 has called 'the nation's pastor', the Reverend Billy Graham, a longtime family friend and spiritual adviser. 'Graham', Bush 43 said, 'planted a seed in my heart and I began to change' (Romano and Lardner 1999).

As his faith began to take root, Bush found he could still play the part of pledge master as he had in the elite world of Skull and Bones (a club at Yale University) without the aid of alcohol. The very aspects of his personality that made 'Dubiya' the guy everyone wanted to sit next to at dinner—the nervous energy, the sly humor, the impulsiveness and lack of structure—were also the parts of himself that Bush wanted to seize control of but not lose. 'I think if...you become more spiritual, you begin to realize the effect of alcohol over-consuming because it begins to drown the spirit', he said (Siker 2003). From daily dipping in alcoholic spirits, Bush soaked himself in the revivalist spirit of his bottle-fed faith.

Bush takes pride in saying that he never went into a substance abuse program such as Alcoholics Anonymous, but indicated that he was guided by the broader AA philosophy of placing one's faith in God. 'If you change your heart, you can change your behavior', Bush has said frequently, parroting the self-help gurus reaching out from every TV box. Bush 43 has crafted perfectly the sincere persona of the evangelical believer whose primary connection is with his God, and whose faith encourages public confession. It is widely reported that Bush is the stereotypical anti-intellectual populist Texan. He has told reporters with a grain of testiness that he doesn't watch TV news and the only part of the

3. A full description of Bush 43's prophetic call from God appears in autobiographical *A Charge to Keep* (2001). For an analytic description of this inspirational call, see Siker 2003.

newspaper he reads is the sports section. 'He may skim the front page', an aide admitted, 'but Laura reads the papers and alerts him' (Auletta 2004).

It seems ironic that a confessional politician with God on his side would sweat so profusely under the warm lights of the press. In December of 2002, Bob Deans, then president of the White House Correspondents Association, sent a letter of complaint about access to the President to his chief of staff Andrew Card. The President 'has not taken a single question from the White House Press Corps in two weeks and has held substantially fewer press conferences, interviews and other media events than either Bill Clinton or George H.W. Bush in their first two years in office'. Deans's complaint went unanswered.[4] Clearly even Bush 43's advisers are uncomfortable with Bush's stumbling prose style, which does not mix so well with the press as it does with his evangelical constituency.

Guns, God, and Oil

It was oil not God that brought his father to Texas,[5] in partnership with his cousin George Walker. In 1948, a youthful Bush 41 moved to West

4. Auletta counts eleven solo press conferences in the three years since the Bush 43 inauguration in January 2001. In a comparable period during their first terms, the post-Truman Presidents possess much higher numbers. Eisenhower held 74, Kennedy 65, Johnson 80, Nixon 23, Carter 53, Reagan 21, Bush '41' 71, and Clinton 38.

5. After graduation from Yale, Bush 41 went to work for Dresser Industries, an oil-field supply company. He was a co-founder in 1953 of the Zapata Petroleum Corporation, and in 1954 he became president of its subsidiary, the Zapata Off-Shore Company. When the firm's subsidiary became independent in 1958, Bush moved its headquarters from Midland to Houston, Texas. He served as Zapata's president until 1964, when he became active in politics, and as its chairman from 1964 to 1966, when he sold his interest in the company.

A quick thumbnail of the father/son parallels and sharp angles. At Andover and Yale, the elite schools where his father was a star athlete and student leader and seemed suffused with special grace, George 43's academic record was mediocre, his achievements modest. While his father rushed to volunteer during World War II and returned a hero, George 43 never flew in combat, and his enlistment in the Air National Guard at the height of the Vietnam War raises the question of whether he sought to avoid front-line service. While his father did well early on in the oil business, George 43 never made money. Rescued by family members and friends, he then was offered a new opportunity in baseball, where he finally succeeded on his own. In public life, his father moved seamlessly from one significant job to another, despite early frustrations running for office; George 43 lost the only campaign he attempted before becoming successful in his bid for the Governorship of Texas. Taking such a perspective of the father and son emphasizes the well-worked story of George 43's turn around by faith after his fortieth birthday (Romano and Lardner 1999).

Texas to take a job working for a subsidiary of Dresser Industries, a company in which his father was heavily invested. The president of the company had been his father's best friend at Yale, and the young Bush had grown up calling his future employer 'Uncle Neil'. Before that entrepreneurial opportunity, for more than two centuries, the family had been traditional Protestant stock, hop-scotching the Northeastern US. A quick look at the genealogy of the Bushes confirms the Puritan remonstrance that God does not bequeath children to the ungodly. The family history could have been written by American novelists Sinclair Lewis, Theodore Dreiser, or John Marquand. The book jacket might have read: 'How generations of high finance and Ivy League breeding led to a presidency handed from father to son'. Perhaps the story is closer to John Cheever. A quick plot summary: Reverend James Smith Bush was born in Rochester, New York, 15 June 1825. He was ordained an Episcopalian clergyman in 1860. Reverend Smith died 11 Nov 1889 in Ithaca, New York, at 64 years of age.[6] His wife lived more than twenty years in Boston after her husband's death. And thus began the Bush begats: Their son, the grandfather of Bush 41, Samuel Prescott Bush, was born in Brick Church, New Jersey, in 1863. The Bush family's ties to oil date back to this steelmaker and railroad equipment manufacturer's relationship to Standard Oil that began about a century ago in central Ohio.

At this point in their Northeastern patrician history, the Bush men began to earn their money not by work, but rather by their connections, both familial and political. While we are all used to reciting the failures of George 43 in business and sports management (he traded Sammy Sosa, batting ace, to the Chicago Cubs), one must recall that George 41 lost two Texas Senate races before he was politically rejuvenated by political ally Richard Nixon with appointments as ambassador to China and then CIA director. While this statement might sound like the statement of an overwrought liberal, let me defer to political pundit Kevin Phillips, who agues that the Bush family was 'built on the five pillars of American global sway: the international reach of U.S. investment banking, the emerging gigantism of the military-industrial complex, the ballooning of the CIA and kindred intelligence operations, the drive for U.S. control of global oil supplies, and a close alliance with Britain and the English-speaking community'.[7]

6. His father, Obadiah Newcomb, was born in New York State, but his dates are disputed in various account.

7. Phillips' (2004) book bristles with rage. It is hard to tell what offends Phillips the most: the Bushes' systematic deceit and secrecy, their shady business dealings,

Grandfather of George 41 was a close advisor to President Herbert Hoover, and was the father of Prescott Bush. Father of George 41, Prescott became a partner in the renowned Harriman family business ventures in 1930. After the firm's 1931 merger with the British–American banking house Brown Brothers, Prescott Bush became managing partner of the resulting company: Brown Brothers Harriman. This was ultimately the largest and politically the most important private banking house in America. Like his father, Prescott Bush was a banker and corporate director, but he became a true political player, elected Senator from Connecticut, where he served from 1952–63. His son, George 41, was born and grew up in Greenwich, Connecticut. Then this blossoming branch of the Bushes headed to Texas.

The Southern Born Again populist role is new to the Bush clan. In the popular biographical material about the forty-third President, there is a studied lack of emphasis upon Bush's blueblood genealogy, his Eastern Brahmin roots. He does not trade on his Patrician establishment lineage, except for the occasional visit to Yale, a university from which he graduated as a third-level legacy. If his father was the imperious 'read my lips', Bush 43 was more the Southern good old boy, 'read my knuckles' Bush. His political ancestors were not the liberal southern presidents of the twentieth century, but rather the reactionary Southern senators and representatives who dominated the Democratic Party from the early nineteenth century until the New Deal, and who took over the Republican Party in the Nineties.[8] The culture that shaped Dubiya was more Texan than generalized Southern. This culture was not the world of earlier Texan President Lyndon B. Johnson, or the 'man from Plains' Jimmy Carter. If Carter was elected by the folks in the country churches, George 43 depended upon similar Evangelicals along with country club capitalists.

In his pre-victory book, *A Charge to Keep* (2001), Bush and his doppelganger collaborator, Karen Hughes, tap-dance lightly over the young Bush's incorrigible sense of play. Hazing, petty thefts, prodigious bouts of

their cronyism, or their family philosophy that privileges the very wealthy and utterly dismisses all the rest.

8. Lind argues convincingly that rural over-representation in the form of the Electoral College, which exaggerates the weight of the small-population states, along with the Conservative majority on the Supreme Court, is what delivered the 2000 Presidential election to George W. Bush. In contrast to the arithmetic of the counties and small towns, which is magnified in the Electoral allocations, in the 2000 election the combination of popular votes for Al Gore and Ralph Nader 'produced the highest popular vote majority for the center-left since 1964' (2003: 76).

drinking are all rendered through a Brooks Brothers lens. As a boy, Bush worshiped in both Presbyterian and Episcopalian churches without any seeming effect. After he married, he switched to the Methodist denomination, the church of his wife, a woman modeled directly upon the *'ashet hayil* of Proverbs 31 (see Chapter 6). Under the influence of his valorous wife, George 43 blossomed in his faith and attended men's Bible study groups. After his life-changing experience with Reverend Graham, Bush's biography reveals that the future President began to take the Scriptures more seriously, reading the Bible cover to cover more than once. As the story goes, Bush was seized by a thirst for 'deeper spiritual meaning' in his life. As his public manner and ramrod rhetoric underscore, his faith has given him a strategy for expressing an uncontestable version of the truth. Once a WASP prince, Bush morphed into a NASCAR dad.

And Then Came 9/11

If time is distance measured in the mind, the world has moved mental light years away from its position on 10 September 2001. There is not a writer or journalist whom I know who has not written the words 'On the morning of September 11'. Whether the felling of the World Trade Center towers should be considered the worst disaster to befall the United States, whether the terrorists hate freedom, or whether AlQaeda has a connection to the former government of Iraq is a disconnected mélange of political, rhetorical, and religious perspectives. In the first few weeks following the 9/11 disaster, religious rhetoric clogged the print and electronic media, irrevocably connecting the mind and will of God with American interests. On the streets of New York City, people eagerly clutched prayer cards from street prophets and apocalyptic preachers. Religion once again fortified American spirit and determination. Attendance at church services rose by 10 per cent all over the nation. The language of comfort mixed with the rhetoric of revenge. 'And let Osama bin Laden and whosoever shall rise against this nation understand that we have not dropped to out knees because we are defeated', vowed a Protestant minister, 'but we have dropped to our knees because we are armed and dangerous and ready to fight the good fight of faith. Glory to God.' The dropping to our knees metaphor became overworked within days. Billy Graham, who was quoted more frequently than Jesus Christ during the first week of post 9/11 media life, offered hope and a not so veiled threat of vengeance to be led by the God of battle: 'While the terrorists may have intended to bring America to its knees, perhaps they did not realize how fitting an analogy that would be. It has driven the nation to prayer. Those perpetrators who took this on to tear us apart, it has worked the other way.' If September 11 would always be known as the day New York fell down, it would not be seen as defeat, as ashes, ashes, all fall down, but an intentional kneel down on one's prayer bones in order for God to raise up the city of cities in triumph. The rhetoric of redemptive violence had become the national anthem.

In the days following the September 11 attack on America, '*pray!*' became the rallying cry on street corners all across the nation—and topics of religion and faith surged front and center in the news. Jerry Falwell asked people to visit his website and promise to join 'this mighty prayer effort'. In return, he would send them a flag lapel pin bearing the slogan 'Pray for America' and place their names on a list that he vowed to present to Bush in the near future (Lincoln 2001: 46). In a collection of uplifting prayers and reflections one learns that 'Religion girds us for action and commitment to a righteous cause. Going to church has always been one sure signal that Americans were beginning to put aside their differences and were starting the process of joint commitment' (Cortada and Wakin 2002: 242). Even secular newspapers sold prayer. *USA Today* featured a full page ad—'To help America speak to God with one voice: A Prayer by the Nation, For the Nation'—co-sponsored by the National Association of Evangelicals (NAE), America's National Prayer Committee, the National Day of Prayer Task Force, and the Mission America Coalition. Fortunately advertisers pay to speak with one voice, so the invocation to God does not raise the question of whose god that might be.

America turned up the volume on righteousness to an ear-splitting level. One Washington commentator noted, 'No one is asking for atheists they can interview on their talk shows'. Fox News reported less than a week later, 'We've seen a resurgence of public religion—Americans are rediscovering the power of faith'.[9] Perhaps nothing so vividly symbolized that public resurgence as when the members of Congress stood shoulder-to-shoulder and sang *God Bless America* on the Capitol steps.[10] To relieve our own pain, we must squeeze the enemy's throat.

9.   Taken from <www.Beliefnet.com>, an online collection of essays, prayers, etc. from the weeks following 9/11.

10.   In her book, *Britons: Forging the Nation, 1707–1837*, historian Linda Colley (1992) has argued, 'A number of European monarchs start appealing to the people to carry out the Protestant Reformation', Colley wrote, 'You can see it very graphically in England in the 16th century, where they get rid of holy images in the church and replace them with the royal coat of arms. So you don't worship images of the saints, you worship the monarch as the head of the church. A lot of countries—Britain,

With an unblinking version of the facts the Administration ignored nuances and presented half-grasped truths as absolutes. The task was to excite Americans with the gee-whiz technology of our war toys and the inevitability of our victories. Since the 9/12, the media has stayed on the Administration's message. Not until June 2003 did former General Wesley Clark assert his corroboration of a little-noted CBS Evening News story that aired almost a year earlier on 4 September 2002. As correspondent David Martin had reported:

> Barely five hours after American Airlines Flight 77 plowed into the Pentagon, the secretary of defense was telling his aides to start thinking about striking Iraq, even though there was no evidence linking Saddam Hussein to the attacks. According to CBS, a Pentagon aide's notes from that day quote Rumsfeld asking for the 'best info fast' to 'judge whether good enough to hit SH at the same time, not only OBL'.[11]

The media let Martin's story go cold throughout the Countdown to War, the Road to Baghdad, and the American troops great success. The road to peace wound slowly through the staging area of Kuwait, and finally through Basra and Baghdad. All day and all night we watched ancient stone ruins and modern palaces with faucets of gold tumble down into the desert. Four months after the Coalitions' mass destruction in Iraq, during the media-tagged 'Quagmire in Iraq', the press began in fits and starts to grumble about weapons of mass destruction that seemed to elude the CIA and the CNN cameras. It was time to book Clark on *Meet the Press*. Instead of cheerleading US efforts in Iraq, General Clark told anchor Tim Russert that Bush Administration officials had engaged in a campaign to implicate Saddam Hussein in the September 11 attacks— starting that very day. Clark said that he'd been called on September 11 and urged to link Baghdad to the terror attacks, but declined to do so because of a lack of evidence:

> CLARK: There was a concerted effort during the fall of 2001, starting immediately after 9/11, to pin 9/11 and the terrorism problem on Saddam Hussein.

Sweden, and Holland—see themselves as the new Israel, the holy nation. The American colonies inherit this tradition as the City on the Hill.'

11.   The initials SH and OBL stand for Saddam Hussein and Osama bin Laden. Tracking the neutral reporting of the mainstream US media is done by FAIR, a national media watch group that documents criticism of media bias and censorship. This study has used much of the reporting from FAIR that has exposed mainstream media practices and neglected news stories.

RUSSERT: By who? Who did that?
CLARK: Well, it came from the White House, it came from people around the White House. It came from all over. I got a call on 9/11. I was on CNN, and I got a call at my home saying, 'You got to say this is connected. This is state-sponsored terrorism. This has to be connected to Saddam Hussein'. I said, 'But—I'm willing to say it, but what's your evidence?' And I never got any evidence (Transcript, *Meet the Press*).

Fast-forward two years: there is still no evidence.

For a *Sources* report that GOP Senate Intelligence Committee members Olympia Snowe and Chuck Hagel have privately questioned the Administration's handling of pre-war intelligence.[12] More of the same tepid treacle had trickled in during the end of June 2003. *Sources* indicated that Congressional Intelligence committees *may* question the CIA analysts who briefed Cheney, and these hearings *might* lead to calling Cheney's hard-line aides and *perhaps* Cheney himself to testify. The shelf-life of this story was shorter than that of a Krispy Kreme donut, or General Clark's subsequent entry into the Democratic run for the Presidential Nomination during the winter of 2004. While Clark was campaigning, he lowered the volume of accusations about 9/11, moving instead to the fertile arena of the military mistakes the Bush Administration had made in Iraq. By July 2004, the cat was out of the Senate bag. No longer were unattributed comments the newsbite of the day. The Senate Intelligence report had substantiated that the weapons had been overstated, the dangers exaggerated by the CIA. After releasing its devastating report on Iraq intelligence failures, the Senate Intelligence Committee is already forging ahead on a much more politically sensitive follow-up investigation that will examine pre-war statements by President Bush and other Administration officials. At the time of writing, members of the Senate panel have been asked by the committee chairman, Pat Roberts (R-Kan.) to submit lists of claims made by White House officials and other policymakers that would be scrutinized to determine whether they were exaggerated or unsupported by intelligence assessments available before the invasion of Iraq. Where were the investigative reporters during this almost three-year period?

Resisting the responsibility of the Fourth Estate, our 'free press' has been laying out jumbo helpings of junk food prose day after day since 9/11. From the flames in New York to the flames in Baghdad, the TV

---

12. See particularly the *Time Magazine* article of 29 June 2003 emphasizes the mystery angle of the missing proof of weapons, but is lacking in investigative reporting, citing 'sources' in a vague imprecise manner.

tapes keep the fires of nationalism alive. Required to fill dead air in order to serve up all news all the time, Cable TV has garnished the tasteless tapes of the Twin Towers in flames and the Pentagon's movie of the week footage on Jessica Lynch with outraged politicians, pontificating military experts, smug security experts, sleepy-eyed historians, and a supporting cast of former Pentagon officials, and anyone else with a half-recognizable credential. According to FAIR, the media watch group, official voices, including current and former government employees, accounted for 63 per cent of overall sources. 'Former military personnel, who often appeared in longer-format in-studio interviews, rather than in sound bites, characteristically offered technical commentary supportive of US military efforts.'[13]

With the press supporting the Administration's version of vengeance as nationalism, America went after the terrorists, all or nothing, God vs. the devil. Verbs changed markedly: pray became attack. The President addressed a joint session of Congress on 20 September 2001, and ended with these words, spun from a Puritan heritage:

> The course of this conflict is not known, yet its outcome is certain. Freedom and fear, justice and cruelty, have always been at war, and we know that God is not neutral between them. Fellow citizens, we'll meet violence with patient justice, assured of the rightness of our cause and confident of the victories to come. In all that lies before us, may God grant us wisdom and may He watch over the United States of America.

After the televised horror of the destruction in New York and Washington on September 11, the media showed us who we were, and even more specifically, who *they* were. During that week, we became a community, a 24/7 TV nation. In stop-time when horror had become fact, and fact a script from a Jerry Bruckheimer film, the message was too overloaded even for 'seen it all' New Yorkers. With Air Force jets zooming over Manhattan and dark warships plowing the waters of New York Harbor, newscasters presented unthinkable destruction with the backdrop of a thousand action films. But the action had lost its fizz. A fictive Wall Street broker who had escaped from the inferno spoke to the ever-present cable news microphones. These particular microphones belonged to satiric publication *The Onion*. 'If the world were going to suddenly turn into a movie without warning, I wish it would have been one of those boring, talky Merchant-Ivory ones instead. I hate those movies, but I sure wish we were living in one right now.'[14]

13. 'Amplifying Officials, Squelching Dissent', *Extra!* (May/June 2003): 12.
14. *The Onion* 37 (26 September 2001).

While the disconsolate broker may have been a figment of someone's imagination, it seems appropriate to situate this tragedy among styles of filmmaking. After all New York City has been the City on the Hill in worldwide fantasies for at least a century. *Bring me your tired; your poor, your huddled masses longing to breathe free...* Bring me your jeans, your big Macs, your ten-gallon hats. The eye candy of films that immortalize almost every street in New York City, from the gritty stoops of Harlem to the slender towers and soaring shafts of midtown commercial buildings, yes! New York is a wonderful town. People who have never been to New York City are familiar with its mansions, tenements, brownstones, and lofts; with its subway system, Grand Central station, and waterfront. As Jean Baudrillard observed,

> [There is a] feeling that you get when you step out [of a movie theater] a city that seems the very reflection of [that which] you have just seen, as if the city had come out of the film and not the other way around. An American city seems to have stepped right out of the movies. To grasp its secret, you should not, then, begin with the city and move toward the screen; you should begin with the screen and move outward toward the city.

Even if one has not actually walked down Fifth Avenue, everyone can experience Breakfast at Tiffany's. Similarly those living thousands of miles from northern New Jersey are familiar with Satriale's pork store and the other urban landscape of an HBO-invented Jersey City through the weekly repetition of the opening minutes of Sopranos.

Add to the worldwide audience that has created their own New York City of the imagination, there is the powerful American homerun rhetoric of sports and Christianity. Called muscular Christianity or Sportsianity, a term coined by *Sports Illustrated* writer Frank Deford, the men-first Jocks for Jesus rhetoric has been popular for even longer than the celluloid mysteries. The muscular Christianity of the late nineteenth century added a moral and spiritual dimension to the fitness movement— which may explain the self-righteousness that so often afflicts its followers. Similar to the earlier connection between nationalism and religious fervor, Sportsianity is the creation of political leaders who have understood religious passion as the one popular emotion that could bring masses of people into the streets. Or the stadium. At the Notre Dame football stadium in South Bend is a large mural known as Touchdown Jesus. At the Cathedral of St John the Divine in New York there is a side altar, dedicated in 1928, which mingles sports figures from baseball and football teams in New York City with such biblical athletes as Jacob wrestling with the angel. We are used to weekend News footage of Presidents jogging, leading the Press Corps, looking fit enough to lead the Free World.

Marjorie Garber argues that the muscular Christianity phenomenon is rooted more in evangelical Christianity than in mainline Protestant denominations because the confessional, 'God is my coach' rhetoric and overt witnessing is more common to the born-again tradition. She cites the sports–religion–patriotism connection made by the Reverend Billy Graham, who proclaimed during the Vietnam War, 'People who are carrying the Vietcong flag around the country are not athletes. If our people would spend more time in gymnasiums and on playing fields, we'd be a better nation' (Garber 1999: 284-85).

Like his crusading mentor, George 43 uses the terminology and glory of the sports page to clothe the gospel in true grit and total victory: a home run, a touchdown, a knockout.[15] Within weeks of 9/11 the World Series was staged with phalanxes of firefighters, police, emergency medical techs and other safety workers, and military brass filling the field from home plate to second base. America's war machine began to flex its muscle as soon as the Twin Towers fell down. The sports metaphor was continually invoked: 'We must strike out their side'. Bush himself played the role of the closer, the go-to pitcher who would assure the win for our team. Since that time we have not had time to exercise restraint. I think our bullpen is overworked.

Trading in Souls

In the years since 9/11 a group of prominent evangelical Christian ministers has sought to capture the Islamic faithful and convert them to Christianity. Incendiary comments about Islam from religious leaders like Franklin Graham, Jerry Falwell, Pat Robertson, and Jerry Vines have drawn rebukes from Muslims and Christian groups alike, but many in the grass roots of evangelical Christianity have absorbed their leaders' antipathy for Islam. In Evangelical churches and seminaries across country, lectures and books promoting strategies for Muslim conversions are gaining

---

15. Sports-as-business has continued in the family up through Bush 43's adult life. His great-grandfather, Herbert Walker, headed a syndicate that rebuilt Madison Square Garden in 1925 as the modern heralded 'Palace of Sport' and in 1930 became New York State Racing Commissioner. Herbert Walker bred racehorses at his own stable, the Log Cabin Stud. He was president of the Belmont Park race track and his son George Walker, Jr, George 43's uncle and financial angel in Texas, co-founded the New York Mets and was the baseball club's vice president and treasurer for 17 years until his death in 1977. President Bush 43 was co-owner of the Texas Rangers baseball club during his father's Presidency. It has been widely reported that his goal is to become the commissioner of baseball.

currency.[16] The rhetoric is not new, although its specific application to
the faithful of Islam instead of those who are vacillating Christians may
be unusual. The urgent faithful vision, as described by Falwell and Franklin, is to extend the vision, to evangelize the world for Christ. No longer
is bringing America back to God enough of a task, now the non-Chris-
tian world must be converted. The biblical truth, as these interpreters
understand it, is for all of us to be one in Christ, even those who understand themselves to be faithful to the God of the Book.

Many of these groups view the US military and its wars in the Muslim
world as the perfect vehicles for missionary work in the difficult '10/40
Window'. The 10/40 Window is evangelical Christian-speak for the
rectangle with boundaries of latitudes 10 and 40 degrees north of the
equator; encompassing most of the Muslim world. Director of his father's
group, The Evangelical Association, and Chairman and CEO of his own
missionizing agency, Samaritan's Purse, Franklin Graham explained the
evangelical reasoning to an interviewer:

> Many people after 9/11 said that 'The Muslims, they worship the same
> god we do, they just have their way to God. Christians have their way to
> God. But it's the same God'. No, it's not. Now they recognize Jesus, but
> they don't recognize his deity. They've even taken excerpts out of the
> Old Testament and New Testament, and thrown it into the Qur'an, to
> sprinkle a few Bible verses throughout to give it validity. But the Qur'an
> is not the word of God. The Holy Bible is God's word.[17]

Franklin has replaced his ailing father in leading the huge Billy Graham
organization. You may wonder about religious ministries being handed
down like fifteenth-century dukedoms, but the practice is fairly common
in America, and several of the nation's big ministries—the type of outfits
that might be characterized as Las Vegas Showstoppers for Jesus—have
been handed down in this fashion. This happens in American politics,
too. The second-generation Bush beat out the second-generation Gore,
at least in the electoral college.

Mincing no words, journalist Mas'ood Cajee describes Graham as a
'spiritual carpetbagger and war profiteer who trades in souls' (Cajee 2003).
Reacting to negative publicity, Graham struck back in an *Los Angeles
Times* editorial:

> Thirty years ago, I visited Baghdad for the first time. Today, our Christian
> relief organization, Samaritan's Purse, has a team of Americans, Cana-
> dians, Iraqis, Jordanians and Lebanese positioned in Jordan, just a few

16. The *New York Times* (27 May 2003).
17. See <www.Beliefnet.com> (search Franklin Graham).

hours' drive from the Iraqi border, waiting to provide aid to the thousands of victims, regardless of religion, race or politics. Why do we do it? Like Livingstone, Mother Teresa and millions of others throughout the ages, we draw our motivation for such work from the greatest physician and relief worker who ever lived, Jesus Christ.[18]

Arab International Ministry, a group that has lead crash courses on Islam for six years, claims to have trained 4500 American Christians to proselytize Muslims, many of those since 2001 terrorist attacks.[19] Their basic presumption is that world's two largest religions are headed for confrontation, with Christianity representing what is good, true, and peaceful, and Islam what is evil, false, and violent. Recently softening their tone and renaming their group the Crescent Project, the group offers missionizing trips to the Middle East, online prayer groups, and printed materials and VHS tapes for organizing church groups in the US. Their argument begins: 'Do not lose heart! Do not quit praying for the Muslim world! Reach out to Muslims everywhere with the transforming message of Christ.' The Project continues to emphasize the word *fanatic* as a reminder of 9/11. 'Fanatics of any religion do not worry the church. The most famous fanatic is Saul of Tarsus, who was transformed by Grace to the Apostle Paul.'[20]

The Crescent Project has an active website which witnesses to their success in their Sahara challenge in missionizing the gospel in the Middle East. A personal witness from one of the evangelizers reads as follows:

> The things I learned in the *Sahara Challenge* definitely helped me talk to and understand the people I was with. Many of the people I met had little or no knowledge of Christianity, and as long as I didn't push them to agree with me, they wanted to hear about what I believe. I didn't have all the answers to their questions, but I was able to share the Gospel with them in a way they understood. One instance that I remember was when I was trying to explain to a Palestinian man that Christians, contrary to

18.   The *Los Angeles Times* (3 April 2003).

19.   See the response to the article in the *New York Times* (27 May 2003), from AIM: 'The *New York Times* article sought to discredit us and other Evangelical groups by including negative comments about Islam made by religious leaders in the past. Arab International Ministry does not endorse any of the critical comments made by these leaders about Islam'. Regardless of the group's outrage, they end their response to the *Times*, with their credo, a clear self-indictment: 'We have an open mind and heart to all people, races and religions, and we have a message of hope to both moderate and militant Muslims—that true peace comes through faith in one God and one Savior Jesus Christ'.

20.   <https://www.arabim.org/saharachallenge.html>.

Muslim beliefs, do not believe in three gods. Fouad had told me that when trying to explain this aspect of Christianity, not to use the favorite verse of Christians, John 3.16. This verse calls Jesus the Son of God and is a problem for Muslims because they do not believe that God can have a son. Instead, use John 1.1, which calls Jesus the Word of God. I used this verse and explained that if Jesus is the Word of God then he had to have been with God since the beginning of time or God would not have been able to communicate, and that same idea with the Spirit of God.[21]

If one does not have the time or desire to preach the gospel, one can distribute products designed to sell Christ to one's Muslim friends and neighbors. One has a choice of purchasing the New Testament in Farsi, Arabic, or Turkish. An Injeel (New Testament) can be had in Arabic, Farsi, or Turkish for about $3 per copy. There is a video called *The Loving Answers* for $30. It is a mellow, mindless infomercial about the benefits of Christian belief, available only in English. In both Arabic and English versions is a biopic; the 'Jesus' Film that can be ordered in bulk.

On a Saturday in May 2003, in a fellowship hall at Southwest Grace Brethren Church in Grove City, Ohio, evangelical Christians from several states gathered for an all-day seminar on how to woo Muslims away from Islam. According to a *New York Times* reporter, one speaker/teacher used passages from the Koran, which he claimed *proved* Islam is regressive, fraudulent, and violent.[22] Following the inner spirituality of the national security state, the Good News or Gospel of this group is not the unconditional love of enemies but their elimination. Salvation is a successful foreign policy.

Most of us probably recall listening to Bush throw down his Gunsmoke-Terminator-007 ultimatum to Saddam Hussein. 'We are a peaceful people', Bush said with his half smile. 'The greatest power of freedom is to overcome hatred and violence and turn the creative gifts of men and women to the pursuits of peace.'[23] Then he warned Saddam that he had 48 hours to get out of Dodge. Americans preened at this 'take no prisoners' line in the sand. Cable networks proclaimed war months before the troops crossed into Iraq. The only suspense was when the troops would leave their camps in Kuwait, accompanied by embedded reporters and camera crews, and enter Iraq. Nightly primetime TV hummed like an

21. This witness is signed 'melissa', at <https://www.arabim.org/sahara.html>.

22. *Religion and Ethics Newsweekly*, citing an interview with Kim Lawton which took place following the publication of Graham's 2002 book, *The Name*. Taken from <http://www.pbs.org/wnet/religionandethics/week549/news.html> (page no longer accessible).

23. Quoted in Jackson 2003.

arms bazaar. Americans were comforted by the TV war; like all made-for TV violence, it would end with the good guys as winners. God is not neutral. God is on our side. The President ended each of his public speeches with the 'May God continue to bless America'. This phrase should be read as more powerful than clichéd. Historian Bruce Lincoln warns, 'Although those so inclined may dismiss Bush's closing words as obligatory, gratuitous, and virtually devoid of meaning, others will rec-ognize them as the tip of a vast subtextual iceberg' (2001: 42-44). Fortu-nately for the Bush team, the American public's long-term memory is about two weeks in duration. For a media-soaked culture, a daily dose of excitement is more vital than pondering the quixotic issues of invasion and destruction.

In the first months after 9/11, the Administration's ruthless exploita-tion of the atrocity was a choice, not a necessity. The natural instinct of the nation to rally around its leader in times of crisis had pushed Mr Bush into the polling stratosphere, and his re-election seemed secure. He could have governed as the uniter he claimed to be, and would probably still be wildly popular. But Mr Bush's advisers were greedy; they saw 9/11 as an opportunity to get everything they wanted, from another round of tax cuts, to a major weakening of the Clean Air Act, to an invasion of Iraq. And so they wrapped as much as they could in the flag. And sealed the package with piety and prayers.

For a religionist, the promise of 'shock and awe' bombing is a bold restatement of *herem*, the 'leave nothing standing' strategy of the battle-fields of ancient Israel. The obligation for Israelites to practice *herem*, or genocide in contemporary terms, is found throughout the warring texts and laws of the Hebrew Bible; it is spelled out in Deuteronomy 20, which instructs on the only acceptable way to conduct warfare: when your [Israelite] army approaches a distant city, enslave *all* its inhabitants, *if it surrenders*, and kill *all* its men and enslave its women and children and steal their cattle and everything else if *it does not surrender*. The *herem* is imperative if the town is a place of infidels, that is, a town that believes in false gods. Nothing should be left alive if these people do not believe in YHWH. Carrying out with precision such a military strategy, exhibiting faithfulness to the Lord, his Commander in Chief, rewarded Joshua with biblical narrative approval. A few chapters later, side-stepping the law of *herem* resulted in the downfall of Saul.

The attack on Afghanistan did not release the tension in the United States. Vengeance still tugged at the American psyche. In the year and a half since its creation, the Department of Homeland Security has never set the security alert lower than yellow, a persistent reminder that we live under a significant risk of a terrorist attack. The Administration has given us an orange alert for Christmas, checkpoints on highways, and in the spring of 2003, a simulated bio-attack on Seattle, played out in front of the TV cameras. Our anxieties have also been enflamed by the duct tape hysteria, forbidding air traffic to fly over Disneyworld and over stadiums during major sporting events. The press has become a lot less shy about pointing out the Administration's exploitation of 9/11, partly because that exploitation has become so crushingly obvious. President Bush has invoked 9/11 not just to defend Iraq policy and argue for oil drilling in the Arctic, but in response to questions about tax cuts, unemployment, budget deficits, and even campaign finance. As *The Washington Post* pointed out while reflecting upon the observance of 9/11/2003, 'the crudity of the Administration's recent propaganda efforts, from dressing the president up in a flight suit to orchestrating the ludicrously glamorized TV movie about Mr Bush on 9/11, have set even supporters' teeth on edge'.[24] And perhaps the most cynical focus on 9/11 will be the Republican Party Convention, which has been rescheduled to September 2004, drawing a taut line between supporting our leaders and the fear of terrorism.

Further, there is the Administration's use of the Other, the immigrants, to show the strength and resolve of the real Americans. More than 13,000 of the Arab and Muslim men who came forward in the winter of 2002 to register with immigration authorities—roughly 16 per cent of the total—may now face deportation. Only a handful have been linked to terrorism. But of the 82,000 men older than 16 who registered, more than 13,000 have been found to be living in this country illegally.[25] Many had hoped to win leniency by demonstrating their willingness to cooperate with the campaign against terror. The government has initiated deportation proceedings, and in immigrant communities across the country an exodus has already begun, in what is the largest wave of deportations after the September 11 attacks.

The justification for abandoning civil rights when 'necessary' is found in the daily repetition of demonizing the enemy, those 'evil ones who recognize no barrier of morality'. In this newest American fusion of politics and propaganda, the strategy remains the same: staying on message. How do we explain the enemy? By reducing cultures different from our own mythically unified America into easy-to-swallow sound bites. While there is lip service to Islam as a fine religion, there is a barrage of

24. *The New York Times* (13 September 2003).
25. *The New York Times* (6 June 2003).

photographs in all the popular media of nefarious Muslim men: disheveled, unshaven, menacing. Through visualizing the sharp differences between baseball-capped Americans and kaffiyah-draped Muslims, we can stage-manage history. Cold war, Commies, axis of evil. How many people even remember that both the National Council of Churches and the Conference of Catholic Bishops argued passionately against the US initiating a war against Iraq?

Sometimes a date is like a sharp knife cutting through history. The date of the first Coalition of the Willing 'surgical strike' bombing of Baghdad was the night of 21 March 2003.[26] Perfect for the morning news in the Eastern time zone. In October 2004, the number of Coalition war dead continues to climb: 1071 Americans (929 of these deaths have occurred since President Bush declared the end of major combat operations on 1 May 2003; 608 since the capture of Saddam Hussein), 68 from the United Kingdom, and 70 'Other'.[27] According to Nancy Lessin, co-founder of the group Military Families Speak Out,

> One does not need to be a historian to know that the image of dead Americans, returning day after day in body bags, helped turn America against the war in Vietnam. This Administration has gone to great lengths to prevent a repeat by keeping images of lifeless and broken bodies away from the cameras and the consciousness of the American people. Mr. Bush has not yet attended a single funeral for anyone killed in Iraq—*not a single one*. Spain and Italy held state funerals for their countrymen who died in Iraq, but the Bush Administration's policy for our own war dead is to hide them.[28]

The US does not count Iraqi casualties.[29] However, Iraq Body Count (IBC) does. A volunteer group of British and US academics and researchers, IBC compiles statistics on civilian casualties from media reports and has estimated that between 13,086 and 37,000 Iraqi civilians have died

26. For those who are interested in the rhetoric of destruction, the Associated Press account of that night: 'Central Command is calling it a historic strike—with B-1, B-2 and B-52 bombers joining in. The command says it's the first time in history that long-range strike aircraft have hit the same area at the same time. The attacks targeted leadership and command and control centers in the Iraqi capital. The missiles ignited a fire at the Iraqi Information Ministry—yards away from a shopping mall named for Saddam Hussein.'

27. <http://www.icasualties.org>, accessed 20 September 2004.

28. <http://www.alternet.org/story.html?StoryID=18030>.

29. On the first anniversary of the beginning of the Coalition bombing of Iraq, the following data was available about Iraqi casualties. Combatant casualties range from 7600 to 10,800. Civilian dead range from 7581 to 10,430. Various reporting sources are Associated Press, United Press, the *New York Times*, and *The Plain Dealer*.

through acts of war or other violence; estimates vary. Accurate numbers for the Iraqi military are difficult to find. The Brookings list indicates that 750 Iraqi police have been killed since January 2004. There an estimated 40,000 insurgents remaining in Iraq.[30]

Myth of Redemptive Violence

Around Memorial Day of 2004, the White House announced that President George Bush had been given a pistol, one that had special significance and makes him very proud. It was taken from Saddam Hussein when he was captured by US Army Delta Force team, the day they trapped him in a spider hole near Tikrit in December 2003. The military had the pistol mounted, and it was presented to Mr Bush privately by some of the troops who ferreted out Saddam. Mr Bush now takes select visitors to see the pistol in a small study next to the Oval Office, which gives the weapon the importance of an icon, a trophy of power.

Though it was widely reported at the time that the pistol was loaded when US troops grabbed Saddam, Mr Bush has told visitors that the gun was actually empty—and that it is still empty and safe to touch. Like a child with a wondrous new toy, Bush shows the mounted pistol to 'select guests'. In the Freudian world, sometimes a gun is more than a gun. This observation is not the only psychoanalytic interpretation to Mr Bush reverencing his enemy's gun. According to Stanley A. Renshon, psychoanalyst and political science professor at City University of New York, 'It's the phallic equivalent of a scalp—I mean that quite seriously' (Bumiller 2004). The icon of defeat becomes in the Oval Office an icon of triumph.

As a biblical scholar, I find it impossible not to connect the pistol with the kinds of prizes biblical war heroes seized from their defeated enemies. One could compare Mr Bush's delight in Saddam's gun with David teasing the doomed Saul with his own spear, proof that David had the power to kill him outright, but would wait until the victory of which God had assured him. Military victory, then as now, allows historians to validate whatever the victors 'had to do' to ensure success.

---

30. These figures are generally confirmed by the website Iraq Body Count <http://www.iraqbodycount.net/>. One can get demonic about counting the dead. The estimate of Iraqi military is 4895 to 6370, although the US does not publish the list of Iraqi military, insurgent, or civilian dead. See also <http://www.antiwar.com/casualties/> which counts Iraqi civilian deaths, approaching 15,000. See <http://brookings. edu/iraqindex>, which is updated each week. It carries data on everything from number of functioning electrical plants by area to number of translators killed (50 since January 2004).

The authors of Deuteronomy make clear the laws of the *herem* or ban: God's people had to destroy every material remnant of the enemy. The logic of this ban seems to revolve around temptation. Do not be tempted to wage war by what your enemy has because you will not profit from his material possessions. Joshua struggles with materialistic Israelites and Saul himself does not seem emotionally able to kill his equal, the king of the Amalekites: 'Now go and attack Amalek, and utterly destroy all that they have; do not spare them, but kill both man and woman, child and infant, ox and sheep, camel and donkey' (1 Sam. 15.3).

While I find this divine order shocking on its face, I think it is a theological solution to maintaining the covenant, which awards God's chosen people the land, while retaining at least a shred of human humility. Niditch understands the ban to be a way 'to assert God's judgment, a defense of the faith, in short a crusade' (1993a: 64). Her view is probably closer to the ongoing view that we are God's chosen people and must defend the faith through violence and destruction. While some Christians may play down the authority of the so-called Old Testament, the appeal to biblical infallibility is a fundamental pillar of evangelical Christians.

Throughout the wars that the Israelites wage against their enemies, there is the insistence that God is the ruler to whom all the spoils will be dedicated. In a confrontation with Joshua, YHWH blazes in anger against the Israelites, who have sinned: 'they [Achan and his family] have transgressed my covenant that I imposed on them. They have taken some of the devoted things; they have stolen, they have acted deceitfully, and they have put them among their own belongings' (Josh. 7.11). Does this imply that if one were to take a strict interpretation of the book of Joshua, a faithful person would destroy the pistol hanging on President Bush's wall? If the keeping of banned booty, even a goat or a silver earring, is enough to incur the wrath of God, then war profiteering such as the Halliburton smoke and mirrors, would surely bring down the wrath of the biblical deity. He insisted on a ban of Achan and his family for just such narcissistic activity

For those of the Christian evangelical world who treasure Bush 43's pride in his confessional connection with Jesus, one might dwell for a moment of time on a scene from the Good Book. Prowling the desert, it was the Evil One who tempted Jesus with unparalleled power and wealth: 'And the Devil took him up to a high place, and showed him all the kingdoms of the world in a moment of time, and said to him, "To you I will give all this authority and their glory; for it has been delivered to me"' (Mt. 4.4-6; Lk. 4.5-8). With the gun hanging upon his wall, Mr Bush has chosen the symbol of death, over the symbol of life. In our name he has chosen the law of force over the force of law.

6

AND GOD CREATED WOMAN:
MARKETING WOMEN FROM PROVERBS TO FIRST LADIES

> He spoke to those that would live perfectly;
> And, masters, by your leave, such am not I.
> I will devote the flower of all my age
> To all the acts and harvests of marriage.
> > —Chaucer, *The Wife of Bath's Prologue*, ll. 111-14[1]

> I'm so proud that you're first lady, Nancy,
> And so pleased that I'm sort of a chum
> The next eight years will be fancy
> As fancy as they come.
> > —Frank Sinatra, *Nancy with the Reagan Face*

The focus of this chapter is to try to trace a trajectory from the biblical origins of female stereotypes through their current existence in the American mass media. Our current media create as much as reflect reality, and their process of selection and interpretation is culturally significant. In the evolving story of American politics, the candidates and the women who surround them (mothers, wives, daughters), media imagery is not a reflection of the news. It is the news. How the media have transformed and perpetuated certain cultural ideals can be traced back to several biblical paradigms: the matriarchs in the Hebrew Bible and the unnamed wife in the final chapter of the book of Proverbs.

The ideal woman changes within each swirl of modern popular culture, almost as frequently as her hemlines. In spite of the obvious differences, however, there seems to be a continuous thread from the ideal woman in the Hebrew Bible to the point women of political husbands. There is a parallel between the ideal woman in our own time, and the ideal wife/ woman of the ancient Mediterranean world. While it may appear to some readers that too many boundaries are disrupted by comparing fictive characters with real women, I have been struck by how direct the connection

---

1.   All quotations from Chaucer are from the 1988 Riverside edition.

is between early gender representation and its contemporary echo. The contemporary women is too often required to conform, or allows herself to be constructed, into the stereotype originally put forth in biblical texts. The pattern of the presentation of First Ladies is to borrow the appeal and the acceptability of these ideals precisely because they are still accepted within large portions of our mass culture.

Powerful women, especially rich and powerful women in the public eye, are usually cast as stereotypes: Jackie Kennedy or Hillary Clinton, diva or opportunist? When women are married to men in power, they are not expected to engage in philosophical tours de force. Rather, they are supposed to be a backdrop against which are projected the activities of their husbands. The necessity of soft-focusing wives can be explained through theories of spectatorship, which usually imply a one-to-one correspondence between the spectator position and gender identity (Bal 1999; Doane 1987; Erens 1979; hooks (1993); Kaplan 1983; Modleski 1992). However, if we think of the reader as the spectator-shopper of the mass media, then there is a pleasure to be had with trying on the identity of the First Lady, which simultaneously allows one to escape her own physically bound identity. When one mass-market image becomes shopworn, one can discard it with the next wave of election mania.

Unlike the successful woman in Proverbs 31, the political wife/woman are not portrayed as efficient, compared with a merchant fleet. That extraordinary woman is not created by the same vision as the matriarchal models in the Genesis narratives: Sarah, Rebecca, Leah, and Rachel. The matriarchs are primarily concerned with procreation, and much closer to the First Ladies of today's US candidates. Like good mother/woman drawn from biblical models, these women are breathtakingly predictable in the characterizations or stories presented in the media. They are primarily the First Consumers, and the media preserves all their brand loyalties, encouraging these women to preen in all their consumerist prowess. As First Consumer the woman becomes the object in the window, subject to the critique of other female consumers, familiar with selecting products and returning the blank gaze of the mannequin.

Clearly, ideal woman is ideal only through a particular focus. The dichotomy of seeing and being seen has usually implied the male as the subject of the gaze and the woman as the object. Being the permanent object of popular media gaze, the First Lady model must continually watch herself, to display herself as a biblically modeled good woman. Doane has argued that the woman functions like the inmate in Bentham's prison, in Foucault's Panopticon: 'For defined in terms of her visibility, she carries her own Panopticon with her wherever she goes, her self image a function of her being for another' (Doane 1987: 14). In her own panopticon does Hillary Clinton see herself as an attorney, a senator, or the husband of Bill, the mother of Chelsea? Her own autobiography delivers that answer, as she writes of the joys of campaigning (for her husband in his first race for Governor of Arkansas) with a diaper bag on her shoulder and small Chelsea on her hip. In her own self-survey, Clinton writes more of her marriage, her daughter, her maternal feelings for children and theories of child development than she does of her legal career.

First Ladies with their own careers, Rosalynn Carter, Hillary Clinton, and Laura Bush (although Mrs Bush has not worked as a librarian since the birth of her twin daughters 22 years ago), have without overt complaint put their careers on hold, as have candidates' wives Teresa Heinz Kerry, a philanthropist, and Elizabeth Edwards, a bankruptcy attorney. Whenever possible these women turn the interviewer's attention back to their husbands, trying to obscure the camera's direct gaze. Perhaps they are flinching under the panoptic gaze, and are trying to stick with John Berger's oft-quoted feminist observation: 'men act, women appear'.

Designing Women

The biblical narrators' story of God's creation of the universe, of the man, of the woman, of the laws of the Garden, have in our culture taken on the force of natural law. The creation of the woman as a companion for the man is a theme that runs through much of our own popular culture. The male dream of controlling creation, including the creation or construction of the woman, continues to drive the underlying plots of many popular narratives, as well as the outlook of the media and the heartbeat of evangelical religion. 'Wives obey your husbands' is a mantra still heard in much of the heartland. By identifying the codes of contemporary American social and cultural ideologies found in both films and print ads from the Forties and Fifties, one learns both how idealized images of people are constructed and how the people are positioned in the social hierarchy. Too often the relationship between the creator and the female object of the gaze is based upon the relationship in the Garden. The producers of commercial discourse continuously struggle to define a target female, believing that she will succeed in offering their products to compliant consumers as she did in the Garden to the unwitting male. The situation has become more diffuse as women have penetrated the predominantly male advertising industry.

Two American cultural icons combine to portray the woman from Genesis 3 in both her guises: Snow White and the Varga pin-up girl. As

Mr Disney's mother of us all, Snow White grows up to become the idealized wife of postwar America, depicted both in films and most stunningly in advertising. Popular images leave little doubt about what makes the woman 'good', this wife-woman the deity might have created as the perfect companion for the man, once upon a time in a misty Garden. The solitary American woman is often pictured with equipment: refrigerator, stove, bathtub, and of course that serpentine instrument of housewifely delight, the Hoover hose vacuum cleaner. Thus, we have the category of woman set within her social context: the home, which is her companion while the husband and children are away. She is always smiling and never confounded by the way the machinery of her world operates.

She is the American girl, who instinctively knows how to clean, cook, and make a house a home; her lineage is reflected not only in advertisements but in that didactic tool: the feature length cartoon. Walt Disney used Snow White to teach the young women who would grow up to clean those houses of the Fifties how to whistle while they worked. If Snow White taught us anything, it was that it is as easy to keep house for seven as one. Clearly she is a woman who lives out the concept of the punished woman from Genesis 3: she will work hard (remember those seven little boy-men on whom she practices her skills) and her desire will be for her husband (Gen. 3.16)—the prince. She is fulfilled doing the work of the household.

From the other side of the tracks come the Varga pin-up girls, who tempt the American male to forget the rules of the game. With pale gold hair, blood red nails and lips, and a sinuous body, each one is a visual mix of the woman and the serpent. Dangerous but compelling, she exudes sexuality from the safe distance of the printed page. Vargas was a commercial artist who painted delicate pastels of glamorous showgirls and well-known movie stars. The Varga girl appeared in advertisements for such diverse products as mayonnaise, shampoo, and Old Gold cigarettes. In 1941 the Varga girl calendar, published by *Esquire* magazine, outsold any calendar published up to that time.[2] While these pin-up girls were

2. Alberto Vargas was probably the most famous and prolific commercial artist, creating glamour girls and pin-ups for the mass market. His work appeared in magazines, in theater lobby posters, and in consumer ads. His first major work was distributed widely in the Thirties by Hollywood studios and the Ziegfeld Follies. Vargas became known worldwide during the years of World War II, where his Varga girl pin-ups appeared on the fusillages of bombers, on soldiers' lapel pins, and on barracks walls. Although he had a full schedule of work for *Esquire* magazine during the war years, he often accommodated special requests from soldiers to paint mascot pin-ups. Vargas' work, both in the monthly magazine and the yearly calendar, was eagerly

overtly sexual, their sexuality did not seem offensive to the mass media. What the Varga ads show, and the multitude of sexually based ads that followed her, is the fierce determination to plumb and predict the female shopper's psyche.

The fantasy of the male being able to create for himself the perfect woman is transformed into a gothic warning in the *Bride of Frankenstein* (1935) and other cinematic dreams of technology aiding modern man's desire for what Shelley's monster shyly hopes will be created as 'friend for me'. The man of science misuses the collective wonders of electricity, chemistry, and transplants in a vain attempt to elevate his abilities to the creative level of the divine. All Frankenstein gets for his trouble is a monstrous imitation of a woman, perhaps all that his ego clay will permit him to shape.

A third variation on the theme of male creating woman is found in the rash of Hollywood films of men pretending to be women, and indeed in the cases of Dustin Hoffman in *Tootsie* (1982) and Robin Williams in *Mrs Doubtfire* (1993), they are better at exuding compassion than women themselves. Of course there is also the comfort that underneath the latex and lashes they are still men. These women-men offer answers to Rex Harrison's despairing question to stodgy Colonel Pickering in *My Fair Lady* (1964), 'Why can't a woman be more like a man?' First planted in the Garden, the dream of perfect companionship persists. The desire to affix the essence of woman drives much of literature and provides the locus for popular music, advertising, film, and TV narratives. The slippery goal of controlling through one-note definition slides just out of the creator's grasp, showing the constructedness of gender roles and the absence of intrinsic or contained gender identity.

The Perfect Wife in the Bible

Perhaps the most telling point about the concept of wife in the Hebrew Bible lies in the Hebrew word for wife, *'ishshah*, the word used both for

---

awaited. *Esquire* (at the urging of the US Army) allowed Vargas to do a series of patriotic pin-ups for William Randolph Hearst's *American Weekly* magazine, the only other magazine work permitted him during the *Esquire* years. Vargas continued to paint Hollywood stars while he worked for the magazine. His 1941 movie poster of Betty Grable in *Moon Over Miami* was a great success; among the other leading ladies he painted were Jane Russell, Ann Sheridan, Ava Gardner, Linda Darnell, Marlene Dietrich, Loretta Young, and Marilyn Monroe. The Varga pin-up girl has not disappeared from the collective commercial consciousness: there are more than 40 entries on eBay for Vargas collectible items in the summer of 2004.

adult woman and wife.[3] As I and other scholars have noted, in the view of the ancient Israelite world, women were viewed primarily as the adjuncts to their husbands. Abigail is labeled the good-sense wife, the embodiment of *sekel*, in contrast to her husband Nabal (the Hebrew form for whose name means fool. The connection to the book of Proverbs where the use of the word *sekel* is the most extensive is direct. The portrait of Abigail can be read as a narrative interpretation and expansion of the qualities attributed to the good wife of Proverbs 31, who provides food, clothing, and comfort to her household. She is a 'model of benevolent constancy and brings him nothing but good and gain' (McKane 1970: 666). Not surprisingly traditional interpretations of the story of Abigail have consistently focused upon Abigail's good-sense works as advantageous to the men in the story, as appeasing David in his anger, thus saving the lives of her husband, Nabal's workers, and of course by providing enormous quantities of food for David and his men. Narrative analysis is silenced by the unit of Proverbs 31, which is more a list of qualities than a narrative showing the life of the woman/wife.

A composite reading of the two texts gives a fuller sense of the wife/woman. Providing us with some of the details of the daily life of an upper-class wife, Proverbs 31 offers an expansion to Abigail's many accomplishments. She (the good woman/wife) considers a field and buys it; she perceives that her merchandise is profitable; she spins; she takes care of the poor; she makes all manner of garments and sells them. Clearly she does not eat of the bread of idleness (when would she have time?) while her husband sits in the gates of the city. Not surprisingly her children call her 'blessed'. She is rated far more precious than jewels. We can only ponder about whether this description at the end of the book of Proverbs is a male fantasy about a wife who can be trusted to manage and increase his property while he does the work of the community, as one of the elders at the gate. For Abigail the payoff for her virtue is connecting herself to a better husband, one as beautiful and pleasing to God as she is herself. It is not the province of this study to analyze in detail the narrative unit of 1 Samuel 25 or the moral narrative of the acrostic model of wife in Proverbs 31. My focus is to bridge the narrow gap between the ideal ancient woman of biblical narrative and today's media version of the ideal woman.

As the biblical authors have created the ideal women, so the contemporary popular media have played the spin of First Ladies as ideal wife. Of

---

3. The Hebrew terms for women follow their sexual rites of passage: there is a virgin (*betulah*) or unmarried woman, a wife-woman (*'issah*), and a widow.

course it is not a great leap from the traditional biblically driven paradigm of the perfect wife to the pattern of First Ladies, who direct the White House staff and support their husbands' political work. The major difference between the Proverbs wife and Abigail composite and its modern-day counterpart, the First Ladies, is that the modern women are not expected to produce wealth. In the days of feminist or postfeminist thought, it is a continuing surprise that a First Lady today is valued for her cookie recipes more than for her entrepreneurial or intellectual qualities.[4] The maternal wife, with freshly baked cookies to tempt the electorate, is a passive version of wife/woman in contrast with the dawn to midnight wife created in Proverbs 31.

At about the same time, across the Mediterranean, in his compilation of moral advice to farmers, *Works and Days*, Hesiod suggests to those men who might be looking for a wife, 'First of all, get a house, and a woman and an ox for the plough—a slave woman and not a wife, to follow the oxen as well' (ll. 405-13). Here Hesiod distinguishes between a slave and wife/woman, that is, a slave woman is the link between the house and the ox; there is no consideration given by Hesiod to the wifely attributes that will produce children. Later in the work, however, Hesiod suggests that a man

> Bring home a wife to your house when you are of the right age, while you are not far short of thirty years nor much above; this is the right age for marriage. Let your wife have been grown up four years, and marry her in the fifth. Marry a maiden, so that you can teach her careful ways, and especially marry one who lives near you, but look well about you and see that your marriage will not be a joke to your neighbors. For a man wins nothing better than a good wife, and, again, nothing worse than a bad one, a greedy soul who roasts her man without fire, strong though he may be, and brings him to a raw old age (Hesiod, *Work and Days*, ll. 695-705).

4. Every First Lady from Martha Washington to Laura Bush has made available her own cookie recipe. According to a recent cookbook called *Presidential Cookies*, Martha Washington liked Jumbals, a butter cookie flavored with orange rinds. Even Hillary Clinton atoned for her famous remark that she 'could have stayed home and baked cookies and had teas' but instead chose to pursue her law career. She later entered a *Family Circle*-sponsored bake-off against Barbara Bush. Both women entered a chocolate chip cookie recipe. Mrs Clinton's won. In 2004, Laura Bush's 'Texas Governor's Mansion Cowboy' cookie, featuring chocolate and cherries, went up against Teresa Heinz Kerry's spiced pumpkin cookie. For these recipes see <http://www.familycircle.com/marketing/04_cookie_cookoff/index.html>. According to *Family Circle*, whichever candidate's wife wins the bakeoff, brings the election home for her husband. At the time of writing, the 2004 cookie winner has not been announced.

The bad wife, who 'roasts her man without fire', is a devastating description of the warnings women present to incautious men, but again, a nonsexual warning. Comparing Hesiod with biblical moral warnings given to young men in the final chapter of the book of Proverbs shows how similar the focus was. Both are concerned with wife/woman as entrepreneur, as the most valuable of all property, for she will increase her husband's barn, she will extend his other property. First Lady Hillary Clinton learned how the handling of money, with an eye toward increasing your husband's barn, can cast a cold eye of suspicion on your activities. Clouded by the events of the Whitewater scandal, there were loud drubbings of the First Lady, who was often accused of wearing the trousers in the family.

At the other end of the narrative spectrum from the asexual good wife in Proverbs 31 is a medieval created woman more than willing to talk about her five husbands, her lusty sexual pleasures, and offer shrewd advice for the men who would be husbands. The Wife of Bath seems aware of men's suspicions about the perfidies of wives:

> You say that oxen, asses, horses, hounds
> Are tried out variously, and on good grounds;
> Basins and bowls, before men will them buy
> And spoons and stools and all such goods you try.
> And so with pots and clothes and all array;
> But of their wives men get no test, you say,
> Till they are married, base old dotard you!
> And then we show what evil we can do.
> —Chaucer, The Wife of Bath's Tale, ll. 291-96

Chaucer's Ironic Women

As an antidote to the immediate conclusion that male creations of women are always resolved in favor of men, one need only look to Geoffrey Chaucer. In the Prologue to The Canterbury Tales, Chaucer praises conventional ideas of female virtue, while in each of the tales, particularly those of the Wife of Bath and the Prioress, Chaucer demonstrates a humorous skepticism, certainly influenced by the rigid hierarchical culture within the fourteenth-century English society in which he lived. Davenport finds the Wife's Prologue particularly unusual, as it reflects Chaucer's independence by refusing the literary designs accepted in other medieval tale collections (Davenport 1998: 21-34). Political power was concentrated in the king and his court and the Catholic Church retained all authority in spiritual matters. The basic conceit of the tales is that a heterogeneous group of pilgrims travel together on a 60-mile trip to the shrine of Saint Thomas à Becket, who was martyred in Canterbury in 1170. The frame of the narrative involves an Introductory Prologue, in which the narrator, called Chaucer, gives a sketch of each of the travelers. Then, to pass the time on the pilgrimage, each of the characters will tell a story or fable. While Chaucer intended each of the thirty pilgrims to tell two tales on the initial trip and two tales on the return trip, he did not live to finish this ambitious plan.

Although each of the tales contains elements borrowed from classical models, Chaucer's stories are all dramatically altered to reflect a new perspective, rather than a repetition of an old pattern. One may compare the narratives in the book of Genesis, familiar from ancient Near Eastern myths. Both the biblical authors and Chaucer have taken the familiar and twisted them to create a new thing. As many biblical critics have noted, the myths in Genesis 1–11 have been told slant to ensure the biblical readers that their God, YHWH, is now in charge of the cosmos. Chaucer does more than upturn his stories, however. There is a gendered tension, particularly in the tale of the Wife of Bath, and her revelations about female sexuality and desire, and an ironic spin of the overly pious Prioress, whose own Prologue is a mellifluous hymn to the Virgin Mary, while her story is weighted down with violence and religious triumphalism.

The tale of the Wife of Bath begins with a garrulous Prologue, much longer than the romantic fairy tale she eventually tells. Immediately her lusty voice distinguishes her from the other female travelers. It is a challenge for the Wife to tell a tale, even a familiar one. Her own life is of much more interest to her. Until the other travelers finally interrupt her sassy narrative of her own marriages and her views about relations between men and women, the ebullient Wife talks of intimate matters, particularly sexual pleasures. She defends at length the moral righteousness of people who marry often, as long as their spouses are dead, quoting the Bible as only stating that sexual abstinence is preferred but not required. According to this experienced wife, the sexual organs have one God-created function: sex. She supports her view with a quote from the book of Proverbs, 'Man shal yelde to his wyf hire dette' ('Man shall yield to his wife her debt', ll. 130).

However, her straight-forward honesty is contrasted with the soft-focused tale she finally tells from the days of King Arthur, a legendary era even in Chaucer's time. The characters are a knight, his queen, and a lovely young maiden. The knight came upon a maiden walking beside the river one afternoon and raped her, an act for which he was condemned to death. The queen interceded, asking her husband the king to spare the knight. In order to have his death sentence revoked, the knight must answer the central question: *what do women want?*

The knight goes off on a quest for a year to find the answer. The Wife of Bath relates several of the answers he received, including the one she favors, which is that *women want to be flattered.* On the day he was to return from his quest, the knight came across several dozen women in the forest. When he approached them, they vanished, leaving (predictably) a crone in their place. She told him that the answer was that *women wanted equality.* Having run out of time and knowing that his life was at stake, the knight repeated the old woman's answer to the queen. Equality was the right answer. The queen spared the knight's life. As in most fairy tales, the knight had to pay up: he was obliged to marry the crone.

The final stanzas of the narrative expresses the Wife's fears about aging, no longer being attractive to men—and then, reflecting her optimistic nature as well as the narrative genre, there is a happy ending. On their wedding night, when the knight would not perform his husbandly duties, she talked to him about the difference between being born noble and being truly noble. Underneath the words about nobility is her fixation on sexual attractiveness, her desire is for him to see beyond her withered body:

> Do with my life and death as you like best.
> Throw back the curtain and see how it is.
> And when the knight saw verily all this,
> That she so very fair was, and young too,
> For joy he clasped her in his strong arms two,
> His heart bathed in a bath of utter bliss;
>
> A thousand times, all in a row, he'd kiss.
> And she obeyed his wish in everything
> That might give pleasure to his love-liking.
> And thus they lived unto their lives' fair end,
> In perfect joy; and Jesus to us send
> Meek husbands, and young ones, and fresh in bed,
> And good luck to outlive them that we wed.
> And I pray Jesus to cut short the lives
> Of those who'll not be governed by their wives;
> And old and querulous niggards with their pence,
> And send them soon a mortal pestilence! (ll. 1251-70)

I quote these final words from *The Wife of Bath's Tale* because it is impossible to imagine them in the mouth of one of our First Ladies. Could Laura Bush or Hillary Clinton survive politically if she were overheard wishing, 'I pray Jesus to cut short the lives of those who'll not be governed by their wives'.

Another of Chaucer's superb female creations, the Prioress, the superior of a monastery of nuns, is attended on the pilgrimage by four of the other characters: the Nun, the Monk, the Friar, and the Priest. Chaucer describes her in the General Prologue with all the qualities that we still think the perfect woman would possess. The Prioress is smiling, modest, very pleasant, and amiable. With tongue in cheek, Chaucer devotes a quatrain to extolling her remarkable table manners.

> And never let morsels from her lips fall,
> Nor dipped her fingers deep in sauce, but ate
> With so much care the food upon her plate
> That no drop could fall upon her breast (ll. 128-32).

There may be no more ironic description of the weepy lady, tender at the fate of a mouse, who then projects that gentleness into the violent retelling of the miracle story in which a Christian child's throat is ripped open by a Jew:[5]

> That she would weep if she but saw a mouse
> Caught in a trap, whether it were dead or bled.
> She had some little dogs, that she fed
> On roasted flesh, or milk and fine white bread.
> But sorely she wept if one of them were dead,
> Or if men smote it with a stick to smart (ll. 144-49).

When the modern reader has finished the Prioress' tale, one will reject the obvious connections between Prologue and tale, substituting what Booth refers to as 'intended instabilities', that resist the obvious meanings of the text. The individual reader will determine whether the irony is leveled at the female character, at all sanctimonious women in Orders, at the Church itself. Ironies can thus be layered, piled up, rendering meaning as individual as the reader identifying the ironies (Booth 1974: 94).

5. In brief, the Prioress' Tale relates a hagiographic narrative, a very common vehicle in the Middle Ages. In her miracle story, the Prioress tells of a young Christian boy who lived in a predominantly Jewish village in Asia. After the child learned *Alma redemptoris*, a song praising the Virgin Mary, he walked home from school singing this prayer. Angry at his pious devotion, the Jews slit the boy's throat, leaving him in a cesspool to die. The child's mother searched frantically for her son, and when she found him he was not yet dead, for the Virgin Mary had placed a kernel on his tongue that would allow him to remain alive until it was removed. When this was removed, the boy immediately ascended to heaven. The story ends with a lament for the young boy and a curse for the Jews who perpetrated the heinous crime. The modern audience considers the pious nun to be a shocking anti-Semite, but the Chaucerian audience probably did not flinch, as the anti-Jewish Christian perspective was commonplace and virtually unchallenged.

Creating distinct characters with subtly shaded personalities was not of interest to the biblical writers. After all, neither Lady Wisdom nor the Strange Woman seem to have personalities, that is, we have no anecdotes or no narrative units that expand upon the models of women expressed in the book of Proverbs. If character is flat, then there is not the same opportunity for layering ironies. Even Claudia Camp, the doyenne of scholars writing about the two figures, Wise Woman and the Strange Woman, must confine her analysis about the characters to their metaphoric persona. Certainly it is the biblical authors, not Camp, who cast the female figures within tightly controlled categories: a riddler, a trickster, a mother, what Camp refers to as a 'paradigm of opposing images' (2000: 92). The reader must set one character against another in the biblical text in order to create a narrative tension.[6] Chaucer provides those layers within each character, creating a thickness of narrative description absent in biblical narratives.

Contrast with the biblical women the forthright voice of the Wife of Bath:

> A woman wise will strive continually
> To get herself loved, when she's not, you see.
> But since I had them wholly in my hand,
> And since to me they'd given all their land,
> Why should I take heed, then, that I should please,
> Save it were for my profit or my ease? (ll. 216-21)

As anyone who reads print media or listens to on-air journalists knows, the cult of personality is the meat and potatoes of popular journalism. However, even on-air TV shows avoid the thickness of description of creative literature. George 43 has proudly assured his supporters, 'I don't do nuance'. He is praised for his lack of introspection, lauded for his firm resolve. Familiar dichotomies are the norm: strength against weakness, rich against poor, clumsy against fit, educated against dumb.

In covering the First Ladies in the mass media, narrative arcs are inevitable: rich and pampered women are not as likeable as their privileged

---

6.   An example of adjectival character formation that tries to fill the gaps, turning the reader's gaze into a stare, is to be found in the prose of columnist Ann Coulter. In characterizing the women at the Democratic Convention in 2004, she wrote: 'My pretty-girl allies stick out like a sore thumb amongst the corn-fed, no make-up, natural fiber, no-bra needing, sandal-wearing, hirsute, somewhat fragrant hippie-chick pie wagons they call "women" at the Democratic National Convention'. *USA Today*, which had hired her to write commentary on the Convention, refused to run the column and quickly replaced her with a less colorful Conservative. She ran the offending column on her website <http://www.anncoulter.org/>.

counterparts. Thus, a skeptical press equates Teresa Heinz Kerry with her wealth, rather than praising her as an Abigail-type wife, a Proverbs 31 entrepreneur. Rarely do commentators point out that she is a philanthropist, whose focus is upon supporting social and environmental causes. Rather than being impressed with her good work, political writers raise the question of her wealth presenting a conflict of interest should she become First Lady. Personality is confined to staying on-message, reducing textured speech to a few catch words. While I am not suggesting that there is conscious imitation of biblical speech patterns, I think the familiarity of good and bad characters, evil enemies and loyal wives, is extended to real women, who are forced to fit into a paradigm of Good Wife.

Mass Culture, Movies, and Mrs President

Mass culture was boosted if not created by the technical expertise of mechanical reproduction. Fashion styles could be printed daily in newspapers, creating desire in spectators as well as market value for the producer. Movies were the great mass image maker. Walter Benjamin's classic article, 'The Work of Art in the Age of Mechanical Reproduction', reflects a method that seems to be cinematic, although Benjamin does not privilege film over other visual images. He does suggest, however, that each still or shot is neutral until it is placed in juxtaposition to another image. It is the progression that generates meanings to the viewer. The resulting montage is one way to define narrative film.

The first 'moving pictures' made their appearance in the 1890s. While Thomas Edison is generally credited with inventing the medium, several men were instrumental in giving birth to this process, including the brothers Lumière, who invented the first portable movie camera, and George Eastman, who created film for motion pictures. The first movies lasted only minutes and had no sound. Nonetheless, they created a sensation. By 1910, the Eastman Company had perfected the technology of fashioning and developing vast lengths of film. Within a matter of years going to the movies on Saturday was a part of our culture. 1916 marked the emergence of costume design in cinema. Up until that time actors usually supplied their own clothes, if the story was contemporary, or directors rented outfits from costume companies, if the film was a period piece. But Parisian-born director Louis J. Gasnier had a particular 'look' in mind when he was working on a movie with serial queen Pearl White. He summoned a tailor and had him assemble an outfit for the female lead consisting of a black suit, white blouse, loose tie, and velour beret. The result? Secretaries of the day made this ensemble standard business dress for urban working women—the style remains popular in varying degrees. Now we call it power dressing. It was the first emergence of Hollywood celebrity fashion.

Edith Head was arguably the most famous costume designer, creating clothes for more than 1100 films during her six-decade career at both Paramount and Universal studios. She gowned Elizabeth Taylor, Audrey Hepburn, Grace Kelly, and Barbara Stanwyck, and started fashion trends (stampedes?) with her sarong for Dorothy Lamour in *The Jungle Princess* (1936), Elizabeth Taylor's strapless white gown from *A Place in the Sun* (1951) and the shoulder-tied boatneck for Audrey Hepburn in *Sabrina* (1954). Today, few movie costumers are well known outside of the industry, and none create a star's signature celebrity fashion look as they once did under the studio system. With few exceptions, most contemporary costumes are bought off the rack, while period costumes are either made, bought or rented from costume companies.

Cinema fashion and the glamour of the celebrity woman have kept the traditional elements of women's lives at the forefront. As Hollywood chic has given way to the 'fashionistas' of the new millennium, pressure on celebrity women for a positive fashion identity has increased. First Ladies are always meat for the Style and Fashion reporters. A good fashion sense, a good haircut, and an adoring support of her husband are the elements of success for a First Lady. Usually the public glimpses a First Lady for the first time when her husband is declared a candidate. Pictures of their wedding, details of their courtship are released to the press, the more conventional the better.

Without the conventions particular to First Ladies, a woman might imagine that whether she keeps or changes her name is a private, personal choice. This issue broke open in national politics with Hillary Rodham, and the choice whether she should become Clinton or not become Clinton, which was blown into a reflection of the woman herself. Former President Clinton remembers the issue as an ongoing nagging sniping at his wife, for being a professional lawyer while he was governor of Arkansas and keeping her Maiden name (W. Clinton 2004: 255). The concern with a woman's preserving her name or taking the name of her husband has hit the 2004 election period square on with Theresa Heinz Kerry and Judith Steinberg (uh, Dean).[7]

---

7. Evangelical Christian women are faced with the same kinds of decisions as less religiously identified groups. Until recently the overt position of evangelical Christians was to leave the matter of finding a marriage partner to God. According to the Evangelical Publishing Association, the number of Christian-themed books on single

'Without First Ladies, American women might believe that they are liberated, that modern marriage is an equal partnership, that the work they are trained for and paid to do is important whether or not they are married, and that it is socially acceptable for adult women in the year 2004 to possess distinct personalities—even quirks!' So wrote feminist columnist Katha Pollitt, in an article bristling at the negative treatment given to Dr Judith Steinberg, the wife of Howard Dean, while he was a candidate for the Democratic nomination for President in 2004.

The chatter about Teresa Heinz Kerry, the wife of the Democratic candidate John Kerry, has been snowballing as the campaign rhetoric thickens. According to the style media, Heinz Kerry is 'too outspoken', 'too opinionated', 'slightly zany', 'eccentric and unpredictable', 'the queen of direct', and, the final blow for an ideal woman, 'says what she thinks, when she thinks it'. Her background speaks more of the entrepreneur wife than the exotic seducer. A philanthropist who oversees a foundation that gives tens of millions to causes like the environment, healthcare and early education,[8] Heinz Kerry appears in interviews to reflect intellectual range, as well as the expected compassion and humor. Yes, she is indeed unabashedly open with her opinions on everything from the war in Iraq ('I would never have gone to war this way') to George Bush ('fazed by complexity') to Botox treatments (she's had them). But isn't that what we claim to want from those in public life? Or are we comfortable with authenticity only when it's a contrivance manufactured to appear authentic?

'When it comes to spicing up the political dessert tray, Teresa Heinz Kerry is one of the most flavorful and compelling public figures to hit the national stage in decades', gushes newly minted Democrat politician

living sold in the United States has risen by 35 per cent since 2002, and the number of books specifically on dating 21 per cent. Demographers claim that up to 90 per cent of these books are bought by women, reinforcing the concept that it is a woman's issue to move from single to married status. In 2002 the online bookstore Christianbook.com offered 59 titles directed at singles; it now sells more than 300, according to the *New York Times* (19 July 2004).

8. The Capital Research Center (CRC), a conservative, Washington-based organization that studies the spending of nonprofits, has been spinning the danger of a Prov. 31 wife in our current time. The United States has never had a wealthy spouse overshadow its president. But Teresa Heinz Kerry leads and funds philanthropic foundations and she sits on the board of directors of highly political nonprofit groups that receive her foundations' support and that can advance or frustrate the policies of her husband, should he become president. That's unprecedented political power. More public scrutiny of Heinz Kerry's public role is in order. While there is still time.

Ariana Huffington.[9] Peggy Noonan, a former Reagan speechwriter, compares Heinz Kerry to Clinton, concluding that both are too powerful;
both women are aggressive and eager to convince the public that electing
their husbands will be a shopper's bonus: 'two for the price of one' (2000:
11). Noonan's description is contemptuous and indicates that Clinton
and Heinz Kerry are threatening. However, if we return to the paradigms
of women in antiquity, two for the price of one is the precise definition of
marriage in Genesis, as the two become one, as well as the intention of
the paradigm of Proverbs 31 and Hesiod in *Works*.

The Fifties were a time of vast relief in the US. The war was over, the
economy was soaring, and women were back in the kitchen. Not the ugly
Depression-era kitchen, but one that signaled the fun of acquisition and
enhanced the pleasures of ownership. Refrigerators and stoves came in
bright colors, frozen dinners could be heated up and consumed in front of
the TV, two-toned cars heavy with chrome waited at the curb.

In contrast to the homespun Bess Truman, Mamie Eisenhower wanted
sparkle and pizzazz, just like the women at home, watching her on TV in
a dreadful ball gown for the inauguration of her husband. Her dresser's
idea of femininity embraced girlish innocence, taking the form of a sugar-
pink dress that would have been more suitable to a debutante than to the
General's wife. To perk up the bouffant gown, Mrs Eisenhower insisted
on having the designer (Nettie Rosenstein) add panels of fullness and
2000 rhinestones to the skirt. To be sure the Mamie look was popular in
the Fifties; indeed, there were Mamie dolls and figurines, each one dressed
in the pinkly *peau de soie* ballgown with matching pinkly gloves, shoes,
and evening bag. The fashion shot that told the country that Mamie and
Ike were winners was her full-length mink coat. Because the inauguration
and presidency of Eisenhower was the first to be followed daily by the TV
cameras, Mamie was a walking compendium of the marketplace. She was
the woman next door, with her tinkly gold charm bracelet.[10]

Between the Fifties' wifely wife/woman and the equal mates who
helped their husbands with substantive matters, including Rosalynn

9.   <http://www.alternet.org/columnists/story/19301/>.
10.   For those readers who may not remember the days of Ike or wonder why I am
discussing mink, let me add that in his renowned Checkers speech, Richard Nixon
attempted to clear himself of charges that he had a tapped a secret slush fund by
exploiting that symbol of decadent luxury, the mink coat. His wife, Nixon boasted,
did not own a mink coat, but rather she owned 'a respectable Republican cloth
coat, and I always tell her that she would look good in anything'. One can only imagine the discussion between Nixon and his superior, President Eisenhower, on the
issue of furs on wives, when Mamie upgraded publicly the idea of Republican fashion.

Carter and Hillary Clinton, there was a film that reviewed the ground rules for the Perfect Wife: *The Stepford Wives*.[11] The movie focuses upon an upscale community, Stepford (which screams Martha Stewart Connecticut), where all the husbands have beautiful, robot-like wives who devote their lives to cleaning their houses and satisfying their husbands. One is watching either a horror film or updated Snow White fantasy, depending on the spectator's point of view. The film's ideal woman is a compendium of the Proverbs 31 wife and the biblical model wife Abigail. Before their revolt, the Stepford women of the Seventies are faceless, expressionless zombies, who are pleasant, malleable, and ignorant. Here, the husbands are completely in power. Do not think that a 30-year-old film is 'dated', and buried in the dust of the collective unconscious. The Stepford women returned in the summer of 2004. Once again the dream is that men can replace bumptious wives with compliant robots. The dream of the perfect wife will not die. Her identity as a compliant servant of her husband has been delicately woven into the First Homemaker style since the days of Mamie Eisenhower.

During the summer of the new *Stepford Wives*, there have been a number of women trying to reinterpret the Perfect Wife, but not too much. Following in the steps of one of the more controversial first ladies in history, Laura Bush lives in the White House during a tempestuous period in US history. According to her biographer, Ann Gerhart, Mrs Bush hints at things, never declares them: 'She is the play-doh first lady: Mold her whatever shape you want, then stamp her back down into a pile of putty for her next audience' (2004: 125). As Gerhart acknowledges, her passivity is not deliberate.

At a time in our culture when women are encouraged to be intellectual and strong, particularly as it benefits their husbands, Condoleezza Rice is more the Proverbs 31 wife/woman than Laura Bush. There is no mention of her personal relationships, only a list of her praise-worthy accomplishments. Unmarried, without children, she is the asexual woman who has reassured interviewers, 'I don't do life crises'. Choreographing state dinners, keeping President Bush sound and grounded, that is not the province of the highest ranking woman in the Bush Administration.

11. *The Stepford Wives* (1975), directed by Bryan Forbes. Adapted from a novel by Ira Levin, who also wrote *Rosemary's Baby* (made into a film in 1968, directed by Roman Polanski). Both novels share similar treatment of wives as objects of husbands, which may help to explain their position as bestsellers. In *Stepford Wives* the women are replaced by robotic imitations who are compliant and content to serve their husbands' wishes. In *Rosemary's Baby* the compliant girl is chosen to deliver the son of the Satan. The remake of *Stepford Wives* (2004) was directed by Frank Oz.

Having no personal life, no details of dailiness, Rice became George W. Bush's national security adviser, having directed an oil company, managed a multi-million-dollar university, and served as a Soviet expert in Washington during the collapse of the Soviet Union. When this resumé belongs to a talented male advisor, the media does not mention the gender of the individual. But try to apply these attributes to a woman in politics and the media start acting like it's 1958—they suddenly don't know how to handle smart, professional, complex women who are the legal wives of the President or candidates for the highest US office.[12] Judy Dean wasn't glamorous or supportive enough, Hillary was too smart and too strong, and Teresa is too loose-lipped and too unpredictable. So it really isn't much of a surprise that the political wife the media seem most comfortable with is the plastic Laura Bush, who has chosen to take on the image of the perfect Fifties sitcom housewife. As for Condi, both her race and her gender are the subtext of her narrative.

Laura Bush's values, image and opinions are not just fodder for fashion magazines or Beltway buzz about whether she supports abortion rights or disagrees with her husband's opposition to embryonic stem-cell research. Laura Bush has been updated. The Betty Crocker hairdo has been replaced by a sleek coif with streaks of blonde. According to *USA Today*, 'Her toenails, peeking out from comfy espadrilles, are bright red. She still prefers to talk about education and reading, her pet issues and avocations, but she can dish up justifications for the war in Iraq, too' (30 June 2004). There is not much difference between Laura and Mamie Eisenhower, the wife who was the proof of the good life of fame and success. Women are still the kinder, gentler side of their world-leader husbands, who must be tough. As Laura Flanders observed,

> the First Lady, as well as the women appointed to the inner circle of the President's Cabinet and sub-Cabinet—provide an alternative facade.

12.   In fairness to the media and the spin they give to high-profile women, when the *New York Times* ran a story on the 46-year-old Professor Condoleezza Rice, it didn't discuss her views on national security until the twenty-seventh paragraph. The subject cropped up near the end of the *Times'* long feature, which was dominated by talk of her dress-size, her hair, her 'just below the knee' hemline, and her place of birth. I offer here a taste of the prose introducing the primary national security aide to the President to the newspaper of record: 'She eats either a bagel or cereal every day for breakfast. She is always impeccably dressed, usually in a classic suit with a modest hemline, comfortable pumps and conservative jewelry. She keeps two mirrors on her desk at Stanford, apparently to check the back as well as the front of her hair ("I do try to make sure everything is in place", she explained)' (18 December 2000).

They are cast as harmless, moderate, irrelevant or benign, and their well-spun image taps into familiar stereotypes about women and people of color, while their political and corporate records remain conveniently out of sight—thanks to a mostly oblivious media (2004: 6).

Political spouses do not shift many votes, but their styles and personalities help fill out voters' perceptions of the candidates. Teresa Heinz Kerry, 65, is opinionated, often blunt, a practicing Catholic, and a very visible part of her husband's campaign. Laura Bush, 57, is all Texan. She was born in Midland, the only child of a Methodist family of modest means. She's more ordinary than exotic, but she's becoming more visible. In 2000 she made only a few solo appearances, sticking for the most part by her husband's side. After 9/11 she became more accessible to the media, following her mother-in-law's advice to wear more vivid clothes. In 2004 she raised $5.5 million for her husband's campaign for re-election. There are clear differences in the women's management styles. Both Teresa and Laura have delivered primetime speeches at their respective party conventions (late summer 2004). The contrast between the two, and what this contrast says about the men in their lives should be stark. Out on the campaign trail, Teresa is given to in-depth discussions about health care and global warming. Her faith is not woven into the interview unless she is asked specifically about her Catholicism. Laura tends to say things like: 'I'm not privy to the policy disputes. I'm not over there at the table where everyone is actually formulating specific policy.'[13] Her strict southern Methodist faith is credited with not only bringing her husband to Christ but also keeping him away from alcohol.

First daughters Jenna and Barbara Bush have chosen the gentle fashion press to launch their public personas as they begin campaigning for their father. The twins appeared in an extreme makeover from their usual jeans and tee-shirt garb in the August 2004 *Vogue*, just in time for saturation before the Republican convention. Reinventing the Bush twins as the perfect embodiment of wholesome American values makes perfect political sense to the President's campaign managers. In a somewhat clumsy attempt to smother the controversial behavior for which the twins have been known since their father became President, the young women now proclaim that one wants to teach in Harlem, the other wants to work with HIV/AIDS babies in Africa.

Last year, to little fanfare and few sales, *Washington Post* journalist Ann Gerhart published a biography of the First Lady. *The Perfect Wife: The Life and Choices of Laura Bush* (2003) was innocuous and bland as a

---

13.   <http://www.alternet.org/columnists/story/19301/>.

good-wife press release except for a devastating chapter which dealt with the lives and recent times of Barbara and Jenna Bush. 'They are girls born rich, blessed with intelligence, good looks, trust funds, loving parents, boundless opportunities, freedom from many of life's daily challenges', Gerhart wrote. And she continued:

> ...they persist in seeing themselves as victims of daddy's job...they have not appeared to engage in any of the pressing issues their generation will inherit, nor shown empathy for the struggles facing their mother and their father, the president of the United States. Once George sought political office Laura's guiding principle in mothering become 'they didn't ask for this', as if Jenna and Barbara were forced into some disastrous, bumpy detour from the normal smooth path toward adulthood. Their struggles are her only regret (2003: 136).

There have been a couple of arrests of the girls who didn't ask for this, some wild-child behavior that Gerhart contrasts with their traditional, bland mother. In spite of media reports of their grandmother Barbara Bush trying to pull them into line, to understand the *oblige* that goes with the *noblesse*, the twins continue to behave in a less than perfect manner. Although stumping for their father, they continue to encourage popular irritation. While riding in the presidential limo with her father, Jenna stuck her tongue out at the waiting photographers.

That bratty pose reminded me that women are complicit in their image-making. Instead of staring into a mirror, they stare into camera lenses, while simultaneously staring inward, driving their own portrayal. Such bifurcation is required by the daily performance of the gender spectacle. Such a rip in the *politesse* expected from First Ladies, the media connects such rude behavior with the President's arrogance, not with the First Lady, who is meant to soothe her husband when the world becomes too threatening. Like Gerhart in her *Perfect Wife*, the popular media feel free to jab at the daughters, but not at the mother. While covering Jenna's first political stump trip with her father, the *Washington Post* chuckled, 'speaking in the steamy Lapp Electrical Service headquarters in Lancaster, Pa., Bush made eye contact with her [Jenna] as she sat in the front row, and she seemed to signal that he should feel free to wrap it up'.[14]

Anyone writing about mass culture, especially as it unfolds day by day, spun by the press, advertisers, and other cultural producers for an audience in which we are all included, runs the risk of being caught up in the

---

14. <http://www.washingtonpost.com/wp-dyn/articles/A39877-2004Jul9.html>. Note that Mike Allen, the author of this article, is a colleague at the *Washington Post* of Ann Gerhart, the author of *Perfect Wife*.

spin. I hope that I have shown that from the earliest attempts at female image-making right into our daily cable coverage of 'real' First Ladies, it is hard work to play the vehicle, to reduce oneself to the popular culture's newest view of the Perfect Wife. She must win the sweepstakes of accept-ability. Otherwise they laugh.

7

YOU DO NOT SEE ME: RESISTANCE FROM RIZPAH TO WOMEN IN BLACK

> Sometimes we drug ourselves with dreams of new ideas. The head will save us. The brain alone will set us free. But there are no new ideas waiting in the wings to save us as women, as human. There are only old and forgotten ones, new combinations, extrapolations and recognitions from within ourselves—along with the renewed courage to try them out.
> —Audre Lorde, *Poetry is not a Luxury* (1986)

Across time, legend and history have mythified the beautiful frail woman who dies while protecting her innocence. The specter of women's bodies mortified by male violence is used to create fear in women. Feminist critics have exposed physical and emotional brutality against women in one literature after another. We have come to understand that rape is not so much a sexual crime as it is a means of physical, mental, and spiritual domination. So powerful is the impulse for feminists to identify violence against women, even within literary texts, that feminist literary critics have inscribed what Adrienne Rich has determined is 'more than a chapter in cultural history', but an actual physical strategy, 'an act of survival' (1979: 90) in the process of analyzing rape narratives.

Analyzing Rape Narratives?

These are the terms of the scholar, the theorist. In a now classic essay, J. Cheryl Exum challenged the biblical authors with her suggestion of female figures being raped by the pen—if not the penis (1993: 171-202). While this suggestion may seem to exist totally within the realm of metaphor, such interpretive passion is more than a tour de force. Because reading is an intimate experience, its form of violation is almost as frightening as a physical experience. Reading with outrage has been the stance of most feminist critics, and biblical violence has been vilified frequently, from the pens of Mieke Bal, Susan Niditch and Lori Rowlett, among others. As women march through city streets to 'take back the night', so feminist critics have also taken back the texts, or at least recognize what is at stake in the process of representing rape and war in the act of reading violence. An oppositional reading, speaking for the female victim, asserts the scholar's right to read representations of violation critically, skeptically, to refuse to remain the victim of the narrative force of the biblical narrator.

In this chapter I want to focus upon two kinds of biblical narratives: one in which a woman is strong and 'safe' from the violence of men, and several connected stories in which women are victims of mass rape and violence. Since the acts of bravery of women and violent submission of them have not ceased in the millennia since these stories originally circulated, I have used some modern political narratives of brave women and shattered women, veiled women and women with voice, as the echoes of the biblical characters who struggled and suffered against the patriarchal state so long ago. While not all these real women are theologians or present overt claims to faith, they all fight the myth of redemptive violence, which defends the belief that violence saves, that war brings peace, that might makes right.

Where in the biblical narratives are the strong women who defend themselves and their people successfully against bodily assault? How do we restore honor to male victims of violence within the Bible. Scholars identify bloodguilt, such as the divine displeasure with Saul's ruptured pact with the Gibeonites. To restore peace and transform drought into rain, famine into food, King David orders the seven sons of Saul impaled, their bodies left as a reminder of the cost of breaking alliances, be they divine or human. But for a few drops of prose, the story would end here, with rain and reconciliation.

But what about a woman who sits it out, defying the actions of men merely by her presence? This woman performs no spectacular act, like Judith cutting off Holofernes's head, or Esther cutting deals to protect her people in the royal realm of power. Not committing any physical act, just sitting out the wrath of men, one woman becomes a fulcrum for peace in the land—Rizpah. Her name means 'glowing coal', and she kept vigil for months, burning like a sun each day and glowing like a human flame against the night. Rizpah demanded honor for the vulnerable and the dead.

Reading Rizpah's Wordless Witness Against Violence

Reading silence? One way to reclaim power as a reader, to take back the text, is to follow a synchronic strategy of reading. Synchronic approaches give the reader a great deal of latitude in making connections between texts. One might term this synchronic strategy reading like Persephone, interpreting part of the year in the land of Ceres, source of seeds and verbal production, and then slipping into the comfort of academia, companion of Hades, of dark affluence and easy conclusions. Central to such a semiotic theory is that flights from one text to a connection in a second or multiple texts have been made in the unconscious mind. There are so many flights to be made in the area of woman as victim of physical violence that I am exhausted before half the connections have clicked. In an earlier work (1998a), I traveled from accounts of ethnic genocide in Rwanda and in Bosnia through the so-called 'carrying off' of the women of Shiloh in Judges 21. My decision to employ a Persephone reading, then, stems from my desire as an academic to examine two related subject territories: first, biblical texts in which women are sexually threatened or raped, and second, a need to witness when women in Afghanistan, Palestine, Kosovo, Columbia, and New York are victimized. These women gather force in the gaps, margins, echoes, digressions, and ambiguities of a text. The silence about the women of Shiloh, in the biblical narrative and in the interpretations of this text, is as loud as the silence of the women themselves, given no voice or no subjectivity in the narrative. These literary figures have been denied voice by male narrator or storyteller, opposed to their ethnic or gendered identity. Often in the presence of men, even in this broadband era of feminist discourse, women's voices are drowned out and their actions are diluted. As I write in the enfolding peace of my study, weighted down by words and reports of war, I feel the need to connect with women of resistance, women who refuse to be beaten by a male voice or a male body.

My biblical muse who will free me from a lifetime of prose is Rizpah, the silent secondary wife of Saul, whose sons and husband were slaughtered, their bones displayed on the rocky mountainside of Gibeah, bleached white as the rocks on which they were scattered. The resistance of Rizpah challenges the emphasis on women as victims. While victory through physical triumph is a male prerogative that has always seemed incompatible with femininity, Rizpah's triumph is physical; she effects change with her body. A woman triply marginalized (a concubine, widow, and mother without sons) defends a small space in which to resist.

Images of women crouched in caves, staring out of tenement windows, fleeing fire-engulfed buildings create models of private horrors and public violence. I must confess that my inner Persephone refused to make the leap from Rizpah to Uma Thurman in Tarantino's recent bloodbath, *Kill Bill* (2003). I have no desire to unleash furious justice upon my enemies. I am decidedly more Persephone than assassin. But the question remains: How do I move from muse to poet? I am a scholar longing to flee my cultural space, speaking out in words, wondering how in the name of theory I can join women in resistance in various places from Afghanistan, Iraq, and Palestine, to Argentina, Columbia, and Chile. I am mindful of Gandhi's observation that the peacemaker belongs where the war is, not where the peace is.

Admittedly, I am not the only person to be confounded by the tension between theorist and activist. Scholars have long been counting on prose to prove their political viability, and the debate will not be resolved here. Twenty years ago, feminist critic Barbara Christian feared that the vogue of French poststructuralism would condemn us all to stumble through a jungle of jargon and opaque style. Christian argued in the name of African-American writers, who were finally being rediscovered after being ignored and uncanonized by the dominant culture, that the abstract voice of theorists would lead to a monolithic formulation about authenticity. She knew she was in a race with theory.

The concern with canonizing a multiplicity of voices, especially those of the previously silenced, was a first move in cultural studies. Within a few years, the cognoscenti ditched the center for the periphery. Many scholars have embraced the postcolonial theories of Spivak, Said, and the central figure of today's discussions, Homi Bhabha, as a way to effect cultural and political transformation. The cultural critique of Homi Bhabha provides a theoretical link that incorporates Adrienne Rich's 'act of survival' in identifying a people of oppression and initiating their plight into theoretical prose. Bhabha insists that theory is not the province of the elite, of the socially and culturally privileged, and thus claims a piece of the landscape of theory for Third World scholars, who defend their 'isms' against those whom Bhabha characterizes as 'depoliticized Eurocentric critics'. He argues for the political relevance of his bread-and-butter term *hybridity*, a talisman that permits Bhabha to contend that theory is not separate from or opposed to political activism. For Bhabha, hybridity fosters some utopian promise of community without diluting cultural difference; hybridity creates and claims a third space, a hybrid defined by neither the empire nor the colonized. Hybridity is a clever notion, and resolves some of my concern about being counted among the white and privileged. Simultaneously, hybridity protects me from the accusations of claiming or co-opting a space on the crowded margins. Hybridity is the cultural equivalent to reading like Persephone. In my view, hybridity works as theory because the concept applies to privileged postcolonial intellectuals who have gained their success and scholarly acceptance on Western campuses. Even if the reader can claim a safe space within Bhabha's Third Space, the problem is exactly that the space is safe, static. In spite of his claim that hybridity unites political and literary intentions, there is no element of risk in the virtual space of hybridity.

Can theorists ever inscribe more than a chapter in cultural history? It seems essential for the scholar, protected by the bricks and mortar, towers and turrets of the academy, to throw off the matrix of American normality: violence edited for the Nightly News, Internet reports of daily emergencies. Does theory provide the moral cover for us to fly inward, to rest among questions of narrative provenance and presence, to blank out the reality of wordless pain? We are somewhat routinized in our mimetic practice of theory: we never pretend that we are objective; we claim to be live within the thickness of things, never above the fray. But are we anywhere near the thick of it?

Perhaps it is as simple as recognizing that the University is too safe to identify as a political Third Space, not the arena to resolve the tensions between theory and praxis, between comfort and want, between routine and risk. In one of his more generous moods, Edward Said shrugged off the problem that at other times was central to his work:

> Most of us in the literary or humanistic fields don't have a very good sense, let us say, of the limits and possible kinds of synchronizations between reading a literary text and politics in the international sense. These are very different things. Most people make a jump that cannot be made... I mean, how do you modulate between literary interpretation and international politics? (1993: 181)

The final verse in the biblical text of Rizpah needs just such modulation. The power of Rizpah's bold protest against death shames David—and ultimately transforms his heart. As the soft, Fall rain descends on the land David orders the bones of Saul's descendants, Rizpah's two sons and the five sons of Merab, to be gathered up and buried with honor, at last. 'After that, God took pity on the country' (Judg. 21.14).

After what? After David gives Saul's sons over to the Gibeonites? After he buries the house of Saul properly? Or after Rizpah's witness to the dignity of life? The narrative remains ambiguous. We are left hanging by an unclear reference that skirts the distance between literary interpretation and political reality. Reading like Persephone, we traverse the newly drenched land, grateful for rain, but mindful of our time in the underworld.

How does one animate well-tempered prose, shake up semiotics until it throbs with action, delineating movement between literary and real resistance? Whether the resistance takes place on the page or on the street, the agent acts today with an understanding that the harvest will be tomorrow. It is re-iteration of purpose and perspective that forms the narrative of resistance. Just as great literary characters hold the reader in thrall when they revel in the gap between intention and expression, so the human individual employs both social and political agency within that gap. In the midst of war, I need to shed the burqa of theory, to join the company of ordinary women who are propelled toward resistance. On the record, written from the microcosm of private existence, I shall focus upon the actions of Women in Black in 'eretz Israel and the occupied West Bank. Witnessing within the same landscape as Rizpah, these activists are reiterating outrage, as the barrel of time bursts apart again and again, leaving only a moment of resistance.

Well, who is Rizpah and what did she do? Even some biblical scholars blank on the name. A secondary wife of King Saul, Rizpah has a fleeting narrative existence, marked by a murdered husband and murdered sons. She possesses a name and little else. Unlike the unnamed women in the book of Judges who suffer violence at the hands of men, Rizpah is a witness to violence, not its direct victim. Silently she defends a generation of Saulides with her body, protecting the dead, dishonored bodies of her loved ones from the animal predators who desired them. Rizpah challenges the arrogance of God's beloved, David, who would leave the remains of Saul and his sons as a reminder of his own preferred status. Sitting amid the bones of the dead, Rizpah becomes a symbol of the fragility of power. Her act is without words, stubborn, soundless. Her witness forces David into behaving properly, if only for a moment. Her strategy is a discourse of silence, speaking to power through her body. In order to rescue the bodies of her men, impaled and displayed by the political allies of David, in the blazing sun of Gibeah, she puts her living body in the midst of their decaying flesh.

Sitting in the heat of the day and cool of the night, keeping away the natural predators who would feed upon carrion, Rizpah's resistance is as steady as the spring rain. After all the violence of men in ethnic and civil wars, she presents a unique picture: singular, silent, patient, waiting for transformation, of David's arrogance, of rain to end the drought. As rain brings life to the land of Israel, Rizpah enlivens the moral climate of her people. Although Merab lost five sons in the same debacle,[1] she did not come to Gibeah to protest their humiliation; instead, Rizpah, a lesser

---

1. I read with LXX (Septuagint version) against the MT (Masoretic version) in assuming that Merab is the correct daughter of Saul, identified in this story, since the narrator has reported Michal to have been childless (2 Sam. 6.23). Further, in 1 Samuel Merab is identified as the wife of Ariel (1 Sam. 18.19).

wife to Saul, protected the bones of her sons and those of Merab equally. Rizpah becomes an icon, linking women who stand today in public places in silent, non-violent vigils that honor all victims. These women call themselves Women in Black.

Being Rizpah

'Women in Black' was inspired by earlier movements of women who demonstrated on the streets, making a public space for women to be heard—particularly Black Sash in South Africa, and the Madres de la Plaza de Mayo, seeking the 'disappeared' in the political repression in Argentina. But WIB also shares a genealogy with groups of women explicitly refusing violence, militarism, and war, such as the Women's International League for Peace and Freedom formed in 1918, and the Greenham Common Women's Peace Camp in the UK and related groups around the world opposing the deployment of US missiles since the Eighties. WIB demonstrations are solely women, usually wearing black, standing in a public place, silently, witnessing, at regular times and intervals. These images take me back to Rizpah, a still-small figure witnessing in the arid landscape of ancient Israel, silent with the bones of the dead until King David relented and buried them with attendant ritual and respect. Within her narrative she never meets David, never gets the chance to speak truth to power, but succeeds in rescuing the bodies of her dead family. As we watch nights of war unfold on CNN, we see that recovering the bodies of the dead is no small victory. Soundbites of keening women and men staggering under the weight of litters are intercut with the cheer of the sports report. Behind my eyelids remain the life-giving images of WIB, silent amid the tumult of people pressing into the streets, across borders, tearing down boundaries, are reminders of righteousness within a world refusing to acknowledge that bloodguilt breeds more bloodguilt. Revenge is a continuous Moebius strip that keeps the military in business.

Rizpah: Speechlessness Crying Out

Women in Black was reborn in 1988 in Israel, not far from Gibeah, where Rizpah had first practiced non-violent protest. Participants in vigils wear black as a sign of mourning for all that is lost through war and violence. In response to violence against Palestinian citizens, Israeli Jewish women began to stand in weekly vigils in public places, usually at busy road junctions. Starting in Jerusalem, the number of vigils in Israel eventually grew to almost forty. In the north of Israel, where the concentration of Arab communities is greatest, Palestinian women who are Israeli citizens stood with WIB groups. Many local WIB groups made contact with women across the Green Line engaged in support work, for example, visiting Palestinians in Israeli prisons.

At WIB vigils, women from different ethnicities and religious traditions carried placards saying 'End the Occupation' and closely related messages. The focus is quite precise, in order to be able to draw in a wide group of women. The vigils are predictable: same site, regular intervals. The women wear black. They are seen by, and provoke reactions from, many passers-by on foot and in vehicles; some heckle and abuse them, both in sexualized terms ('whore') and for their politics ('traitor'). Their policy is not to shout back but to maintain silence and dignity. The dilemma of speechlessness compounded by femaleness has inspired the group. Their policy, like that of Rizpah, is to challenge the performance of bloodguilt, male revenge that restores the balance of political power, and too often the instrument of reconciliation with the deity.

In other places, including Canada, the USA, Australia, and many European countries, WIB vigils were organized in support of those in Israel. In Berkeley, California, WIB has been standing weekly since 1988. In 1998 and 1999 WIB groups everywhere had occasion to demonstrate against a sequence of military engagements by the USA, sometimes partnered by the UK, or in the context of NATO.[2] These groups do not participate in direct action but use the resistance of their silent, often veiled, bodies to 'speak' truth to power.

One of the best-known groups is the Revolutionary Association of the Women of Afghanistan (RAWA), founded in Kabul in 1977 by one woman, Meena, who was assassinated in 1987. Determined to present the faces of veiled women to the world, she traveled throughout Afghanistan organizing these invisible women and later throughout Europe and the Soviet Union to create an independent political and social organization of Afghan women fighting for human rights and social justice. Using their bodies as ghostly reminders of human rights, Meena and her kind

---

2. These included continued sanctions and bombing raids against Iraq, the bombing of Sudan and Afghanistan, and the bombardment of Belgrade and other Serbian cities. It was the Latinas of *Mujeres de Negro* who first understood the central importance of information technology was in linking WIB groups in anti-war action. They were the ones to take the step of setting up an electronic list-serve for WIB, at first in Spanish, eventually in English. By the end of 2000 they set up a system of 'country coordinators', thus effectively turning WIB into a worldwide net. Women with similar intentions to practice non-violent resistance, though using different names and organizational approaches, are also linked through the list.

were directly involved in the war of resistance against the Soviet Union in the Eighties. She was assassinated by the KGB in 1987. Her work continues. Faceless, without human voice, the Internet bears witness to the Rizpah women, who will not be intimidated by power. Wrapped in the anonymity of broadband burqas, women have organized worldwide in solidarity with RAWA.

The renewal of the Palestinian intifada, in late September 2000, after the Al-Aqsa mosque slaughter, returned WIB to their witness in Israel. By mid-November women were standing at six sites (Nazareth, Acre, Haifa, Tel Aviv, Jerusalem, and the Nachson junction) and this activism continues today in fifteen simultaneous vigils.[3] Groups of women, primarily from *Donne in Nero* but also from London WIB have been visiting Palestine and Israel to strengthen links with Israeli women peace activists. As the Israeli oppression of the West Bank and Gaza intensified, Israeli WIB and the Coalition called, in June and again in December 2001, through worldwide e-mail coordination, for a day of simultaneous protest. Through this and similar international actions, beginning in prose and ending with a swelling of the body politic, it is estimated that there are more than 150 WIB groups in at least 24 countries. Israeli Women in Black won the Aachen Peace Prize (1991), the peace award of the city of San Giovanni d'Asso in Italy (1994), and the Jewish Peace Fellowship's 'Peacemaker Award' (2001).[4]

In the year before her assassination, Meena wrote a poem that she spoke at rallies when she traveled abroad. Her words give voice to the silence of Rizpah:

> I'm the woman who has awoken
> I've arisen and become a tempest through the ashes of my burnt children
> I've arisen from the rivulets of my brother's blood
> My nation's wrath has empowered me.

3. November 2000 also saw the formation in Israel of the Coalition of Women for a Just Peace, which brings together all the WIB vigils in Israel as well as nine other women's peace organizations. Dressed in black, these women have carried out direct action (e.g. placing a 'closure' on the Israeli Defense Ministry by blocking traffic to it), in addition to holding mass WIB vigils twice a year, with thousands of women participating.

4. WIB locally and internationally have received a number of awards in recognition of their work for peace. The worldwide network were awarded the Millennium Women's Peace Prize sponsored by the NGO International Alert and the UN agency UNIFEM (the United Nations Development Fund for Women), and the following year the network was a nominee for the Nobel Peace Prize. *Donne in Nero* was awarded the Gold Dove of Peace, an Italian prize, in 2002. WIB was honored by Church Women United, USA, in 2002.

To break together all these sufferings all these fetters of slavery.
I'm the woman who has awoken,
I've found my path and will never return.

Reading Rape in the Good Book

Another kind of message is sent by the sexual violence committed by the
Israelites in order to get wives for the men of the tribe of Benjamin.
Judges 21 depicts two kinds of rape: the sexual rape of women of Shiloh,
and, by extension, the economic rape of their fathers and brothers, who
are by ancient standards the offended parties. There is collective violation in both acts. While an event of rape is not acknowledged openly in
Judges 21, it is encoded within the ambiguity, the indirections of the
text. The result is to naturalize the rape. By reading against the grain of
the writers' intention to narrate the carrying off of women as wives for
the men of Benjamin as necessary and natural, one sees how the biblical
authors, men who possessed both benevolence and reason, could inscribe
a rationale for oppression, violation, and exploitation within the very
discourse of the biblical text.

In this reading of Judges 21 I inhabit the border life of the text,
rubbing the friction between the narrative in chs. 19–20 and against the
one in ch. 21, not privileging one over the other. My initial move is to
scrutinize the cultural ideology that supports rape as a stock narrative
device for disorder in the biblical narrative. Literary critics from various
fields are currently engaged in a polemic over the function and meaning
of rape in its textual representation.[5] Readers, like texts (and for that
matter characters within texts), are always sites where pluralities inter-
sect. The friction between the biblical concept of rape, or more usually
'not-rape', and our own intense feelings of abhorrence at the violation of
the female body provides a major site for my reading. Reading Judges 19–
21 as a single narrative unit allows me to follow the progression of violence from the representation of one violated female figure (*pilegesh*) to
the representation of a violated tribe of females (daughters of Shiloh),
thus raising the specter of the tribes of Israel as guilty of a brutal male
assault an act of gynocide.[6] It seems almost automatic to fill the gaps in

---

5.   There is a growing scholarly literature on rape, reflecting the consciousness of
real-life rape as well as literary and metaphoric rape. See especially Brownmiller's
classic *Against Our Will* (1975). For literary rape, see discussion in Bal 1988a, 1998b;
Barthes 1973; Exum 1993; de Lauretis 1987; Dimen 1989; and Harris 1984.

6.   To the reader who thinks the term gynocide is an over-reading, an exaggeration, of the act of 'carrying off' the young women of Shiloh, I can say only that

Judges 21 through the rape camps recently uncovered in Bosnia, and to fill the female silence in the one text with the witness from the other.

Depicting, narrating, or representing rape certainly does not constitute an unambiguous gesture of endorsement. The consciousness of what constitutes rape is very different now from what it has been in earlier times. One advantage of a synchronic analysis is that the reader can move forward or backward through time. Foucault is correct that 'the lateral connections across different forms of knowledge and from one focus of politicization to another [makes it possible] to rearticulate categories which were previously kept separate' (1980: 127). Thus, a synchronic reading cognizant of cultural theory needs to inhabit both the insular territory of the biblical world and other cultural arenas where the practice of sexual violence has been represented, such as the genocide in Bosnia. When a woman is raped in the Hebrew Bible, who has lost respect, who is the offended party? The biblical narrator does not raise a literary eyebrow at either the Levite in Judges 19 or Lot in Genesis 19 for using women's bodies as shields to defend themselves against sexual violence. Nor does the Bible characterize as rape 'carrying off' women to become the wives of the remaining men of an offending tribe in Judges 21. So the Foucauldian story of rape as evidence of ubiquitous domination is suppressed. The threat of homosexual rape is averted in Genesis 19, but sexual violence toward the *pilegesh* in Judges 19 is *doubly* suppressed; its homosexual element is disavowed by the Levite in his retelling of the story and the corpse of the *pilegesh* is defiled by the Levite himself after her ravaged body has been returned to him.

A standard cultural myth is that rape is an unavoidable consequence of war. Looking solely at modern times, we remember that rape was a weapon of revenge as the Russian army marched to Berlin in World War II. Rape flourishes in warfare irrespective of nationality or geographic location. 'Rape got out of hand', writes Susan Brownmiller, 'when the Pakistani Army battled Bangladesh. Rape reared its head as a way to relieve boredom as American GI's searched and destroyed in the highlands of Vietnam' (1975: 32). Of course in modern times rape is outlawed as a criminal act under the international rules of war. Rape is punishable by death or imprisonment under Article 120 of the American Uniform Code of Military Justice. Yet rape persists as a common act of war.

Since the focus of this chapter is to be the interweaving of modern gynocidal activities of war with narratives of rape and one of gynocide,

we shall never know how the women characters in the text perceived their predicament. The silence of the women in the text will be filled by each reader.

let us look at the mirror story of a gang of men in Genesis 19 and Judges 19.[7] When one reads each of these stories as a linear narrative, emphasizing its beginning, middle, and end, one concludes that such a narratologic strategy is far from innocent. Viewed schematically the beginning of the story focuses the reader upon the details it offers and suggests that other details or reality is insignificant (e.g. the reactions of Lot's daughters to the pounding on the door or to their father's magnanimous offer); the events of the beginning of the story lead to the middle and set up a causal inevitability (the threatened Levite thrusting the *pilegesh* outside the door); and finally the story's end appears as the unique result of all that has come before. Most important in this seemingly logical progression of a linear narrative is that it creates a sense of order, as though the conclusion (i.e. the rape and torture of the *pilegesh*) is the only possible outcome. Unless the reader listens for the woman's story muffled in the gaps and silences of the male narrative, the reader becomes a voyeur, complicit with the orderly retelling of the story. While listening to the silence is one effective narratological strategy for moving outside the power of the text, the reader can also examine narrative elements that aid the storyteller in the representation of rape.[8]

One narrative element provides a first clue: night, *laylah*, the dark time of abandon. The two parallel stories of men threatening men occur at night: the men of Sodom call out to Lot, 'Where are the men who came to you *tonight*' (Gen. 19.5). The Benjaminites also come knocking at night. They 'know' the woman all through the night, a continuous connection of nighttime horror, when men turn into ogres. As Bal so memorably characterizes this scene: 'she dies several times, or rather, she never stops dying' (Bal 1998a: 2). But the classification of even this rape, which seems so explicitly violation to a modern reader, is not clearly rape in the

---

7. I have resisted supplying a name for the *pilegesh*, as Bal and Exum have done. Bal calls her Beth; Exum Bath-sheber. The anonymity of her namelessness creates a problem for the reader trying to identify her in a retelling of the narrative. This very difficulty underscores the gap or silence created by the biblical storyteller. By referring to her as *pilegesh*, I hope to maintain the narratorial vagueness and lack of subjectivity that anonymity of a character presents in a story.

8. Another subtle reference to rape comes from the mother of Sisera (Judg. 5.30) standing at the window, waiting for her son, triumphant in war. She waits for him to bring her 'spoil of dyed stuffs embroidered, two pieces of dyed work embroidered for my neck as spoil'. And without a shiver, she wonders about her son and the other victors: 'Are they not finding and dividing the spoil?—A girl or two for every man; spoil of dyed stuffs for Sisera?' The irony of the text as traditionally interpreted comes from the fact that Sisera is dead, not that a woman is serenely imagining the rape of other women.

context of ancient law. Remember, the Levite *gave* the woman over to the mob. Compare another night scene earlier in the book of Judges: a Gazite mob lay in wait all through the night for Samson at the city gate, but they do not try to kill him 'until the coming of the dawn'. The difference between the two situations is twofold: the Gazites' plan to capture Samson fails, and second, they evince no sexual designs upon Samson. The male victim is also the male hero. He survives, indeed, he triumphs.

Night is not always a sign in biblical texts for dangerous, loathsome acts. Night is figured as the time for important dreams, from the wrestling of the Jacob with the angel to the apocalyptic dreams of Zechariah: 'In the night I saw a man riding on a red horse!' (Zech. 1.8). The medium at Endor has her visions at night. But the dreams of Zechariah and the woman at Endor are embedded with symbols of death. Usually it is the horrors of battle that occur in the light of day. Needless to say these are usually victories for Israel, not negatively signed acts. The taking of the young women of Shiloh in Judges 21 occurs in the daylight. Thus, one has the first indication of difference between the individual occurrences involving Lot and the Levite from the unified act of the Benjaminites taking wives from the virgins of Jabesh-Gilead and of Shiloh. Getting wives for Benjamin is a victory for Israel: not against a foreign enemy, but a triumph that reunites the tribes, the men of Israel.

It is crucial to ask of a historical period whose literature is given over to the covenant between its members and God: How rape can function as a stock device and what is the relation this genre bears to gender? While several female characters are raped in biblical narrative—Dinah, David's daughter Tamar, the unnamed *pilegesh*—the rape least dwelled upon narratively by recent interpreters is the national rape of the daughters of Shiloh, initiated by the tribes of Israel. The text does not even name the action rape. It is figured as a political necessity, not a sexual crime. Indeed the elders have created a problem for themselves through an ill-conceived vow: 'What shall we do for wives for those who are left, *since we have sworn by the Lord* that we will not give them any of our daughters as wives?' (Judg. 21.7). To understand the cleverness of this surface-seeming foolish vow, one must look at the double misreading of the Levite, who both covers up sexual violence (to himself) and uncovers it (to the *pilegesh*). It is up to the reader to recover the reading that denigrates women. Through a rereading of ancient narratives about male brutality towards women, I believe it is possible to envision rape as more than a symptom of war or even evidence of its violent excess.

Ovid's *Metamorphoses* offer an example of another ancient Mediterranean text built upon the representation of sexual violence. The

Latin text retells the rape or attempted rape of many individual mythic women, among them Daphne, Europa, Syrinx, Arethusa, Thetis, Galatea, Pomona, Persephone, and Callisto. Unlike the narrator/storyteller of the biblical rape events, Ovid's narrator systematically focuses on the victim's pain, horror, humiliation, and grief. Ovid highlights the cruelty of sexual violation, showing the part of violence and degradation as clearly as the erotic element. Curran observes that rape is sometimes used by Ovid as a strategy to remind the reader that 'whatever else is going on in the foreground, rape is always present or potential in the background' (Curran 1978: 216). I would counter Curran's support of Ovid's depiction of rape with the caution that the goddesses and mortal women who were victims of these rapes rarely suffered serious consequences beyond getting pregnant and bearing a child—serving to move the storyline forward. Lest the reader be left with the idea of great sensitivity to rape in ancient classical myths, it is important to note that Ovid also wrote in his version of the rape of the Sabine women, 'Grant me such wage and I'll enlist today', adding a flippant but not unheard-of note to his other descriptions of rape in ancient Rome.

In contrast to the use of rape as a metaphor for social dissolution or for male warrior caodes are Greek mythic texts in which rape is often used as a device to portray the enormous sexual prowess of the gods. Even when Semele is immolated after being penetrated by Zeus's lightning bolt, the mortal woman's pain and fear are not part of the story. The male-focused story continues, as does the life of her unborn fetus, Dionysus, who is brought to term in his father's thigh. The immolation is blamed on the jealousy of Hera; the nurturing and birthing of Dionysus is attributed to Zeus.

In medieval French romances rape is not presented as the malevolent act pictured by Ovid, but rather is mystified and romanticized. Rape is viewed as a permissible act of manhood, woman as warrior's booty. Chrétien de Troyes, for example, systematically shifts away from the literal representation of the female experience of violence toward the moral, erotic, and symbolic meaning rape holds for male characters. While Chrétien admittedly tends to rosy up rape in the *Yvain, le Chevalier au lion*, he embeds the legal codification of rape evidence: the woman fought back, she tried as hard as she could to get away, she resisted—such are the proofs required of a woman prosecuting a man in medieval rape trials (Gravdal 1991: 42).

Returning to the biblical stories of rape or attempted rape, let us see if any of these proofs are evidenced. Annette Kolodny describes a critical position that corresponds to mine in comparing rape narratives in the

Hebrew Bible: 'The power relations inscribed in the form of conventions within our literary inheritance...reify the encodings of those same power relations in the culture at large' (1975: 97). Women do not fight back, they do not try to get away; indeed, the women's struggles and pain are not narrated. Women, even the violated ones, are as silent, compliant, as uninvolved as the narrator understands them to be. For, in biblical law, rape is a crime against the father or husband of the woman. A woman has no right to initiate a trial. While Dinah's brothers exact retribution from Shechem and Tamar's brother Absalom from Amnon, there is no articulated remorse on the part of biblical rapists. There is only one woman who screams 'rape', and retells her story quite volubly and graphically to her husband and to her servants. One remembers from Genesis 39, through the narrative of the wife of Potiphar accusing Joseph of raping her, that a woman in the Bible is supposed to be hysterical and outraged at rape. While the Egyptian woman behaves in the accepted manner, her histrionics are all a sham, as the audience knows full well that the woman is lying about rape. And we remember her as the narrator wants us to, a seductive woman asking for sex.

Writing Hatred upon the Body Politic

As I have noted, what I am referring to as rape in Judges 21 is not referred to as such in the Hebrew narrative. Instead of creating disorder in the biblical narrative as similar acts have in Latin or medieval narratives, these biblical instances of sexual violence are misread by interpreters as political exigencies. Finding enough virgins to wive the men of Benjamin is a political problem that men need to solve. Jabesh-Gilead has been defeated in battle, so carrying off their daughters requires no justification.[9] The arena of war (whether it be holy war or civil war)

---

9. The classical interpretation understands the carrying off of the women of Shiloh as part of a 'holy war', sanctioned by YHWH and a reflection of the tribal confederation. The amphictyony theory has been discredited by most scholars. However, much of this scholarship has remained unchallenged in relation to the narratives in Judg. 21, being part of a holy war, and thus inevitable and justifiable. See von Rad's foundational study of holy war in which he argues that an amphictyony-type confederation of the Israelite tribes is both political and cultic (*Der heilige Krieg im alten Israel* [1991]). Smend's study (1970) modifies von Rad's theory, assuming that the amphictyony before Samuel was solely cultic and neither political nor military. For a review of the many views of holy war in the ancient Near East, see Weinfeld 1983. Niditch (1982) questions the amphictyony theory but settles for half a cake, reading Judg. 19–21 as 'the acting out of this sort of justified holy war situation in a

provides men with the perfect psychological backdrop to give vent to their contempt for women. Whether narrative rape or actual gynocidal violence, rape in war is a familiar act with a familiar excuse.

If this argument seems too harsh, look at the narrative, the male explanation for male action. The only narratorial concern at the outcome of the Shiloh incident is that the act of taking these nubile young women must not be misunderstood by the males of the clan. So the elders instructed the Benjaminites, saying, 'Go and *lie in wait* in the vineyards, and watch; when the young women of Shiloh come out to dance in the dances, then *come out* of the vineyards and each of you *carry off* a wife for himself from the young women of Shiloh, and go to the land of Benjamin' (Judg. 21.21). The verbs '*rb* ('ambush') and *htp* ('carry off') are violent physical actions that contrast sharply with the whirling of the women's celebratory dance. The verb '*rb* embodies both physical harm and action against an enemy; it is used to describe the Philistines lying in wait to ambush Samson until Delilah successfully binds him (Judg. 16.2). The narrator relates that Joshua must ambush Ai and its king as he did at Jericho; 'when Joshua and all Israel saw that the ambush had taken the city' (Josh. 8.21). Both these uses of '*rb* differ from its use in Judges 21 in that ambushing a national enemy is the context in the Samson and Joshua texts. It is the women of Shiloh who are to be ambushed in Judges 21. This ambushing of women goes back to the model of the heroic rape, where the desire for women and violence against women go hand in hand. The elders of Israel need not have worried. The act of taking these young women was not misunderstood.

The only other biblical use of the verb *htp* is found in Psalm 10 ('they lurk in secret like a lion in its covert; they lurk that they may carry off the poor', v. 9). In Psalm 10 *htp* is also used in combination with '*rb*. Both scenes evoke images of violence performed by a powerful party onto a poor or helpless one. In the Psalm God is expected to intercede against the jackals terrorizing the poor. Presumably the women of Shiloh have no need of rescue; they have the Benjaminites as husbands.

It is a struggle to sympathize with the men of Israel even if their confederation is endangered. For the men of Israel in Judges 21 are never the ones who are in danger. Indeed, wiving the Benjaminites is a problem on account of another of those foolish male vows that results in women being sacrificed to protect male honor. As the Israelites conceive their

symbolically charged, rich narrative medium' (p. 375). A concise review of the scholarly chain of argument appears in Ben Ollenburger's Introduction (pp. 1-34) to the English translation of von Rad's *Holy War in Ancient Israel* (1991).

plan, 'if their fathers or their brothers come to complain to us, we will say to them, "Be generous and allow us to have them; because we did not capture in battle a wife for each man. But neither did you incur guilt by giving your daughters to them"' (Judg. 21.22). The traditional understanding is that the Israelites had to be united as twelve tribes to keep their covenant with God. Since they had vowed not to give Benjamin their daughters as wives, how could they then ensure that the tribe would survive? After annexing the virgins of Jabesh-Gilead there is still a shortfall. To tidy up the mess, the men devise a plan to wive the girls of Shiloh. Dancing perhaps the same ritual as the friends of the daughter of Jephthah, who had suffered mortally from a father's foolish vow, now the girls of Shiloh are to be sacrificed, not killed but taken as wives. Taken *as wives*—the escape clause that naturalizes the violent action and even lets their fathers off the hook, since they had not offered them as wives to the offensive but still 'men of Israel' Benjaminites. Once again women have been the victims in a male shell game of sexual violence.

What may be interpreted by a modern reader as the nefarious plundering of the females ripening in the vineyards at Shiloh is obliquely connected by the biblical narrator to each man doing what was right in his own eyes. Perhaps the repetition of this phrase is meant as a pro-monarchic statement studded with sarcasm. Perhaps the phrase is a clear-eyed assessment of the importance of inter-tribal loyalties with a wink at sexual politics. At best the reader is nudged toward an interpretation unfriendly to the tribes' resolution of their problem. But can a feminist critic let the biblical narrator soothe the reader as easily as he plans to soothe the fathers and brothers of the maidens of Shiloh? The well-known call to arms of Helene Cixous to act obliges readers, 'Language conceals an invincible adversary because it is the language of men and their grammar. We must not leave them a single place that's any more theirs alone than we are.' From a feminist viewpoint the biblical understanding of rape and its punishment serve to show an asymmetrical relationship between women and men, coding sexual violence in ways that make it culturally acceptable. A second hint that the foolish vow resulting in the carrying off of the Shiloh women may not have been so foolish. The narrative raises the question of rape or seizing of women as an expected outgrowth of war. Triumph over women by rape is also a way to measure victory, 'part of a soldier's proof of masculinity and success, a tangible reward for services rendered' (Brownmiller 1975: 33). The neat resolution of the entire story reading Judges 19–21 also helps to bury deep within the literary unconscious the memory of homosexual attack.

Men Raping Men

One more category of rape augments my intertextual reading of Judges 21. In the minds of the male formulators of the story and their ideal audience, the horror of homosexual rape is far greater than that of a male violating a female. Substituting the violence done to himself with violence to the *pilegesh* explains the Levite's rage. Unharmed himself, he retains honor and standing within the community, enough to be able to incite the other tribes to violence against Benjamin. Unsanctioned male sexual appetite can ignite the proper rage of all Israel and does result in the vow to cut off the tribe of Benjamin, that is, to ensure that Benjamin loses its power among the tribes. But had the Levite himself been the victim of rape, the shame and humiliation would have been too great for him to relate his story publicly as he does in Judges 20. Further, it would have been unthinkable to readmit Benjamin as a tribe had its crime been a taboo that smashed sexual boundaries instead of merely stretching them.

The key semes that generate this reading are those of substitution, of offering the woman in place of the male in both Genesis 19 and in Judges 19, of offering the Levite's version of the story in Judges 20 in place of the one the reader has just witnessed in stunning detail in Judges 19. The version of the homosexual attack in Genesis reveals some important clues about the nature of the offer and of the substitution. Lot goes out the door and shuts the door after him, so he is on the same side of the door as the men. The door is clearly a sexual boundary. Then he pleads with the men: 'I beg you, my brothers, do not act so wickedly' (Gen. 19.7). He offers his two virgin daughters in place of himself, but the bedeviled men press hard against him. Their nefarious act is stopped by the angels. Divine intercession restores Lot to the proper side of the door and rescues him at the last moment from narrative destruction. The divine narrator sends a strong symbolic message by blinding the men who would look and lust after what is forbidden to them (19.11). Nowhere in this Genesis text is a female substituted for a male. It takes divine intervention to halt homosexual intercourse. God responds furiously by destroying the Sodomites who would break through that door, that taboo that binds men in community in the Hebrew Bible.[10]

10. I would like to call attention to Wilson's (1995) reading from a queer perspective. She emphasizes that the sin of Sodom is not that of homosexual threat, but rather that of ethnic and sexual violence (pp. 168-69). Her suggestion that the 'same-sex male-appearing angels' at the door in Gen. 19 are gay, and thus, are the potential victims of the story, is an intriguing example of gap-filling with one's ideological position.

What is the situation in Judges 19? The Levite and his host were enjoying themselves much as the Levite had recently enjoyed himself with the father of his *pilegesh*. The men of the city, a perverse lot, surrounded the house, and pounded on the door. They said to the old man, the master of the house, 'Bring out the man who came into your house, so that we may have intercourse with him'. The Levite made no move. The Ephraimite went outside, as had Lot, to try to deal with the men: 'No, my brothers, do not act so wickedly', pleads the Ephraimite, 'since this man is my guest do not do this vile thing' (Judg. 19.22-23). The repetition is intentional; the one text recalls the other. Men threaten other men by pounding on the door. The door that leads to death is the boundary, the shield. In this account the Levite never risks death by going outside the door, but rather, the Levite seizes his *pilegesh* and 'pushes her outside' to the waiting mob on the other side. Can we consider the Benjaminites' act rape if the Levite handed her over to them?

In the version of the story that he tells in Judges 20, the Levite states that the men of the mob intended to kill him, so he gave them the *pilegesh*. But there is a piece missing: there is a lack of logic that is unquestioned by the other men, the narrator, or most interpreters. Why was the mob satisfied by the offer of the *pilegesh*? In Genesis 19, the mirror of the story, the mob rejected the offer of the daughters. It took divine intercession to protect Lot from homosexual rape. Divine intervention was not afforded the Levite.[11] Perhaps that explains the Levite's murderous rage. Could the rape of one woman initiate total tribal warfare in Israel? (Keefe 1993). Is the ensuing battle an uniterated *herem* as Niditch suggests (1993a: 69-71).[12] Perhaps the Levite knew the confederation could not cut off Benjamin as easily as he could cut up the *pilegesh*. Perhaps the Judges version of the story has been inverted to protect the

11.   One has the same narratological pattern in parallel stories in Gen. 22, where divine intervention halts child sacrifice of a male child, and Judg. 11–12, where there is no divine intervention to rescue a female child.

12.   I do not claim to reflect the narrator's understanding of 'tribe', nor his view of the situation between the tribe of Benjamin and the other tribes. Niditch notes that the *herem* is considered as an appropriate form of aggression only against outsiders: 'When the ban is used as a technique "to keep ingroup miscreants in line by a nervous and insecure leadership with the power to enforce its will", it becomes devisive' (1993: 70). Clearly this is the situation in Judg. 21. Niditch shares my puzzlement over the designation of tribe in this context, and the situation of exogamous marriage, neither of which has much historical evidence. I suggest that the story does not function historically, but rather serves to suppress the homosexuality in Judg. 19 as well as the violent rape in Judg. 21.

men of Israel from the specter of sodomy. Are there any further textual clues about denying homosexual rape? Back to the *pilegesh*. In the morning she is unable to return to the 'safe' site even after the Levite opens the door. The Levite shows no emotion at seeing her collapsed form on the threshold. He also appears to think she is alive. Why else would he command her to get up? Thus, the violated woman, perhaps by this time a corpse, *nebelah* (n[a]b[e]l),[13] surely a disgrace, a *nabalah* (n[a]b[a]l), has never returned inside, to the place of safety, of life, where the Levite and Ephraimite have remained all through the night. Unlike Lot, the *pilegesh* has no divine messenger to bring her back to the safe side of the door. One reading of the fate of the *pilegesh*, then, is that she has been broken so that the final boundary (the *delet*) could hold firm and protect the Levite against shame and death. She has collapsed on the death side of the door. Another possibility is that her body was the boundary that stopped the mob from committing rape—that is, rape of the Levite. Another woman found on the wrong side of the door is Tamar. After raping her, Amnon called to his servants, 'Put this woman out of my presence, and bolt the door after her' (2 Sam. 13.18). The door becomes the marker between security and danger, honor and shame, life and death. In a lucid synchronic reading that links Genesis 19 and Judges 19–20, Niditch observes that a homosexual rape would have been worse than the rape of the *pilegesh* in the eyes of Israel, and ethically indefensible (1982). Niditch does not, however, address the absence of anger or moral outrage on the part of the narrator. Nor does she explain the rage of the Levite in the following chapter of Judges. Perhaps the biblical narrator has slammed the door on sodomy so effectively that no reader, even a modern one, dares to press up against that door. Like Lot and the Levite, who are exonerated for offering women as substitutes, the reader is exonerated for not wondering if perhaps the Levite had not been the victim after all. But the misreading demands the answers to two crucial questions: Why else the Levite's extraordinary rage? Why else the cutting up of the sacrificial victim?[14] One must account for the Levite transforming

13. The noun *nebalah*, defined in BDB as 'disgraceful folly', 'to do a thing disgraceful according to Israel's standards', is used in conjunction with all the biblical rape narratives; in Judg. 19.24 the term may refer to the threat of homosexual rape; in Judg. 20.6 the term clearly refers to the gang rape of the *pilegesh*; in Gen. 34.7 it refers to the rape of Dinah. For further discussion of the term *nebalah*, see Keefe 1993: 82.

14. Many scholars have noted the similarity between the cutting up of the *pilegesh* and Saul's cutting up of the yoke of oxen in 1 Sam. 11.5-7. In both narratives the pieces are sent to the tribes of Israel to incite them to battle. Niditch (1982: 371) sees the dismembered body as a part of the division of the body politic. Reading

the Benjaminites' threat to sodomize him into a desire to kill him. The shame and horror of sodomy were equivalent to death. Unruly unlawful male sexuality, according to the tale as used in Genesis, does result in the death of the Sodomites. But the Levite has eluded death. He escapes punishment over her dead body. The Levite further vilifies the dead female body by using it to incite his countrymen. Choosing to misread the sign of her body, the men exact revenge on Benjamin. But then, in order to assuage the guilt and anger against their brothers, they amplify the violence done to one woman by violating many women. Each act of violence is justified by hiding the truth behind the door, throwing out lies to distract the spectators. Men's misreadings result in the mistreatment of women. The substitution of women for men occurs in both the story of Judges 19 and in the revenge taken in Judges 21. Gender inversion of the tale becomes the Levite's security.

While the violations of individual women in Genesis 19 and Judges 19–20 have become the subject of earnest debate in the feminist community, the carrying off of the women of Shiloh has been met with near silence. The representation of violence and pain of rape have been lost in a welter of interpretations that talk about reuniting the tribes of Israel, fighting a holy war in YHWH's name, assuring the continuation of the tribe of Benjamin. Male and female commentators alike seem to identify deeply with the portrait of female victimization expressed in the narratives of violence to one woman, but silence greets the genocidal brutalization of the women of Shiloh.

Breaking the Silence of the Women of Shiloh

Feminist criticism combines the personal and the political, and insists on a kind of self-consciousness that is explicit about the origins of one's projects and the position from which one speaks. Undermining the traditional academic boundaries between professional and subjective is an example of the interaction between personal and political. I suspect that it would be impossible for any woman to write about rape without becoming emotionally involved in the work.[15]

through the gender code, Exum argues that 'by leaving her husband the woman makes a gesture of sexual autonomy, so threatening to patriarchal ideology that it requires her to be punished sexually in the most extreme form' (1990b: 181).

15. For riveting descriptions of the scenes of horror in the Bosnia rape camps, see *I Remember = Sjecam Se: Writings by Bosnian Women Refugees* (Zarkovic [ed.] 1996). The memoirs appear in the original Serbo-Croatian, along with English,

The biblical text remains silent about the young women of Shiloh. There are some documented atrocities from the recent gynocidal actions in Bosnia that do speak. The parallel seems strong, for the recent atrocities were committed during an ethno-religious civil war, a war in which men's violence was inscribed upon women's bodies. In both situations there is the strong patriarchal association of the female body with territory, so that raping one and conquering the other come metaphorically to the same thing. For those readers clinging to the 'marriage' element of the Judges 21 text, let me add that what Allen calls 'enforced pregnancy' (1996: 87) was also practiced by the Christian Serbs against Muslim women. The male aggression in Bosnia manifested itself in a way unique from most other wartime rapes, however. In this war, rape was used as a tool for ethnic cleansing through the forced impregnation of women, although this argument does not, however, explain the mass rapes of old women and young girls:

> There is a difference between the kind of genocidal rape that ends in murder and the kind that ends in pregnancy: victims of the second kind of genocidal rape must be able to become, and remain, pregnant. Being a female, therefore, is a necessary condition for receiving this kind of treatment (1996: 121).

The following testimony was offered by a survivor of the Susica camp in eastern Bosnia. The witness was testifying about several young women who had been selected for enforced pregnancy:

> They started selecting young women. The first was only 14, the second could have been 16 or 17... I knew them all, they were from Vlasenica... Then they started yelling, 'We want the muslims to see what our seed is'. The women were never seen again... We know that Dragan Nikolic knows about it very well. That's what he did... He told us himself: 'I am the commander of the camp. I'm your God and you have no other God but me' (Zarkovic [ed.] 1996: 21).

Many of the soldiers were, in fact, following orders, even though this does not excuse their actions. After the war, many army generals testified

---

Spanish and Italian. See also Hukanovic 1997. I recommend these works with the warning provided by Beverly Allen: 'A repetitive serial form may easily hook even a reader disgusted by the events the text relates into wondering at least what comes next. This scene was so horrible, can the next one possibly be worse? And so the reader may keep turning the pages, caught in spite of her or his revulsion in the formal pleasure of repetitive linear narrative' (1996: 32). As I have noted above, this sort of narrative risks placing the reader in the position of voyeur. Also see Allen 1996 and Stiglmayer 1994.

that they ordered their troops to rape women as a way to 'increase the morale of our fighters' (Stiglmayer 1994: 149).

Local soldiers were not the only ones to participate in the violence against women, however; the United Nations, the 'organization of nations pledged to promote world peace and security...and the observance of international law', participated in the rapes and proliferation of pornography, as well. The spectacle of the United Nations troops violating those they are there to protect adds a touch of the perverse—some UN troops are participating in raping Muslim and Croatian women taken from Serb-run rape/death camps: 'the UN presence has apparently increased the trafficking in women and girls through the opening of brothels, brothel-massage parlors, peep shows, and the local production of pornographic films' (MacKinnon 2001: 192). There are also reports that a former UNPROFOR commander accepted offers from a Serbian commander to bring him Muslim girls for sexual use.

What I would like to suggest is that after reading rape accounts such as the one quoted above from the recent genocide in Bosnia, the reader will fill the gaps and silences in Judges 21 with the cries of the victims of ethnic/religious rape of massive proportions. As I have argued elsewhere (1998a) we do not read in a linear fashion. Regardless of the order of one's reading, what is immediately apparent is that female readers will feel an emotional connection between the plight of the Muslim women of Bosnia and the virgins of Shiloh—if readers allow themselves to dwell upon that sliver of biblical narrative. I do not mean to imply that men will not feel horror at these atrocities, but I have searched all the traditional accounts of holy war in Israel, of war suborned by YHWH, of war won by YHWH, and nowhere is there a mention of the carrying off of the women of Shiloh as rape, or even a hint that such a deed might have been divinely sanctioned but *against their will*. Much like violence portrayed in cartoons, the carrying off of the dancing maidens is accomplished without pain, without struggle, without resistance. If the narrative were focalized even for a moment through the eyes of the victims, one would be required to appropriate the female body as a sign of the violator's power. But the women remain as passive signifiers; the biblical storyteller is not interested in representing their experience. Thus, the reader must inhabit the gap, the silence, and through the power of imagination break the silence of the women of Shiloh. Almost a decade later, the crimes against the women of Bosnia still shock: by their magnitude and not their novelty. To leave them in silence is gynocide.

On the Ground in Ramallah

Palestinian women living in the Occupied Territories have had greater opportunities than many other women in the Arab world to participate in the labor force, to vote and hold political office, and to be visible and active in civil society, but the political situation has counterbalanced many of their social gains. In one recent example, the International Labor Organization reported that disruption created by the current crisis made it impossible to implement the action plan for gender mainstreaming in the Ministry of Labor that it had developed in 2000.[16]

According to Amira Hass,[17] an Israeli journalist who lived in the Gaza Strip while posting articles to *Ha'aretz*, since the escalation of violence in September 2000 Israel has imposed and steadily tightened closure and curfew restrictions on the residents of the Gaza Strip, resulting in the most severe restrictions on the movement of Palestinian people and goods since 1967. In her extraordinary piece of personal journalism, *Drinking the Sea at Gaza* (2000), Hass reflected on her reasons for choosing to witness in Gaza. 'In the end', she wrote, 'my desire to live in Gaza stemmed neither from adventurism nor from insanity, but from that dread of being a bystander, from my need to understand, down to the last detail, a world that is, to the best of my political and historical comprehension, a

16. <http://www.womenwarpeace.org/opt/opt.htm>.

17. Amira Hass has been a human rights worker and a journalist. Her publications include *Drinking the Sea at Gaza* (2000) and a collection of articles entitled *Reporting From Ramallah: An Israel Journalist in Occupied Land* (2003). She is a recipient of numerous human rights and journalism awards, including the Bruno Kreisky Human Rights Award, and, in 2003, the UNESCO Press Freedom Award. In the middle of the first Intifada she volunteered in a group called Workers Hotline, who assisted Palestinian workers, mainly, whose rights were violated by Israeli employers. This advocacy group offered active assistance in the sense of approaching the employers either through lawyers or directly in order to get fairness and justice for these people. Her background gives Hass total credibility within Israel, although her own frustration with speaking truth to power is apparent in her columns. Her parents were Jewish Holocaust survivors, members of the Israeli Communist Party. Her mother had been a partisan in Yugoslavia against German occupation, but then she was deported to a concentration camp. In an interview at the University of California, Berkeley, in October 2003, she talked about the ongoing power of that connection to her work today: 'I think I was raised in their personal attempt, an ideological attempt, to compensate for the terrible emotional and ideological vacuum and family vacuum created after the Second World War, with the loss of most of their family and friends, history and life; to compensate this with the hope that you can work on for a better world, where the principle of equality is recognized as a basic for human life'.

profoundly Israeli creation. To me, Gaza embodies the entire saga of the Israeli–Palestinian conflict; it represents the central contradiction of the state of Israel—democracy for some, dispossession for others; it is our exposed nerve' (p. 19).

In November 2002, OCHA (the United Nations Office for the Coordination of Humanitarian Affairs) reported that the combined effects of dozens of permanent IDF (Israeli Defense Forces) checkpoints and an IDF-managed permit system in the West Bank, frequent IDF roadblocks and checkpoints in the Gaza Strip, the construction of numerous bypass roads in the Occupied Territories, and the activities of Israeli settlers (particularly in the West Bank) made mobility difficult, if not impossible, for most Palestinians. Israeli society has learned to live in peace with the following facts. There are 8000 Jews and 1.4 million Palestinians in the Gaza Strip. The total area of the Strip is 365 square kilometers. The settlements occupy 54 square kilometers. Along with the areas held by the IDF, according to the Oslo accords, 20 per cent of the Strip is under Israeli control—that's 20 per cent of the territory for half of one per cent of the population. Women thus face important obstacles in their efforts to provide food and other basic necessities for their families: lack of availability, decreased family income, restricted movement, and subjection to sexual harassment and blackmail.

Palestinian women have become heroes or murderers depending on which side of the Green Line you are living. Increasing numbers of Palestinian women began training to become suicide bombers during the second Intifada. From January 2002 to 14 January 2004, seven Palestinian women conducted suicide bombings and at least four more were arrested before carrying out planned attacks. Secret training courses for 'female martyr brigades', witnessed by *Sunday Times* reporter Hala Jaber in December 2003, offered up to six hours a day of training in such skills as assembling and dismantling assault rifles, study of the 'enemy and its tactics', intensive study of previous suicide bombings, and how to handle explosives. The women's trainers described them as 'Palestinian human precision bombs'.[18]

The words of one of the 'trainees' speaks eloquently and terrifyingly of the mindset of some Palestinian women. I reprint the words here with some concern that some readers may accuse me of glorifying violent death and promoting a cult of martyrdom:

18.   <http://www.womenwarpeace.org/opt/opt.htm>. I realize statistics are as slippery as the people who use them. I have tried to use the information from the Peace Groups whose work I trust.

Yes, I seek revenge. Of course I seek revenge. How can I not when I daily watch people we have grown up with, including our nearest and dearest, being killed for no reason? Marriage? Why? So that in a few years' time I join the long list of Palestinian widows? Motherhood? What—to see my children being killed? Tradition says I should be a homemaker, but why should I build a home that will eventually be destroyed? My only dream and ambition is to become a martyr. I no longer dream of love and marriage. I dream of martyrdom every minute of the day… I would prefer it if only Israeli soldiers are killed and not civilians. But sometimes civilians have to be killed and I say may God rest their souls, but there is no alternative. We have to force them to feel with us, to feel our pain and that means they sometimes have to suffer civilian losses just like us'. 'Nour'.[19]

Hamas used a woman suicide bomber for the first time on 14 January 2004, at the Erez checkpoint, as part of a new tactic designed to counter Israeli security precautions, which the group said had created 'obstacles' for male suicide bombers. Hamas said they would continue to use this tactic to escalate attacks on Israeli targets. The family of Reem al-Reyashi—a 22-year-old mother of two, and only the second mother to become a suicide bomber—are reported to have disowned her for her action. Her brother-in-law was quoted as saying that he condemns her action because he supports peace, but also because 'It's not accepted for a woman to do that. This doesn't exist in our traditions.'

As a result of the 14 January 2004 attack described above, Israel began to treat Palestinian women more strictly when they crossed army checkpoints in the Gaza Strip, especially the Erez checkpoint. A female soldier had been called to carry out a body search of the bomber, who detonated her explosives while waiting for the soldier to arrive. Israel also sealed the Gaza Strip, keeping thousands of Palestinians from their jobs in Israel, and closed the Erez industrial area, where 4000 Palestinians are employed. As I write in the midst of violence and vengeance in Israel and the Occupied Territories, I am mindful of a remark that Hala Jaber made on CNN: 'It takes about ten people who are disappointed with something, angered by something or upset by another to create a cell and to carry out on attack on something'.[20] Ten people, a minyan of horror.

19.   Age 24, this woman offered herself as a suicide bomber after seeing her sister die in an Israeli raid. This Palestinian narrative was written by Hala Jaber. A well-respected journalist, he is the author of *Hezbollah* (1997). Jaber is trusted by the people about whom she writes, his journalistic reputation perhaps heightened by his being a Lebanese Muslim reporter at Britain's *Sunday Times*. Jaber received the Amnesty International Journalist of the Year Award in 2003.

20.   <http://www.cnn.com/TRANSCRIPTS/0305/23/i_c.00.html>.

Another Rizpah woman who held her ground in *'eretz* Israel was 23-year-old American peace activist Rachel Corrie. She did not succeed in protecting the territory with her body; the Israeli Defence Force soldiers did not respond in the way that King David had to Rizpah in the biblical narrative. On the afternoon of 16 March 2003, an Israeli soldier flattened Rachel in the occupied territories of Palestine with an armored Caterpillar bulldozer. Rachel was trying to prevent the soldier from crashing that bulldozer into the house of a Palestinian family in Rafah. There was reason to believe the soldier was going to demolish the house, as the Israeli army has destroyed more than 1000 homes and misplaced nearly 15,000 people in that small town in the past two years.

There are news accounts that claim all the homes in Rafah were hiding tunnels that allow weapons into Gaza from Egypt. Four tunnels have been found—only one of which had evidence of weapons transport. 'What you may not have heard about', wrote Mollie McClain in the *Seattle Post-Intelligencer* on the first anniversary of Rachel's death, 'is the wall the army is building between Rafah and Egypt. In fact, it is all the homes, greenhouses, fields, mosques, schools and shops "in the way" of this wall that have been destroyed.'

The troubles in Gaza and Rafah continue as of this writing. At least 2200 Palestinians have been left homeless as hundreds of homes have been destroyed by the IDF. With precision, Amira Hass describes the desperate exodus of Palestinian families:

> The streets of Rafah were filled yesterday evening [18 May 2004] with horse-drawn carts, trucks and pick-ups, all laden to the brim with any and every item that the town's residents could remove from their homes— mattresses, water tanks taken down from roofs, clothes, blankets, doors and windows removed from their hinges, dismantled beds and closets, school books, tin and asbestos sheeting, baby carriages, refrigerators, gas canisters and more.
>
> The Kishta family has stopped counting the number of times IDF bulldozers, supported by tanks, APCs and helicopters, have demolished homes in the area—maybe five, or six. On one occasion, a bulldozer destroyed their bedroom, from where they now look out onto the steel wall the army is erecting along the border, the Termit outpost, bare concrete houses, and piles of rubble between the sand dunes. Last Thursday, bullets and shells left holes in the walls of their son Abed's home.

The Palestinian human rights group Al Mezan, based in Jabalya refugee camp, found that 81 women were killed by IDF gunfire in the Strip; 344 children under the age of 18 were killed by IDF gunfire; 255 members of the Palestinian security and police forces were killed either at their positions or offices and frequently in battle; 264 were armed men who took part in battles with the IDF or tried to attack military positions or settlers and settlements. In the IDF's targeted assassinations, 46 of those killed were the targets of the attacks—and 80 were passersby killed with 'pin-point prevention'.[21]

Amira Hass has pondered the efficacy of witnessing with the pen: 'This is an admission of failure. The written word is a failure at making tangible to Israeli readers the true horror of the occupation in the Gaza Strip' (2000: 26). Like the activists who count the dead in Iraq, in Afghanistan, throughout Africa, Hass is exhausted by the weight of number, the impossibility of reading about horror from a comfortable chair. 'How would photographs illustrate the following facts?' Hass continues her counting in March 2004,

> …from September 29th up to Monday this week, 94 Israelis have been killed—27 civilians and 67 soldiers, according to the IDF. From that same date up to February 18th this year 1231 Palestinians have been killed—all of them were terrorists? Lacking a central Palestinian agency, there are differences between the data provided by Palestinian groups and none claim to be 100 per cent accurate.[22]

On the Ground in the USA

'Nuclear weapons are legal, right across the board, from making and proc-essing them to running them through Pantex down in Amarillo, Texas and deploying them. You can make it legal, but you can never make it right!', Elizabeth McAlister tells an audience of peace workers. For almost 40 years McAlister has pried open the jaws of violence and imperialism to give peace and compassion a chance. She is a Rizpah figure, but only to a point. McAlister is anything but silent. Time after time she has used her body and her prophetic voice to respond to militaristic action. With clear-eyed calm, Liz has named the evil in the world: pollution of the earth, hunger, and homelessness as the price for weapons systems, defining war as peace, 'these are all forms of practical idolatry, though they com-monly go under more acceptable names like patriotism'. Working through

21. Al Mezan Center for Human Rights is a Palestinian non-governmental, non-partisan organization based in the refugee camp of Jabalia in the Gaza Strip. Al Mezan's mandate is 'to promote, protect and prevent violations of human rights in general and economic, social and cultural (ESC) rights in particular, to provide effective aid to those victims of such violations, and to enhance the quality of life of the community in marginalized sectors of the Gaza Strip'.

22. Hass 2004. For a daily update on the situation on the ground in Rafah, visit <http://www.mezan.org/site_en/rafah/index.php>.

the Jonah House community, which Liz founded with her late husband Philip Berrigan, the multi-generational group continues to bring out under-reported figures and results of the global efforts of 'the American Empire'. The name Jonah House, according to the community's website, has a theological significance directly tied to the book of Jonah: 'If God could use Jonah for the works of justice, there is hope for each of us'. 'Are we not all reluctant prophets?'[23] Reluctant perhaps, but steadfast, and as the media might phrase it, 'continuously on-message'.

The physical location of Jonah House has been Baltimore, Maryland, where McAlister and Berrigan lived in community for 30 years, except when one or both was serving time for peace activities. With the other members of the community, Liz and Phil raised their three children, all of whom have become resisters as adults. During that 30-year period, Philip Berrigan spent an aggregate of more than eleven years incarcerated for peace-making actions. Liz McAlister has served about four years herself, although neither of them has ever conducted business with a currency of righteousness. In spite of the bleak message that she delivers to those who would keep the status quo, Liz has a refreshing certainty, a joy that emanates from her, encouraging those with feet to take a first step. Liz and Phil both have worn their commitment lightly, never making those whose commitment is fragmented, and who come and go in the movement, feel guilty or wrong. Jonah House has always emphasized consensus decision-making. While the names McAlister and Berrigan are well known as American peace activists, the pair have never been star-trippers. In sharing experiences and in planning actions they have always included everyone who chooses to be involved. The spiritual location of Jonah House defies zip codes and national boundaries. As the voice of Amira Hass emanates from the Gaza Strip and from Ramallah and from any other location from which she files her articles for *Ha'aretz*, the voices of American peace activists are not limited by geography.

This faith-based resistance movement, of which Jonah House is a beacon, understands its actions to arise out of the biblical prophecy of Isaiah and Micah as well as Jesus' refusal to engage in battle, even to save his own life. Together with Jesuit activist and poet, Dan Berrigan, and other friends and activists, the Jonah House community has been compelled to perform acts of what some call civil disobedience, what Liz and her family call holy obedience. In 1980 the Plowshares Eight performed the first of the Plowshares actions, entering the General Electric Nuclear Missile Re-entry Division in King of Prussia, Pennsylvania, where nose

23. Visit <http://www.jonahhouse.org/jhbrochure.htm>.

cones for the Mark 12A warheads were made. They hammered on two nose cones, poured blood on documents and offered prayers for peace. Since that time there have been more than 70 Plowshares actions worldwide, each one performed to disarm components of nuclear and conventional weapons non-violently.[24] More than two decades after his first Plowshares action, after 9/11, Dan Berrigan continued to take a counterclockwise turn, disavowing the commodity culture for a life of prayerful non-violence. 'What we have to offer is a literal hope against hope, promulgated in the teeth of the worst times. With a sense of lively contempt, it is up to us to shuck off the victim role; cease to be mute, passive, resigned.' To act non-violently is to be in harmony with God.

Months before the *Washington Post* discussed it, Liz had spoken out about the mistreatment of third-world people on the ground in Afghanistan, in Africa, in Latin America, in Iraq. Now the wider world is aware of the imperial violence that sends the poor to do the work of the Halliburton conglomerate, particularly by a subsidiary called Kellogg Brown & Root Inc. Like other multinational companies, KBR has a multibillion-dollar contract to provide support services for US troops at a fraction of the pay given to US workers. Finally the *Washington Post* reported on this new kind of outsourcing: 'They have been hired through layers of subcontractors and usually get a fraction of the pay, benefits, and sometimes security of Western workers. One group of Indians who worked for Halliburton recalled being tricked into going to Iraq and then not being given flak jackets or sufficient food. 'I cursed my fate', said one former worker, 'not having a feeling my life was secure, knowing I could not go back, and being treated like a kind of animal'.[25]

---

24. By spotlighting these activists I do not mean to exclude the other people in this movement. More than 150 individuals have participated in over 70 Plowshares and related disarmament actions. Add to that number several groups and individuals who were stopped by security and arrested at or near a weapons site before being able to complete their intended disarmament action. Some Plowshares activists have gone on to participate in other Plowshares actions. Plowshares actions have occurred in the US, Australia, Germany, Holland, Sweden, and England. The backgrounds of Plowshares activists vary widely. Parents, grandparents, veterans, lawyers, teachers, artists, musicians, priests, sisters, house-painters, carpenters, writers, health-care workers, students, advocates for the poor and homeless, and members of Catholic Worker communities have all participated in Plowshares actions. Most of those who have participated in Plowshares actions remain actively involved in the peace and justice movement.

25. <http://www.washingtonpost.com/wp-dyn/articles/A19228-2004Jun30.html> (Thursday 1 July 2004), p. A01.

Following exhortations of the biblical prophets, such as envisioning all the boots put on to stamp with and garments of warfare 'burned as fuel for the fire' (Isa. 9.4), the Jonah House resistance community in connection with other peace activists have continued to act, speak, write, and witness—even when their anti-war sentiments are neither reported or the movement supported by a wide majority of citizens, as it was during and after the war against Vietnam. Their message has remained as steadfast as their actions: there is not going to be any real disarmament until there's a disarming of hearts. People are being brutalized or pacified. And so one puts oneself on the line to disarm symbolically the weapons in a hope and prayer that the action might be used by the Spirit of God to change minds and hearts. One puts oneself on the line—at risk and in jeopardy—to communicate the depth of commitment to that hope.

Perhaps it is this spiritual connection, the disarming of hearts, that allows Liz to deliver some of the most poignant and heart-felt information about the American empire. Never one to write with a poison pen, McAlister manages to present the most devastating information about the brutality inflicted on the poor of the earth without losing sight of the promise that the situation can be reversed. Like Rizpah, she has taken her stand and will not be moved.

8

WOMEN'S ALTARS:
LIVED RELIGION FROM NOW TO THEN

I will tell you something about stories
They aren't just entertainment.
Don't be fooled.
They are all we have, you see,
All we have to fight off disaster, dis-ease, and devastation
We don't have anything
if we don't have stories.
>   —Leslie Marmon Silko, *The Storyteller* (1981)

Having excoriated the classicists and biblicists in their unwillingness to redivide the disciplinary pie, I would like to center the idea of women's daily rituals and religious artifacts within the larger context of culture, politics, media, and American religion. Thus, I shall be combining many subdisciplines in the examination of a question involving women's lives in the ancient Mediterranean world and in contemporary American culture/s. With an emphasis on the plurality of those cultures and the popular ritual and images that are created by women, I will try to recreate the taste of a specially baked egg-glazed bread, the sight of a bouquet of brilliant orange marigolds, the aroma of a cinnamon-scented kitchen.

As a feminist scholar, I consider 'the gendered kitchen' as a valid scholarly lens through which to analyze religious traditions; the more medieval recipe collections I have read, the more I have understood what a vast field of inquiry food encompasses. Through stories women communicate the rhythms of dailiness. St Theresa of Avila remarked in several accounts that God was to be found in the 'pots and pipkins'. The Prioress of the Domenican Order of San Tommaso of Perugia kept notebooks in which she not only recorded holy thoughts but also one hundred and seventy recipes.

Since we have so little literary evidence from the ancient world reflecting women's voices, one needs to use a bit of auditory magic to elicit their voices. The more time I have spent listening to women's voices struggling with questions of identity in our contemporary world, the more tempted I have been to link our voices back to the silent women of antiquity. While my own research is based more on literary texts than historical evidence, the anthropologic and historical investigations of other feminist scholars led me to the conclusion that the roundness of a wedding cake plump with nuts and dried fruits has a sacramental value, too often overlooked. Following the trajectories suggested by the theories of lived religions with a dash of sesame-fried dumplings, I have had a delicious time, pushing out the boundaries of what has been termed 'correct' scholarship.

While men surely have been storytellers, they have had law codes and political orations and philosophical treatises from the earliest written times to document their thoughts and reflect their lives. Because the shape of women's lives tends not to be linear, not directed toward a goal, one often finds women's stories to be circular, complex, circumstantial, often cloud-like, seeded with feeling and desire. Some records of dailiness are woven into quilts; some are planted into gardens; others are sculpted into clay, painted onto pottery, inscribed into journals and letters. Women's stories tend to be laden with details—what we ate, what we wore, what we said, each to the other. We have few literary records and few artifacts from the ancient Mediterranean world that reveal women's world through women's eyes. Thus, what is real in our records of women's lives must be imagined in the world of ancient Mediterranean women.

Feminist poet Judy Grahn has expressed the frustration we have with trying to focus on what is not there—words and pictures of the lives of women of antiquity. In her poem 'They Say She is Veiled', which appears in her 1982 collection, *The Queen of Wands*, Grahn expresses the frustration of a woman struggling against the silence of her foremothers:

> They say she is veiled
> And a mystery. That is
> One way of looking.
> Another
> is that she is where
> she always has been,
> exactly in place,
> and it is we,
> we who are mystified,
> we who are veiled
> and without faces.

Even a queen, and a legendary beauty like Helen, had not the power to carve her way through the world in which she lived. While we have splinters of the literary lives of the privileged in this world through male-authored epic texts, we lack the sense of dailiness or intimate contact with the women. Thus we remain veiled, wishing for the power to see and hear across time. Grahn's realization that it is we who are veiled seems right to me. Poets are allowed to spend their days squinting across time. Scholars are meant to devise a method that will reveal that world without a trace of our handprints on the creation. Fortunately, some scholars have been as frustrated as poets, wanting to sense that ancient time, acknowledging that the reified tradition of impartiality and *truth* needs to crumple. The process of tumbling backwards through time is what I think many feminist scholars are trying to refine.

There is a new approach to studying religion and culture that embeds the religious person and community in history, that sees history and culture not as something that religious persons are 'in', but as the media through which they fundamentally are. This method, the study of lived religion, is supported by what Pierre Bourdieu has named the *habitus*—the power of cultural structures and inherited idioms—both to shape and discipline thought and as well to give rise to religious creativity and interpretation. According to Robert Orsi, 'what is called for is the recognition that it is the historicized and acculturated religious imagination that is also the imagination by means of which in Marx's well-quoted expression, the frozen circumstances of our worlds are forced to dance by our singing to them their own melodies.' Orsi is talking about 'lived religion', a method for examining religious practice through the realia and religious imagery that reflect the way people live their religious beliefs as part of their daily lives (1997: 13).

What excited me about this approach of lived religion is precisely what is anathema to many in the discipline of biblical studies, that is, establishing a link between the practices one studies and ones own everyday concerns. As Orsi has noted (and this chapter and its fruits are permeated with Orsi's method and sensibility), 'the acknowledgment of a resonance between our experiences in the present and those of people in the past is so fearsome to historians that they have branded it a heresy and history departments strain to ensure that their neophytes are free of any taint of this notion' (1997: 15).

I have welcomed the taint in order to look at women's altars and shrines as images of visual piety that reflect women's culture, with its domestic locus and fragmented use of everyday objects. One such intellectual leap might look like this: several sixth-century BCE vases from Corinth show scenes of women in a line holding hands. They are clearly involved in some sort of religious ritual. *Dancing, walking in processions, and making offerings*. Southeast of Corinth, across the Mediterranean, to the Phoenician and Israelite cultures, were there women's festivals, similar to the rituals to Demeter and Kore? Were there flowers, aromatic as the marigolds in the Latina Day of the Dead festivals?

I have tried to focus upon Orsi's lived religion scheme, what anthropologist James Clifford has called 'that moment in which the possibility of comparison exists in unmediated tension with the sheer incongruity ...a permanent ironic play of similarity and difference, the familiar and the strange, the here and the elsewhere' (1998: 146), and I have tried, leaning on these two scholars and woman wisdom, not to explain away those missing elements in ancient Mediterranean cultures that render our own culture newly incomprehensible.

An altar of sacrifice, an altar of devotion, an altar tended by a priest to a deity, these are the altars of ceremony, of public religious ritual. But there have been personal or household altars tended by women in each of these patriarchal religions. A domestic altar contains a woman's artistic as well as her religious expression, and therefore bears evaluation purely in terms of its material arrangement and the motives this arrangement reveals. Women's altars promote an aesthetic of relationship. It can be argued that a domestic altar may be the prototype for many of women's domestic arts, such as quilting, needlepoint, and appliqué, that evolve from the art-making process that artist Miriam Shapiro has named 'femmage'. Femmage (a play on collage and assemblage) is women's artistic process of collecting and joining seemingly disparate elements into a functional whole.[1]

The theory of popular religious visual culture advanced here posits that by becoming continual and transparent features of daily experience, embedded in the quotidian rituals, narratives, and collective memories that people take for granted, religious images help form half-forgotten textures of everyday life. As part of the very fabric of consciousness, religious images participate fundamentally in the social construction of reality. It is not the image itself, as an intrinsically meaningful entity, but

---

1. Shapiro is probably best-known for an installation *Womanhouse* from 1971 that she created in collaboration with Judy Chicago and other feminist artists to emphasize the importance of dailiness of women's lives on their artistic output. These artists altered the way we think about 'art' and 'artisan' by examining and challenging what are considered women's crafts, by working with collaborators instead of working in isolation, and creating overtly political statements in explorations of such volatile subjects as female sexuality and the Holocaust. See Chicago, also Guerrilla Girls.

the image as it is articulated within the context of the other visual metaphors present in the shrine that creates and stabilizes the sense of lived religion within the domicile. In both the traditional and spontaneous altars from Oaxaca to New York, religious imagery anchors everyday life to reliable religious routines in the home, and provides historical traces of the worlds they helped to construct. Shrines and altars contain the visual images that help belief work.

In the domestic altars I have analyzed, elements of femmage project women's chosen social and spiritual values. Notably heterogeneous, femmage is still unintentional as it drives a cycle that constantly turns fragmentation to wholeness and then back again. As a sacred, symbolic manifestation of this cycle, the home altar demonstrates the value of fragments, which when linked together, provide a center of focus derived not by imposition, but organically through layering and accretion. Are there markers of women's altars in the Hebrew Bible and other ancient literary texts?

When she fled with Jacob from her father's house, Rachel took her household gods with her. The Greek hearth altar dedicated to Hestia became the Roman one devoted to Vesta. The altar to the Virgin Mary occupying a niche in the home of a thirteenth-century woman of Lucca finds its counterpart in an Italian Catholic home in Brooklyn. An American Buddhist in California tends the Shinto altar of his deceased Japanese father-in-law while his wife constructs a domestic altar of bark and stone to the Great Mother Goddess. My own home altars are varied: dried flowers, carved figures of women amid the flames of Purgatory, the Mexican *anima sola*, the traditional figures of the popular celebration of All Souls Day, next to a peace button on top of my grandfather's childhood Bible resting against a Santos figure of St Francis. The connections that my eye makes to each of these objects narrate a personal story, intimate as prayer, but visible, tangible. For the creator of the altar or shrine, a seemingly random arrangement of objects is orderly and full of meaning; the altar can be read like a lyric poem, with verbal metaphors replaced by visual images. A landscape of memory, a personal altar gives old memories new contexts. Having an altar within the house allows one to integrate the daily world and the shrine world, crossing seamlessly the boundaries between the sacred and the profane. As one continually revises the altar, the reification of belief and the symbols that recall tradition change, keeping the spiritual life reflective of and concurrent with daily life.

A reflection of personal spirituality, the domestic altar is a site of subversion and insistence of the evolutionary nature of institutional religion.

Women's domestic altars have in my opinion changed little across time. As women have reinvigorated old practices with new symbols, the consideration of women's altars as important elements of women's culture can be seen through an examination of hybridized Catholic ritual practices: within altars for Mexican Day of the Dead celebrations, and within Vodou altars from Haiti and the southern Mississippi Delta region. A recent study of American folklore, examining the placement of memorial poetry and photography in local newspapers, concluded that a woman's role is to mark family occasions during the calendar year and the life cycle, and that women regard it as their privilege, as representatives of the family, to report and publicize both joyous and mournful changes in life. Displaying their visual metaphors, altars provide women with a cherished mnemonic devise for discerning a narrative order in their lives. Narrative memory works with popular religious imagery in creating and installing its shrines, and also falls upon devotional images associated with rites of passage. Read through a spiritual lens, then, the primary function of the altar may be to disclose the benevolent and constant presence of God within the house. Read as a proponent of 'lived religion' methodology, one must eliminate the boundaries between people doing religious things in the past and us today.

First, let us look at the evolution of the visual images of the Virgin Mary during the Middle Ages. At the same time that visual messages of the Virgin as perfect mother came to dominate the production of images for the Church, verbal messages pronouncing the innate inferiority of women were part of the traditional Catholic theology. This contrast has been examined by Margaret Miles, who has argued that women's personal interpretations of visual images have produced a strategy for self-empowerment over and against verbal misogyny. Miles (1996) looks at the Virgin and sees not the testimony to her purity and passivity glorified by the Church, but rather an understanding of her freedom from the entailment of marriage and sexuality, and hence her spiritual autonomy. I wonder what items from the practitioners of the old earth-based religions in the Middle Ages, the potions, amulets, incarnations, blessings at births and healings, what part of these elements of lived religion have disappeared, hidden under the weight of established religious propriety.

What arguments are there for envisioning invisible altars, not altars of death and sacrifice, but altars of spiritual connection between the sacred and the profane? Instead of scattering blood and oil, were there altars redolent of spices and perfume, containing household gods, a scrap of silver, a shard of pottery that had personal meaning to the family who walked past it each day. Did women fashion special plates to hold the raisin cakes for the Queen of Heaven? Did ritual objects associated with private devotions fill the spiritual space between what Pierre Bourdieu has called the 'objective order and the subjective principle of organization'.

Were aromatic oils such as cinnamon, spice, incense, myrrh, frankincense more widely used than the biblical texts have mentioned? As I have noted earlier, within the collection of Jeremiah warnings and prophecies the subversive activities of the people of Israel continue to provoke God (Jer. 7.18). The children gather wood, the fathers kindle fire, and the women knead dough to make cakes for the Queen of Heaven; and they pour out drink offerings to other gods. 'What better description can one offer for an entire family worshipping together', wrote Robert Carroll in his commentary on Jeremiah, 'collaborating in their stiff-necked refusal to ignore all gods but YHWH' (1986: 213).

Listen to the female voice in Jer. 44.19: 'And the women said, "Indeed we will go on making offerings to the Queen of Heaven and pouring out libations to her; do you think that we made cakes for her, marked with her image, and poured out libations to her without our husbands being involved?"' Though the prophets cry out against making altars to other gods, though the Hebrew texts continually remind the people of Israel of God's loyalty, we are reminded that both men and women turn to other gods, some of whom apparently delight in raisin cakes.

Were there other foods in the ancient world, foods concocted by women desperate to feed their children, foods that have not been recorded? A few weeks ago I saw a photo in the *New York Times* of a Haitian woman offering some cakes to a group of spindly children. These dirt biscuits of Haiti—called *argile*, meaning 'clay', or 'earth'—are not exactly a final *cri de coeur* against starvation. According to the *Times* the dirt cakes are daily fare, similar to various African fare. The *Times'* assurance that dirt cakes are not comestibles is belied by their providing the recipe: dirt, salt, water, butter or margarine. Mix and bake in the sun. In Malawi, children stand on the roadsides selling skewers of roasted mice. In Mozambique, when grasshoppers eat the crops, people turn the tables and eat them, calling the fishy-tasting bugs 'flying shrimp'. Like the mice in Malawi, they are a staple of the very poor, somewhere between a snack and a desperation measure.

While we search for recipes for the delicacies offered to the Queen of Heaven, we need not wonder about the Haitian cakes:

> Making them has been a regular business for years. The clay is trucked in plastic sacks from Hinche, on the central plateau. Blended with margarine or butter, they are flavored with salt, pepper and bouillon cubes and

spooned out by the thousands on cotton sheets in sunny courtyards that
are kept swept as 'bakeries'. They cost about a penny apiece.[2]

Regardless of the normality of the recipe (like the stone soup New York
kids make in Central Park) delicious prose seems more like cold comfort
to the Western audience reading the story over latté and croissants than
the stomach-churning realization that people eat dirt on a daily basis.
Hunger provides the dark side of the joyous offerings of the raisin cakes.
Compare the dour description of the tasteless dirt cakes with the
delightful prose generated by a gourmet's experience with pigs' tails, also
published in the *New York Times*:

> One evening in late winter, my wife (a far better cook than I am) and I
> made Henderson's crispy pig's tails, and we got a ghoulish thrill from his
> instruction to deal with 'any slightly hairy extremities' by using a throw-
> away Bic razor. The pig's tails are delicious, by the way—the tailbone is
> threaded with flavorful meat that you pick away with your teeth. But
> don't put off tossing the uneaten portion, as we did. Trust me: congealed
> pig's tails aren't something you want to confront in a pan at 8 am on a
> Sunday (Garner 2004: 10).

The contemplation of eating offal, the cooked viscera of butchered
animals, seems almost as debilitating as dirt cakes. These so-called 'variety
meats' have been a part of the human diet since the invention of
cooking, which rendered the otherwise indigestible animal parts edible.
Is it the prose that makes one an act of desperation and one a gastronomic
adventure?

Day of the Dead Altars

There are vibrant examples of women's spirituality vividly interwoven
within religious festivals and rituals. While we have no specific parallels
from the ancient world, it seems clear from looking at differing cultural
ritual shrines and altars, some temporary, others intended to be more

2. A few other examples of hunger-driven human ingenuity: Africans dig up
anthills and termite mounds to sieve out the tiny grains the insects have gathered.
Some seeds, however, provoke fatal allergic reactions. Like Chad's mukhet bush,
wild cassava in tropical regions and baucia Senegalensis in West Africa are poisonous, but can be made edible by pounding and soaking for days. In Bangladesh, a type
of lentil known to slowly destroy the nervous system is eaten when people are hungry
enough. Marula fruit is so tasty that elephants knock trees down to get at it, but in
battered Zimbabwe, once the fruit is gone people may be reduced to eating the tough
seeds by cracking them with rocks and fishing out tiny kernels with a pin. See further
McNeil 2004.

temporary, that the creative impulses motivating women to make shrines or altars in our own times would have been operative in the Mediterranean cultures under consideration. One sense of 'it might have been' comes through the voice of Epiphanius in the fourth century CE. The concern was that Arabian women were baking cakes to the Virgin Mary:

> They prepare a kind of cake in the name of the ever-Virgin. They assemble together, and in the name of the holy Virgin they attempt to undertake a deed that is irreverent and blasphemous beyond measure—they function as priests for women...
>
> For some women prepare a certain kind of little cake with four indentations, cover it with a fine linen veil on a solemn day of the year, and on certain (other) days, they set forth bread and offer it in the name of Mary. They all partake of the bread (*Medicine Box* 78.23, 79).

One of the most exuberant of the modern feasts with women creating and tending impromptu altars occurs on 2 November, the day of All Souls in the Catholic Church: the Day of the Dead as it is celebrated in Mexico and Chicano-America. A quick examination of this traditional holiday illustrates ways in which women have worked to share their resources of food and flowers and household care, which have resulted in a process of hybridization between older pagan or primal religious traditions with the dicta of the Church. A study of the impudent imagery of Day of the Dead underscores its subversive nature and destabilizes our reified expectations about the visual systems of religious value and representation to which we have become attached. I take personal delight in the shock of the uninitiated as they come upon these figures in my house and gaze transfixed at the skeletal heads—blinding them to the comedy of the papier-mâché figures engaged in daily activities, talking on the phone, enjoying a massage, performing dental surgery.

Day of the Dead is a time when Mexican families spend hours at the cemetery, visiting the graves of their relatives. Women clean and decorate the headstones, arrange flowers, especially flowers of the dead (*marigolds*), and light candles. Eating and drinking, surrounded by reminders of the relative's favorite earthly objects, a subversion of the grim threat of death itself. It is also the time to construct special domestic altars dedicated to the spirits of deceased loved ones. Such altars range from the simple to the very elaborate and are usually filled with objects that provided pleasure to the departed person in life, including favorite food and drink. Altars dedicated to the spirits of deceased children often include toys, candy, and other sweets. Because the altars are created by those who knew intimately the dead, the private desires and tastes of the deceased can be heaped on the altars for the living to savor. Although the home altars change and add objects, a few items persist: a holy image, usually of the Virgen of Guadelupe, is situated in the center of the altar; a photograph of the dead relative; and his/her favorite foods.

The altars, or *ofrendas* as they are called, also usually contain objects made from sugar or sugar sculpture known as *alfenique*. These objects may be small animals, such as lambs, miniature plates of food (enchiladas with mole), small coffins, often with pop-up skeletons, and of course, the sugar skull, or *calavera*. The skulls are made by pouring a mixture of boiling water, confectioner's sugar and lime into clay molds, which have been previously soaked in water. The *calaveras* are decorated with paper foil for eyes and a kind of colored icing for hair. Names can be added to the skull and Mexican children often exchange them. While to the uninitiated these wide-eyed skeletal skulls may seem grisly, to those familiar with the ritual, Day of the Dead is a joyous time and the symbols a joking nod to death. If the tradition had not continued through time, the sugar *alfenique* and *calavera* would have dissolved into invisibility, the aroma of marigolds would have left no trace of their peppery scent. And as in the instance of the raisin cakes baked for the Queen of Heaven and the cakes baked by the Christian Arabian women, we would have gleaned crumbs from some report by an unfriendly observer.

Vodou Altars[3]

Vodou is a low-budget religion that thrives on the bits and pieces of daily life. Vodou cycles all of the world that comes its way; its altars move and vibrate like dances for the eyes. If poverty darkens the believers' world, then the glittering figures that evolve into the Vodou altar light their spiritual practices. The plump head of a doll that arrives on an airplane from Miami as a Christmas present may be adorning an altar in Haiti three hours later. Like the Day of the Dead figures, some 'high-art' critics have questioned these personal altars as art. Is it art trouvé? Assemblage? Is it sacred art at all? In Vodou ceremonies, objects are chosen, assembled and dedicated to deities whose tastes are shaped as often by fashion as by tradition. Thus, any object may be sacred if it pleases the deities, since its reason for being positioned on an altar is to summon, appease, contain, or direct divine energies. Just as the skeletal figures that reflect the daily lives of dead ancestors on All Souls Day are considered sacred by the Latinos who create them and are sustained by them, a Vodou practitioner

---

3. I have chosen to spell Vodou with the majority of scholarly sources. The spellings Voodoo and Voodou are also common.

from Brooklyn, clutching a wooden santos of the Virgin Mary, explained to me that any object could do *mystique* if you believe in it. You do some kind of prayer and you touch the objects and the prayer becomes reality.

The shadows of the Catholicism that has dominated the official practices of Haiti for centuries is apparent in the devotion to Mary, similar to the Latina devotion to the Virgin of Guadelupe. The Virgin Mary holds an elevated place that few other beings or symbols have attained in Vodou. There is a strong parallel between these practitioners who depend on Marian worship with the Italian-American working-class women from Harlem that Orsi has studied for so many years:

> When their sufferings as others and wives were most intense, as these women tell their stories, when they felt that no one else could understand their particular agonies, they turned to the one who long ago had appealed to the to the masses of Europe because of her evident participation in humanity's trials (1985: 204).

Like the Haitian practitioners of Vodou, the Italian women in Orsi's study turned to the only religious figure they felt would support them in a time of crisis. The centrality of the Virgin Mary to the poor of Haiti, particularly the women, is born out of desire for comfort. Those with the deepest longings 'turned to the Madonna out of an awareness of the severe limitations of their power and a sense of desperation over their powerlessness' (1985: 207).

To connect the Haitian obeah women with the vital role that material goods—such as the santos figures from Catholic religion as well as the spirits from Vodou—play in the process of meaning-making is to wrap her in scraps of Bourdieu's analyses of the power of the indigenous religion to disaffect the habitus of the dominant faith. Briefly, Bourdieu argues that the success of the dominant religion is based on the degree of difficulty or success the religious hierarchy has in convincing the populace to accept the orthodox religious habitus. The Brooklyn obeah whom I interviewed reflects the extent to which orthodoxy has failed. Uncontrolled by the hierarchal orthodox Catholicism onto which her Vodou habitus is grafted, the obeah has a side business of making miniature altars for home spaces. Built upon a base of canvas, and hand-painted and decorated with the appropriate colors, a mini-altar usually contains candy offerings, a paper talisman with herbs, a tiny chest that opens for tiny offerings, a toy wagon, feathers, sequins. The powerful spiritual creations of this obeah practitioner reflect her skills as a religious consumer in manipulating the dominant religious systems and practices that produce a personal habitus. Ironically, Vodou affords her access to the altar and other sacred practices forbidden her by orthodox Catholicism.

Altars are the ideal form for this syncretistic practice; dolls, glittery objects, and handmade toys are the habitus for all Vodou's sacred arts.[4] They are palimpsests of Haiti's twisted history, made coherent through the eyes of synchronous gods. To look at an altar cluttered with whiskey bottles, satin pomanders, clay pots dressed in lace, sequins, feathers, plaster statues of Catholic saints, laughing Buddha figures, rosaries, crucifixes, bugged-eyed kewpie dolls, is to enter the ghost lives of slaves and free, indigenous and colonial. All the dances for the eyes, conflicting beliefs, traditions, from Dahomey and Kongo, to the country houses of the south of France merge into a statement of belief.

The impact of Vodou altars has been described as visual jazz, constantly reworked and revised, representing the music of time. The aesthetic of these altars is certainly improvisational; they can never be finished. Poet Derek Walcott has described the altars of his homeland in a collage of poetic words.

> Break a vase, and the love that reassembles the fragments is stronger than that love which took its symmetry for granted when it was whole... This gathering of broken pieces is the care and pain of the Antilles, and if the pieces are disparate, ill-fitting, they contain more pain than their original sculpture, those icons and sacred vessels taken for granted in their ancestral places. Antillean art is this restoration of our shattered histories, our shards of vocabulary, our archipelago becoming a synonym for pieces broken off that the original continent (1990: 2).

New York City

If an altar makes visible what has been invisible, there is a small sacred space or altar known to an odd assortment of folk on the Lower East Side of New York City. The 'back yard' of the Catholic Worker house on First Street is not a formal altar; it is not a shrine shaded or protected from the elements, it has no images, flowers, or incense. It is not recommended by a guide book or sanctioned by the Church. For me and the other

---

4. I visited a Vodou practitioner in Brooklyn, New York, but she was very much a product of Haiti. Her spiritual training and perspectives came from her Haitian background. I suspect part of her boldness came from what Mintz (1974) defines as 'being Haitian'. Mintz's research reflects his conviction that the Haitian culture has none of the ethnic divisions of US-American culture: 'Everybody understands and speaks Creole; everybody eats the same kind of food, everybody dances the same way (or knows how to). Hence the content of being Haitian is shared, even if the life and fate of Haitians vary from quite rarefied luxury to terrible misery and suffering' (1974: 83).

members of the community, this six by nine-ish foot space of cracked concrete stained with bird droppings was an ever-changing sanctuary, depending on which person craved a few moments of solitude. The altar afforded respite from the hustle.

About 20 years ago, this space provided a daily retreat space for me. Several large lidded steel garbage cans, sagging black trash bags, lumpy with the detritus of the morning soup line on the ground, a small wrought iron table and two busted iron chairs would not seem to be altar decorations. There was a stack of wooden boxes, stripped of paint from hard winters and brutal summers that held, well, old food. The brick of the back wall of the building was badly in need of pointing; there were slumping, potted plants at each window on the five-story fire escape. In spite of the brick, the few leaves, and the thin-leaved tree next door, one seemed to have entered a world of black and white. Above this urban sanctuary was a great swath of sky.

At that time the concrete space was tended by a man who cared little for people, a man who loved birds. We called him Brother Paul. I do not know where he lived, what his real name was, or, most important, why he loved birds. While we fed the homeless people who came to our door, Brother Paul would stand out in the back yard in winter and summer and take from the refuse of our soup and bread and vegetables enough to fill his pans for the birds. Muttering under his breath, a growly monologue that continued for months, he would take his pans and stride through the Catholic Worker kitchen. On his way to serve the birds.

Brother Paul seemed not to notice any of us. He continued his work, choosing bits of vegetables for a special pan; bread crusts and macaroni curls he tossed into the chipped zinc tub at his right hand. Frequently a man who had finished his soup would go out to the back yard space and look up at the sky, in the odd quiet, in the midst of the city. A volunteer from the soupline would go out for a quick smoke; it never seemed cold or hot or wet out back. People sat out there even in the rain and snow. The snow softened the stone; the rain shined up the fire-escape railings. The sky held. Brother Paul continued his work. Dorothy Day often said that a saint was a person whose life would make no sense if God did not exist. Some days he had a meal with us, and said a few words to a couple of the old timers. He never talked to me.

When I first became interested in the phenomenon of contemporary women's altars, and their analogy to possible ancient domestic altars maintained by women, I had no idea that New York City, the omphalos of my world, would itself become an altar. Suddenly, with no warning, on September 11 2001, its most public spaces would become private; its secular rushing rhythms would become a dirge. The clang of garbage trucks would be replaced by the keening of women and men searching for loved ones, and finding not twisted bodies, but rather twisted steel girders and pulverized concrete. Suddenly, on a cloudless blue-skied morning at the beginning of a new academic year, the sky began to roar. My idea of altars and sacred spaces changed forever. The material has been transformed into the spiritual; the differences between the sacred and the mundane have been erased.

Spontaneous shrines have been widely pictured by the media in the broadband era. Since the death of Diana, Princess of Wales, these mounds of popular grief almost instantly became an expected part of public mourning, flourishing after the deaths of John F. Kennedy Jr and the victims of the 9/11 attacks. Most recently, In June 2004, the telegenic ceremonies for Ronald Reagan have provided us with 21 gun salutes, empty saddled horses, all the icons and ruffles and flourishes Americans have come to expect since the assassination of John F. Kennedy in 1963. Spontaneous altars have sprung up for Reagan at many places. At his boyhood home, at his presidential library, and even on the Hollywood Walk of Fame, those makeshift but de rigueur shrines appeared, as people left flowers, flags, and jars of his favorite candy, jellybeans.

After 9/11, communal grieving for a stranger grants a license to mourn, whether that grief is expressed in person or by watching television. The mass eruption of grief in New York City left behind its own kind of debris. Fences were lined with butcher paper; restaurants in lower Manhattan surrendered their walls and turned them into vast bulletin boards. Sidewalks called out in colored chalk, pleading for peace, insisting on war. Flowers, snapshots, toys, and teddy bears assured broken-hearted people that the world was still there. New York sought to connect the worlds of the human and the divine. Rather than a crucifix, a firefighter's hat was surrounded by votive candles. Rather than a Star of David, a policeman's shield gleamed among hastily scrawled notes: Have you seen my husband, my sister, my neighbor, my friend? One of the extraordinary results of the tragedy of September 11 has been the creation of hundreds of altars, a spontaneous visual creation of religious art, a tangible testament to the terror of separation, the need for comfort and connection.

Often, the memorials drew clusters of people, commuters who paused in their rush to stand in silence and reflect on lives lost on 9/11. These shrines created within small portions of ordinary public space private spaces, set apart, sanctified, silent amid the commotion, by what people had placed there. Such sacred spaces, like the Catholic Worker back yard, bring healing, creating a bridge to grief for viewers to find a form of solace, to be quiet at a time of turmoil.[5]

It is not surprising that we have nothing left of ancient personal shrines. The shrines in New York have already disappeared. The fact that most of the posters have been drenched with rain and sleet, torn by autumn winds, reveals an answer. Like the pans of discarded food reclaimed each day by Brother Paul, decay seems to be part of the life of these spontaneous shrines. Symbols of grief are not designed as instruments of cheer. Candles, for instance, are not prized merely for the flickering vitality of their light. They must also melt and vanish—the flame must consume the flesh, the paper posters will blacken and curl, flowers are offered up because they bloom and rot. But the emotion has neither flickered nor decayed. As Marshall Sella wrote in the *New York Times Magazine* a few weeks after the calamity:

> The second waves of fliers, which cropped up on the weekend after the attacks, were suddenly leaning heavily on detail, ostensibly for the sake of victims' recovery and identification. Photos and text became brutally disconnected with each lovingly chosen photograph came spikes of forensic data. A proud man in a tuxedo, we were told, had 'very distinctive thick brown discolored toenails'. The merry lady with the white dog had 'a tribal tattoo along the lower back above the tailbone' (2001: 48).

In their desperation to find the living person, the secrets hidden in the visual images had to be revealed. The altar memories were being turned into a search for relics, an arthritic finger, a warted toe, any body part that would identify the loved one would be beautiful, sanctified.

A few weeks after the debacle of 9/11 I returned to the Lower East Side to attend a memorial service for the homeless who were not counted among the named dead. Crossing Fourteenth Street, I saw that New York was coming back to life. The gasoline stench of 9/11 had faded, the traffic was again fierce, and of course there were 9/11 tee-shirts for sale. There

---

5. One must note that there is a voyeuristic delight in death that has overflowed recently in the popular culture. There is certainly evidence in pop culture that mourning rituals are being newly embraced. 'Six Feet Under', HBO's popular series about a family of funeral directors, demystifies the rituals and, as the heroes counsel their clients, makes mourning seem a wise idea. That demystifying process ripples through the culture, reassuring people that there is a planned ritual when death happens and there are people to help put it into motion. A&E has the copycat 'Family Plots', a reality show about a family of funeral directors. Event planning to the ultimate degree. The dead body is a subject for extreme close-ups in hit series like CBS's 'C.S.I.', and books like Mary Roach's best-selling *Stiff: The Curious Lives of Human Cadavers* (2003).

were still many spontaneous altars, photos of people with phone numbers scrawled underneath the pictures, still rotting flowers and limp American flags. The used-book guys were back, plenty of folks selling handbags, towels, CDs, cameras. What I had not expected were the war rugs: Afghani woven war rugs. Imagine a hand-woven oriental rug made of traditional colors and seemingly traditional geometric and pastoral patterns, with knotted fringe—but with unexpected icons of war woven into the traditional pattern. Automatic weapons, tanks, helicopters, grenades, bombs.[6] Hot off entrepreneurial looms.

A crowd was beginning to form around the rug display. On the ground was a small rug picturing the planes just about to hit the twin towers. It was woven with wool and cotton threads, a muted palette in shades of taupe, gray, and beige, with crude red letters reading War against Terror. Other rugs had abbreviations floating in a cloudless sky: FDNY—WTC—NYPD. The hip-hop dude selling the stuff gestured to the rug on the ground and assured me that it would be a collector's item, shipped direct from families of weavers in Kabul. As I continued on my way to the small sacred space at the back of St Joseph House, the November wind tossed old flyers and refuse around the Bowery streets. I wondered if any of the men I had spent time with at the house on First Street were among the dead that no one had mourned for, the numberless gathered into the sky.

6. These images, found in *narche jangi*, or war rugs, are the expressions of the Beluchi tribe in Afghanistan, reflecting their country's war-ravaged history. While the Afghan people are feeling the effects of US strikes and bombings today, these rugs represent the scars of the Soviet–Afghan war of 1979–89. To see samples of these rugs, visit <http://www.warrug.com>.

BIBLIOGRAPHY

Abel, Richard
  1988   *French Film Theory and Criticism: A History & Anthology, 1907–1939* (Princeton, NJ: Princeton University Press).
Ackerman, Susan
  1992   *Under Every Green Tree: Popular Religion in Sixth-Century Judah* (Atlanta: Scholars Press).
  1998   *Warrior, Dancer, Seductress, Queen: Women in Judges and Biblical Israel* (New York: Doubleday).
Ahlstron, S.E.A.
  1972   *Religious History of the American People* (New Haven: Yale University Press).
Albanese, C.L.
  1999   *America: Religions and Religion* (London: Wadsworth).
Alexander, George
  2003   *Why We Make Movies: Black Filmmakers Talk about the Magic of Cinema* (New York: Harlem Moon).
Alexander, William
  1981   *Film on the Left: American Documentary Film from 1931 to 1942* (Princeton, NJ: Princeton University Press).
Allen, Beverly
  1996   *Rape Warfare: The Hidden Genocide in Bosnia-Herzegovina and Croatia* (Minneapolis: University of Minnesota Press).
Amberg, G.
  1971   *The New York Times Film Reviews: A One Volume Selection, 1913–1970* (New York: Arno Press).
Amit, Yairah
  2001   *Reading Biblical Narratives* (Minneapolis: Fortress Press).
Andersen, Christopher
  2002   *George and Laura: Portrait of an American Marriage* (New York: William Morrow).
Anderson, Benedict
  1991   *Imagined Communities: Reflections on the Origins and Spread of Nationalism* (London and New York: Verso).
Appel, Willa
  1983   *Cults in America: Programmed for Paradise* (New York: Henry Holt & Co).
Arbuckle, Gerald A.
  1985   'Dress and Worship: Liturgies for the Culturally Dispossessed', *Worship* 59: 426-35.

Armstrong, Karen
    2002   *Islam: A Short History* (New York: Random House).
    2004   'Resisting Modernity: The Backlash Against Secularism', *Harvard International Review* 25: 1-15.

Auletta, Ken
    2004   'Fortress Bush', *The New Yorker* (19 January).

Avisar, Ilan
    1988   *Screening the Holocaust: Cinema's Images of the Unimaginable* (Bloomington: Indiana University Press).

Axelrod, Steven Gould
    1978   *Robert Lowell: Life and Art* (Princeton, NJ: Princeton University Press).

Babington, B., and P.W. Evans
    1993   *Biblical Epics: Sacred Narrative in the Hollywood Cinema* (Manchester: Manchester University Press).

Bach, Alice
    1996a   'Calling the Shots: Directing Salome's Dance of Death', *Semeia* 74: 103-26.
    1996b   *Tracing Eve's Journey from Eden to MTV* (New York: American Bible Society/Paulist Press).
    1997a   'Directing Salome's Dance of Death', *Semeia* 74: 103-26.
    1997b   'Throw them to the Lions, Sire: The Bible as Cultural Artifact in American Film', *Semeia* 74: 1-12.
    1997c   *Women, Seduction and Betrayal in Biblical Narrative* (Cambridge: Cambridge University Press).
    1998a   'Reading the Body Politic: Women, Violence, and Judges 21', *Biblical Interpretation* 3: 2-19.
    1998b   'Whitewashing Athena: Bernal, the Bible, and the Critics', *JSOT* 77: 3-19.

Bach, Alice (ed.)
    1997   *Biblical Glamour and Hollywood Glitz* (*Semeia*, 74; Atlanta: Scholars Press).

Bal, Mieke
    1988a   *Death and Dissymmetry: The Politics of Coherence in the Book of Judges* (Chicago: University of Chicago Press).
    1988b   *Murder and Difference: Gender, Genre and Scholarship on Sisera's Death* (trans. M. Gumpert; Bloomington: Indiana University Press).
    1999   *The Practice of Cultural Analysis: Exposing Interdisciplinary Interpretation* (Stanford, CA: Stanford University Press).

Barber, Benjamin R.
    1995   *Jihad vs. McWorld* (New York: Ballantine Books).
    2003   *Fear's Empire: War, Terror, and Democracy* (New York: W.W. Norton).

Barg, Werner C.
    1966   *Kino der Drausamkeit: die Filme von Sergio Leone, Stanley Kubrick, David Lynch, Martin Scorsese, Oliver Stone, Quentin Tarantino. mit einem Beitrag von Peter Wilckens* (Frankfurt: Bundesverband Jugend und Film).

Barilleaux, Ryan J.
    2004   *Power and Prudence: The Presidency of George H.W. Bush* (College Station, TX: A. &. M. University Press).

Barthes, Roland
    1973   'Striptease', in *idem*, *Mythologies* (New York: Hill & Wang): 84-87.

Bartov, Omer
    1996   *Murder in Our Midst: The Holocaust, Industrial Killing, and Representation* (New York: Oxford University Press).

Bataille, Gretchen M., and Charles L.P. Silet
    1985   *Images of American Indians on Film: An Annotated Bibliography* (New York: Garland).

Baudrillard, Jean, and Sheila Faria Glaser
    1994   *Simulacra and Simulation: The Body in Theory: Histories of Cultural Materialism* (Ann Arbor: University of Michigan Press).

Baugh, Lloyd S.J.
    1997   *Imaging the Divine: Jesus and Christ Figures in Film* (Kansas City: Sheed & Ward).

Benjamin, Walter
    1937   *The Work of Art in the Age of Mechanical Reproduction* (n.p.).

Bennett, William J.
    1992   *The Devaluing of America* (New York: Summit Books).

Benson, L.D., *et al.* (eds.)
    1988   *The Riverside Chaucer* (Oxford: Oxford University Press, 3rd edn).

Berenstein, Rhona
    1996   *Attack of the Leading Ladies: Gender, Sexuality, and Spectatorship in Classic Horror Cinema* (New York: Columbia University Press).

Berlinerblau, Jacques
    1999   *Heresy in the University: The Black Athena Controversy and the Responsibilities of American Intellectuals* (New Brunswick, NJ, and London: Rutgers University Press).

Bernal, Martin
    1987   *Black Athena: The Afroasiatic Roots of Classical Civilisation* (2 vols.; New Brunswick, NJ: Rutgers University Press).

Berrigan, Daniel, SJ
    2002   *Lamentations: From New York to Kabul and Beyond* (Lanham, MD: Sheed & Ward).

Berry, S. Torriano
    2001   *The 50 Most Influential Black Films: A Celebration of African-American Talent, Determination, and Creativity* (New York: Citadel Press).

Berthrong, John H.
    1999   *The Divine Deli: Religious Identity in the North American Cultural Mosaic* (Maryknoll, NY: Orbis Books).

Bhabha, Homi K.
    1990   *Nation and Narration* (London: Routledge).
    1994   *The Location of Culture* (London: Routledge).

Bird, Phyllis
    1989   'The Harlot as Heroine: Narrative Art and Social Presupposition in Three Old Testament Texts', *Semeia* 46: 119-39.

Bliss, Michael
  1995   *The Word Made Flesh: Catholicism and Conflict in the Films of Martin Scorsese* (Lantham, MD: Scarecrow Press).
Bobo, Jacqueline
  1991   'Black Women in Fiction and Nonfiction: Images of Power and Powerlessness', *Wide Angle* 13: 72-81.
  1995   *Black Women as Cultural Readers* (New York: Columbia University Press).
Bogle, Donald
  2001   *Toms, Coons, Mulattoes, Mammies, and Bucks: An Interpretive History of Blacks in American Films* (New York: Continuum).
Booth, Wayne
  1974   *A Rhetoric of Irony* (Chicago: University of Chicago Press).
Bottero, Jean
  2000   *Ancestor of the West: Writing, Reasoning, and Religion in Mesopotamia, Elam, and Greece* (trans. T.L. Fagan; Chicago and London: University of Chicago Press).
Bourdieu, Pierre
  1977   *Outline of a Theory of Practice* (London: Cambridge University Press).
  1993   *The Field of Cultural Production* (New York: Columbia University Press).
Bourne, Peter G.
  1997   *Jimmy Carter: A Comprehensive Biography from Plains to Post-Presidency* (New York: Charles Scribner's Sons).
Boyd, Malcolm
  1958   *Christ and Celebrity Gods: The Church in Mass Culture* (Greenwich, CN: Seabury Press).
Brenner, Athalya
  1994   *A Feminist Companion to Exodus to Deuteronomy* (The Feminist Companion to the Bible, 6: Sheffied: Sheffied Academic Press).
  1995   *A Feminist Companion to the Latter Prophets* (The Feminist Companion to the Bible, 8; Sheffield: Sheffield Academic Press).
Brown, Rita Mae
  2002   *Hotspur* (New York: Ballantine Books).
Brownmiller, Susan
  1975   *Against Our Will: Men, Women, and Rape* (New York: Simon & Schuster).
Bumiller, Elizabeth
  2004   'The President and the Gun: To the Avenger Go the Spoils', *New York Times* (21 June).
Bush, George W.
  2001   *A Charge to Keep: My Journey to the White House* (New York: Harper-Collins).
Butler, Ivan
  1969   *Religion in Cinema* (New York: A.S. Barnes).
Byars, Jackie
  1991   *All that Hollywood Allows* (Chapel Hill: University of North Carolina Press).

Cajee, Mas'ood
    2003   'Franklin Graham: Spiritual Carpetbagger', *Counterpunch* (3 April).
Calasso, Roberto
    1993   *The Marriage of Cadmus and Harmony* (trans. T. Parks; New York:
            Alfred A. Knopf).
Camp, Claudia V.
    1988   'Wise and Strange: An Interpretation of the Female Imagery in the
            Proverbs in Light of Trickster Mythology', *Semeia* 42: 14-36.
    1991   'What's So Strange About the Strange Women?', in Peggy L. Day,
            David Jobling and Gerald Sheppard (eds.), *The Bible and the Politics of
            Exegesis* (Cleveland: Pilgrim Press): 17-32.
    2000   *Wise Strange and Holy: The Strange Woman and the Making of the Bible*
            (JSOTSup, 320; Gender, Culture, Theory, 9; Sheffield: Sheffield
            Academic Press).
Camp, Claudia V., and Carole R. Fontaine
    1993   *Women, War, and Metaphor: Language and Society in the Study of the
            Hebrew Bible* (Atlanta: Scholars Press).
Campbell, Richard H., and Michael R. Pitts
    1981   *The Bible on Film: A Checklist, 1897–1980* (Metuchen, NJ: Scarecrow
            Press).
Carmen, Ira H.
    1966   *Movies, Censorship, and the Law* (Ann Arbor: University of Michigan
            Press).
Carnes, Tony
    2000   'A Presidential Hopeful's Progress', *Christianity Today* (2 October): 64.
Caroll, Noel
    1988   *Philosophical Problems of Classical Film Theory* (Princeton, NJ: Prince-
            ton University Press).
Carroll, Michael P.
    1986   *The Cult of Mary: Psychological Origins* (Princeton, NJ: Princeton
            University Press).
Carroll, Robert P.
    1986   *Jeremiah* (OTL: Philadelphia: Westminster Press).
    1995   'Desire Under the Terebinths: On Pornographic Representation in the
            Prophets—A Response', in Brenner (ed.) 1995: 275-307.
Carson, Diane, Linda Dittmar and Janice R. Welsch
    1994   *Multiple Voices in Feminist Film Criticism* (Minneapolis: University of
            Minnesota Press).
Carter, Rosalynn
    1984   *First Lady from Plains* (Fayetteville: University of Arkansas Press).
Certeau, Michel de
    1997   *Culture in the Plural* (Minneapolis: University of Minnesota Press).
Cham, Mbye B., and Claire Andrade-Watkins
    1988   *Blackframes: Critical Perspectives on Black Independent Cinema* (Cam-
            bridge, MA: MIT Press).
Chicago, Judy
    1979   *The Dinner Party: A Symbol of Our Heritage* (New York: Doubleday).
    1996   *Beyond the Flower: The Autobiography of a Feminist Artist* (New York:
            Penguin Books).

Christensen, Inger
      1991   *Literary Women on the Screen: The Representation of Women in Films Based on Imaginative Literature* (Bern and New York: Peter Lang).
Christian, Barbara
      1995   'The Race for Theory', in B. Ashcroft, Gareth Griffiths and Helen Tiffin (eds.), *The Post-Colonial Studies Reader* (London: Routledge): 457-60.
Clark, Randall
      1995   *At a Theater or Drive-In Near You: The History, Culture, and Politics of the American Exploitation Film* (New York: Garland).
Clifford, James
      1998   *The Predicament of Culture: Twentieth-Century Ethnography, Literature and Art* (Cambridge, MA: Harvard University Press).
Clinton, Hillary Rodham
      2004   *Living History* (New York: Charles Scribner's Sons).
Clinton, Willian J.
      2004   *My Life* (New York: Alfred A. Knopf).
Clover, Carol J.
      1992   *Men, Women, and Chain Saws* (Princeton, NJ: Princeton University Press).
Cohen, Sarah Blacher
      1983   *From Hester Street to Hollywood: The Jewish-American Stage and Screen* (Bloomington: Indiana University Press).
Colley, Linda
      1992   *Britons: Forging the Nation, 1707–1837* (New Haven: Yale University Press).
Collins, Jim, Hilary Radner and Ava Preacher Collins
      1993   *Film Theory Goes to the Movies* (New York: Routledge).
Colombat, André
      1993   *The Holocaust in French Film* (Metuchen, NJ: Scarecrow Press).
Cook, David A.
      1996   *A History of Narrative Film* (New York: W.W. Norton).
Cook, Michael
      2000   *The Koran: A Very Short Introduction* (Oxford: Oxford University Press).
Cook, Samantha
      1992   *Women and Film Bibliography* (London: British Film Institute).
Corn, David
      2003   *The Lies of George W. Bush: Mastering the Politics of Deception* (New York: Crown Publishing).
Cortada, James W., and Edward Wakin
      2002   *Betting on America: Why the U.S. Can Be Stronger After September 11* (New York: Prentice–Hall).
Cozzens, Donald B.
      2000   *The Changing Faces of the Priesthood: A Reflection on the Priest's Crisis of Soul* (Collegeville, MN: Liturgical Press).

Cripps, Thomas
    1971   'The Death of Rastus: Negroes in American Film Since 1945', in A.F. McClure (ed.), *The Movies: An American Idiom: Readings in the Social History of the American Motion Picture* (Rutherford, NJ: Fairleigh Dickinson University Press): 266-75.
    1977   *Slow Fade to Black: The Negro in American Film, 1900–1942* (New York: Oxford University Press).
    1978   *Black Films as Genre* (Bloomington: Indiana University Press).
    1993   *Making Movies Black: The Hollywood Message Movie from World War Two to the Civil Rights Era* (Oxford: Oxford University Press).
Crombie, Deborah
    2002   *And Justice there is None* (New York: Bantam Books).
Crossan, John Dominic
    1991   *The Historical Jesus: The Life of a Mediterranean Jewish Peasant* (San Francisco: HarperSanFrancisco).
    1994   *Jesus: A Revolutionary Biography* (San Francisco: HarperSanFrancisco).
    1995   *Who Killed Jesus?: Exposing the Roots of Anti-Semitism in the Gospel Story of the Death of Jesus* (San Francisco: HarperSanFrancisco).
    1998   *The Birth of Christianity: Discovering what Happened in the Years Immediately After the Execution of Jesus* (San Francisco: HarperSanFrancisco).
Crowther, Bosley
    1960   *Hollywood Rajah: The Life and Times of Louis B. Mayer* (New York: Henry Holt).
Curran, Leo
    1978   'Rape and Rape Victims in Ovid's Metamorphoses', *Arethusa* 11: 213-41.
Dalby, Andrew
    1996   *Siren Feasts: A History of Gastronomy in Greece* (London: Routledge).
Dash, Julie
    1992   *Daughters of the Dust: The Making of an African American Woman's Film* (New York: New Press).
Davenport, W.A.
    1998   *Chaucer and His English Contemporaries* (New York: Palgrave Macmillan).
Davies, P.R.
    1995   *Whose Bible is it Anyway?* (JSOTSup, 204; Sheffield: Sheffield Academic Press).
Day, Peggy
    1989   *Gender and Difference in Ancient Israel* (Minneapolis: Fortress Press).
de Lauretis, Teresa
    1984   *Alice Doesn't: Feminism, Semiotics, and Cinema* (Bloomington: Indiana University Press).
    1987   *Technologies of Gender: Essays on Theory, Film, and Fiction* (Bloomington: Indiana University Press).
    1990   *Film and the Primal Fantasy—One More Time: On Sheila McLaughlin's She Must be Seeing Things* (Milwaukee: University of Wisconsin-Milwaukee, Center for Twentieth Century Studies).

de Lauretis, Teresa, and Stephen Heath
    1980   *The Cinematic Apparatus* (New York: St Martin's Press).

Deikman, Arthur J.
    1990   *The Wrong Way Home: Uncovering the Patterns of Cult Behavior in American Society* (Boston: Beacon Press).
DeMille, Cecil B.
    1956   'Forget Spectacle—It's the Story that Counts', *Films and Filming* 3, no. 1.7.
    1959   *Autobiography* (ed. D. Haynie; Englewood Cliffs, NJ: Prentice–Hall).
Desser, David, and Lester D. Friedman
    1993   *American-Jewish Filmmakers: Traditions and Trends* (Urbana: University of Illinois Press).
Diakite, Madubuko
    1980   *Film, Culture, and the Black Filmmaker: A Study of Functional Relationships and Parallel Developments* (New York: Arno Press).
Dilulio, John, Jr, and Dionne E.J., Jr (eds.)
    2000   *What's God Got to Do with the American Experiment?* (Washington, DC: Brookings Institution Press).
Dimen, Muriel
    1989   'Power, Sexuality, and Intimacy', in A. Jagger, and Susan Bordo (eds.), *Gender/Body/Knowledge* (New Brunswick: Rutgers University Press): 34-51.
Dinnerstein, L.D.
    1995   'Henry Ford and the Jews', in L.D. Dinnerstein and K.T. Jackson (eds.), *American Vistas: 1877 to the Present* (New York: Oxford University Press): 181-93.
Doane, Mary Ann
    1987   *The Desire to Desire* (Bloomington: Indiana University Press).
    1991   *Femmes Fatales* (New York: Routledge Press).
Doane, Mary Ann, Patricia Mellencamp and Linda Williams (eds.)
    1984   *Re-Vision: Essays in Feminist Film Criticism* (Frederick, MD: University Publications of America).
Dodge, Toby
    2003   *Inventing Iraq* (New York: Columbia University Press).
Doneson, Judith E.
    1987   *The Holocaust in American Film* (Philadelphia: The Jewish Publication Society of America).
Dubois, Page
    2001   *Trojan Horses: Saving the Classics from Conservatives* (New York: New York University Press).
    2003   *Slaves and Other Objects* (Chicago: University of Chicago Press).
Dyson, Michael Eric
    1996   *Between God and Gansta Rap: Bearing Witness to Black Culture* (New York: Oxford University Press).
Eagleton, Terry
    2000   *The Idea of Culture* (Malden, MA: Basil Blackwell).
    2003   *After Theory* (New York: Basic Books).

Easthope, Antony
    1993   *Contemporary Film Theory* (London and New York: Longman).

Echols, Alice
    1989   *Daring to be Bad: Radical Feminism in America, 1967–75* (Minneapolis: University of Minnesota Press).
Erdrich, Louise
    2001   *The Last Report on the Miracles at Little No Horse* (New York: Harper-Collins).
Erens, Patricia
    1979   *Sexual Stratagems: The World of Women in Film* (New York: Horizon Press).
    1984   *The Jew in American Cinema* (Bloomington: Indiana University Press).
Ersoz, Meryem
    1998   'Gimme that Old-Time Religion in a Postmodern-Age: Semiotics of Christian Radio', in Kintz and Lesage (eds.) 1998: 211-25.
Everett, Anna
    2001   *Returning the Gaze: A Genealogy of Black Film Criticism, 1909–1949* (Durham, NC: Duke University Press).
Exum, J. Cheryl
    1983a   'The Theological Dimension of the Samson Saga', *Vetus Testamentum* 33: 30-45.
    1983b   '"You Shall Let Every Daughter Live": A Study of Exodus 1.8–2.10', *Semeia* 28: 63-82.
    1985   '"Mother in Israel": A Familiar Figure Reconsidered', in L.M. Russell (ed.), *Feminist Interpretation of the Bible* (Philadelphia: Westminster Press): 73-85.
    1990a   'The Centre Cannot Hold: Thematic and Textual Instabilities in Judges', *Catholic Biblical Quarterly* 52: 410-31.
    1990b   'Murder They Wrote: Ideology and the Manipulation of the Femail Presence in Biblical Narrative', in A. Bach (ed.), *The Pleasure of Her Text* (Philadelphia: Trinity Press International): 45-67.
    1993   *Fragmented Women: Feminist (Sub)versions of Biblical Narratives* (JSOTSup, 163; Sheffield: Sheffield Academic Press; Valley Forge, PA: Trinity Press International).
    1995   'Michal at the Movies', in M. Daniel Carroll R., David J.A. Clines and Philip R. Davies (eds.), *The Bible in Hunan Society: Essays in Honour of John Rogerson* (JSOTSup, 200; Sheffield: Sheffield Academic Press): 273-92.
    1996a   'Bathsheba Plotted, Shot, and Painted', *Semeia* 74: 47-73.
    1996b   *Plotted, Shot, and Painted: Cultural Representations of Biblical Women* (JSOTSup, 215; Sheffield: Sheffield Academic Press).
Exum, J. Cheryl, and Stephen D. Moore (eds.)
    1995   *Biblical Studies/Cultural Studies: The Third Sheffield Colloquium* (Gender, Culture, Theory, 7; Sheffield: Sheffield Academic Press).
Faas, Patrick
    1994   *Around the Roman Table: Food and Feasting in Ancient Rome* (New York: Palgrave Macmillan).

Facey, Paul W.
  1974   *The Legion of Decency: A Sociological Analysis of the Emergence and Development of a Social Pressure Group* (New York: Arno Press).
Farmer, Paul
  1999   *Infections and Inequalities: The Modern Plagues* (Berkeley: University of California Press).
  2003   *Pathologies of Power: Health, Human Rights, and the New War on the Poor* (Berkeley: University of California Press).
Ferre, John P.
  1990   *Channels of Belief: Religion and American Commercial Television* (Ames: Iowa State University Press).
Flanders, Laura
  2004a   'Beware the Bushwomen', *The Nation* (11 March).
  2004b   *Bushwomen: Tales of a Cynical Species* (New York: Verso).
Fontaine, Carole R.
  1997   'More Queenly Proverb Performance: The Queen of Sheba in Targum Esther Sheni', in M.L. Barre, SS (ed.), *Wisdom, You are my Sister: Studies in Honor of Roland E. Murphy on the Occasion of his Eightieth Birthday* (CBQMS, 29; Washington, DC: Catholic Biblical Association of America): 216-33.
Fore, William F.
  1987   *Television and Religion: The Shaping of Faith, Values, and Culture* (Minneapolis: Augsburg).
Forman, Henry James
  1933   *Our Movie Made Children*, with an introduction by Dr. W.W. Charters (New York: Macmillan).
Forshey, Gerald E.
  1992   *American Religious and Biblical Spectaculars* (Westport, CT: Praeger).
Foucault, Michel
  1980   *Power/Knowledge: Selected Interviews and Other Writings* (trans. C. Gordon; New York: Pantheon).
Fowden, Garth
  1986   *Egyptian Hermes: A Historical Approach to the Late Pagan Mind* (New York: Cambridge University Press).
Fox, Stuart
  1976   *Jewish Films in the United States: A Comprehensive Survey and Descriptive Filmography* (Boston: G.K. Hall).
Friedman, Lester D.
  1982   *Hollywood's Image of the Jew* (New York: Ungar).
  1987   *The Jewish Image in American Film* (Secaucus, NJ: Citadel Press).
  1991   *Unspeakable Images: Ethnicity and the American Cinema* (Urbana and Chicago: University of Illinois Press).
Friedman, Regine Mihal
  1983   *L'image et son Juif: le Juif dans le cinema nazi* (Paris: Payot).
Fuchs, Esther
  1982   'Status and Role of Female Heroines in the Biblical Narrative', *Mankind Quarterly* 23: 149-60.

Fuller, Robert C.
    1989   *Alternative Medicine and American Religious Life* (New York: Oxford University Press).

Fusco, Coco
    1988   *Young, British, and Black: The Work of Sankofa and Black Audio Film Collective* (Buffalo, NY: Hallwalls Contemporary Arts Center).
    2001   *The Bodies that Were Not Ours: And Other Writings* (London: Routledge).

Gaines, Janet Howe
    1999   *Music in the Old Bones: Jezebel through the Ages* (Carbondale and Edwardsville: Southern Illinois University Press).

Garber, Marjorie, and Rebecca L. Walkowitz (eds.)
    1999   *One Nation Under God?: Religion and American Culture* (New York and London: Routledge).

Gardiner, Steven
    1998   'Through the Looking Glass and What the Christian Right Found There', in Kintz and Lesage (eds.) 1998: 141-58.

Garner, Dwight
    2004   'Cooking', *New York Times*: n.d.: 10.

Gehring, Wes D.
    1988   *Handbook of American Film Genres* (New York: Greenwood Press).

Gerhart, Ann
    2004   *The Perfect Wife: The Life and Choices of Laura Bush* (New York: Simon & Schuster).

Gilbreath, Edward
    2002   'The Top Tomato', *Christianity Today* 46/11: 94.

Glancy, Jennifer
    1996   'The Mistress and the Gaze: Masculinity, Slavery and Representation', *Semeia* 74: 127-46.

Glassman, Sallie Ann
    2000   *Vodou Visions: An Encounter with Divine Mystery* (New York: Villard Books).

Gordon, Andrew
    1995   'Star Wars: A Myth for our Time', Martin and Oswalt (eds.) 1995:73-82.

Gorsline, Douglas W.
    1969   *What People Wore: A Visual History of Dress from Ancient Times to Twentieth-Century America* (New York: Viking Press).

Gottwald, N.K., and R.A. Horsley
    1993   *The Bible and Liberation: Political and Social Hermeneutics* (Maryknoll, NY: Orbis Books).

Graham, Franklin
    2002   *The Name* (Nashville, TN: Nelson Books).

Grahn, Judy
    1982   'They Say She is Veiled', in *idem*, *The Queen of Wands* (Freedom, CA: The Crossing Press).

Gravdal, Kathryn
    1991   *Ravishing Maidens: Writing Rape in Medieval French Literature and Law* (Philadelphia: University of Pennsylvania Press).
Grayson, Sandra M.
    2000   *Symbolizing the Past* (Lanham, MD: University Press of America).
Guerrero, Ed
    1993   *Framing Blackness: The African American Image in Film* (Philadelphia: Temple University Press).
Guerrilla Girls
    2003   *Bitches, Bimbos, and Ballbreakers: The Guerrilla Girls' Guide to Female Stereotypes* (New York and London: Penguin Books).
Guilmartin, Nance
    2002   *Healing Conversations: What to Say When You Don't Know What to Say* (San Francisco, CA: Jossey-Bass).
Gunn, David M.
    1996   'Bathsheba Goes Bathing in Hollywood: Words, Images, and Social Locations', *Semeia* 74: 75-101.
Hackett, David G. (ed.)
    1995   *Religion and American Culture: A Reader* (New York and London: Routledge).
Hall, David D. (ed.)
    1997   *Lived Religion in America: Toward a History of Practice* (Princeton, NJ: Princeton University Press).
Hansen, Miriam
    1991   *Babel and Babylon: Spectatorship in American Silent Film* (Cambridge, MA: Harvard University Press).
Harding, Susan Friend
    2000   *The Book of Jerry Falwell: Fundamentalist Language and Politics* (Princeton, NJ: Princeton University Press).
Harris, Trudier
    1984   *Exorcising Blackness: Historical and Literary Lynching and Burning Rituals* (Bloomington: Indian University Press).
Hass, Amira
    2000   *Drinking the Sea at Gaza: Days and Nights in a Land Under Siege* (New York: Owl Books).
    2003   *Reporting From Ramallah: An Israeli Journalist in Occupied Land* (trans. R.L. Jones; New York and Los Angeles: Semiotexte[s]).
    2004   'Words Have Failed Us', *Ha'aretz* (9 March): n.p.
Hesiod
    1999   *Theogony and Works and Day: A New Translation with Introduction by M.L. West* (Oxford World Classics; repr, Oxford: Oxford University Press).
Heston, S.
    1995   *In the Arena: The Autobiography* (New York: HarperCollins).
Higgs, Robert J.
    1995   *God in the Stadium: Sports and Religion in America* (Lexington: University Press of Kentucky).

Holloway, Ronald
  1977   *Beyond the Image: Approaches to the Religious Dimensions in the Cinema* (Geneva: World Council of Churches in Cooperation with Interfilm).
Hollyday, J.
  1994   *Clothed with the Sun: Biblical Women, Social Justice and Us* (Louisville, KY: Westminster/John Knox Press).
hooks, bell
  1993   *Black Looks: Race and Representation* (London: Turnaround Press).
Hoover, Stewart M.
  1988   *Mass Media Religion: The Social Sources of the Electronic Church* (Newbury Park, CA: Sage).
Hukanovic, Rezak, Colleen London, Midhat Ridjanovic and Ammiel Alcalay
  1997   *The Tenth Circle of Hell: A Memoir of Life in the Death Camps of Bosnia* (New York: Basic Books).
Hurley, Neil P.
  1978   *The Reel Revolution: A Film Primer on Liberation* (Maryknoll, NY: Orbis Books).
  1993   *Soul in Suspense: Hitchcock's Fright and Delight* (Metuchen, NJ: Scarecrow Press).
Hurston, Z.N.
  1931   'Hoodoo in America', *Journal of American Folklore* 44: 320-417.
  1939   *Moses, Man of the Mountain* (New York: HarperCollins).
  1981   *The Sanctified Church: The Folklore Writings of Zora Neale Hurston* (ed. T.C. Bambara; Berkeley, CA: Turtle Island Foundation).
Insdorf, Annette
  1983   *Indelible Shadows: Film and the Holocaust* (New York: Random House).
Jaber, Hala
  1997   *Hezbollah* (New York: Columbia University Press).
Jackson, Derrick Z.
  2003   'We Trivialize Violence', *The Boston Globe* (19 March: A15).
James, Henry
  1946   *The American Scene, Together with Three Essays from 'Portraits of Places'* (New York: Charles Scribner's Sons).
Jayamanne, Laleen
  1995   *Kiss Me Deadly: Feminism and Cinema for the Moment* (Sydney: Power Publications).
Jenkyns, Richard
  1991   *Dignity and Decadence: Victorian Art and the Classical Inheritance* (Cambridge, MA: Harvard University Press).
Jewett, Robert
  1993   *St. Paul at the Movies: The Apostle's Dialogue with American Culture* (Louisville, KY: Westminster/John Knox Press).
Jewett, Robert, and John Shelton Lawrence
  2003   'The Biblical Sources of the Crusade Against Evil', *Religious Studies News*.
Johanson, Sheila
  1976   '"Herstory" as History: A New Field or Another Fad?', in B. Carroll (ed.), *Liberating Women's History* (Chicago: University of Illinois Press): 400-30.

Johnson, Eithne
    1998   'The Emergence of Christian Video and the Cultivation of Videovan-
            gelism', in Kintz and Lesage (eds.) 1998: 191-210.
Johnson, P.E.
    1994   *African-American Christianity: Essays in History* (Berkeley: University
            of California Press).
Juergensmeyer, Mark
    2000   *Terror in the Mind of God: The Global Rise of Religious Violence*
            (Berkeley: University of California Press).
Kaplan, E. Ann
    1980   *Women in Film Noir* (London: British Film Institute Publishing).
    1983   *Women and Film: Both Sides of the Camera* (New York: Methuen).
    1991   *Psychoanalysis and Cinema* (London: Routledge).
    1992   *Motherhood and Representation: The Mother in Popular Culture and
            Melodrama* (London and New York: Routledge).
Keefe, Alice
    1993   'Rape of Women/Wars of Men', *Semeia* 61: 279-97.
Ketcham, Charles B.
    1976   *Federico Fellini: The Search for a New Mythology* (New York: Paulist
            Press).
    1986   *The Influence of Existentialism on Ingmar Bergman: An Analysis of the
            Theological Ideas Shaping a Filmmaker's Art* (Lewiston, NY: Edwin
            Mellen Press).
    1992   'One Flew Over the Cuckoo's Nest: A Salvific Drama of Liberation', in
            idem, Image and Likeness (New York: Paulist Press): 145-52.
Keto, C. Tsehloane
    1995   *Vision, Identity, and Time: The Afrocentric Paradigm and the Study of the
            Past* (Dubugue, IA: Kendall/Hunt Publishing Co).
Keuls, Eva C.
    1985   *The Reign of the Phallus: Sexual Politics in Ancient Athens* (Berkeley:
            University of California Press).
Kidwell, Claudia Brush, and Valerie Steele
    1989   *Men and Women: Dressing the Part* (Washington, DC: Smithsonian
            Institution Press).
Kilian, Pamela
    2002   *Barbara Bush: Matriarch of a Dynasty* (New York: Thomas Dunne
            Books and St Martin's Press).
Kintz, Linda
    1998   'Culture and the Religious Right', in Kintz and Lesage (eds.) 1998: 3-
            20.
Kintz, Linda, and J. Lesage (eds.)
    1998   *Media, Culture, and the Religious Right* (Minneapolis: University of
            Minnesota Press).
Koch, Gertrud
    1992   *Die Einstellung ist die Einstellung: visuelle Konstruktionen des Judentums*
            (Frankfurt: Suhrkamp).
Kohut, Andrew, John C. Green, Scott Keeter and Robert C. Toth
    2000   *The Diminishing Divide: Religion's Changing Role in American Politics*
            (Washington, DC: Brookings Institute Press).

Kolodny, Annette
  1975   *The Lay of the Land: Metaphor as Experience and History in American Life and Letters* (Chapel Hill: University of North Carolina Press).
Konzelman, Robert G.
  1972   *Marquee Ministry: The Movie Theater as Church and Community Forum* (New York: Harper & Row).
Koosed, Jennifer L., and Tod Linafelt
  1996   'How the West was Not One: Delilah Deconstructs the Western', *Semeia* 74 : 167-82.
Kraemer, Ross S.
  1988   *Maenads, Martyrs, Matrons, Monastics* (Minneapolis: Fortress Press).
  1992   *Her Share of the Blessings* (New York and London: Oxford University Press).
Kreitzer, Larry J.
  1993   *The New Testament in Fiction and Film* (The Biblical Seminar, 17; Sheffield: JSOT Press).
  1994   *The Old Testament in Fiction and Film: On Reversing the Hermeneutical Flow* (The Biblical Seminar, 24; Sheffield: Sheffield Academic Press).
Kritzman, Lawrence D.
  1995   *Auschwitz and After: Race, Culture and 'the Jewish Question' in France* (New York: Routledge).
Krugman, Paul
  2003   *The Great Unraveling: Losing Our Way in the New Century* (New York: W.W. Norton).
Lang, Robert
  1989   *American Film Melodrama: Griffith, Vidor, Minnelli* (Princeton, NJ: Princeton University Press).
Lasine, Stuart
  1994   'Levite Violence, Fratricide, and Sacrifice in the Bible and Later Revolutionary Rhetoric', in M.I. Wallace and Theophus H. Smith (eds.), *Curing Violence* (Sonoma, CA: Polebridge Press): 204-29.
Leege, David C., and Lyman A. Kellstedt,
  1993   *Rediscovering the Religious Factor in American Politics* (Armonk, NY: M.E. Sharpe).
Leff, Leonard J., and Jerold L. Simmons
  1990   *The Dame in the Kimono: Hollywood, Censorship, and the Production Code from the 1920s to the 1960s* (New York: Grove Weidenfeld).
Lefkowitz, Mary R.
  1996a   *Not Out Of Africa* (New York: Basic Books).
Lefkowitz, Mary R., and Guy MacLean Rogers
  1996   *Black Athena Revisited* (Chapel Hill: University of North Carolina Press).
Lewis, C.S.
  1942   *The Screwtape Letters* (New York: HarperSanFrancisco).
  1971   *The Abolition of Man* (New York: HarperSanFrancisco).
Lincoln, Bruce
  2001   *Holy Terrors: Thinking about Religion after September 11* (Chicago: University of Chicago Press).

Lind, Michael
    2003   *Made in Texas: George W. Bush and the Southern Takeover of American Politics* (New York: Basic Books).
Littell, Franklin H.
    1969   *The Church and the Body Politic* (New York: The Seabury Press).

Locke, Maryel, and Charles Warren
    1993   *Jean-Luc Godard's Hail Mary: Women and the Sacred in Film* (Carbondale: Southern Illinois University Press).
Lorde, Audre
    1986   *Our Dead Behind Us* (New York: W.W. Norton).
Lucano, Angelo L.
    1975   *Cultura e religione nel cinema* (Torino: ERI).
Lucas, George
    1977   'Interview', *Rolling Stone* (25 August).
Luciano, Patrick
    1987   *Them or Us: Archetypal Interpretations of Fifties Invasions Films* (Bloomington: Indiana University Press).
Lucie-Smith, Edward
    2000   *Judy Chicago: An American Vision* (New York: Watson Guptill Publications).
Lupack, Barbara Tepa
    2002   *Literary Adaptations in Black American Cinema: From Micheaux to Morrison* (Rochester, NY: University of Rochester Press).
Lyon, David
    2000   *Jesus in Disneyland: Religion in Postmodern Times* (Cambridge: Polity Press).
MacKinnon, Catherine A.
    2001   *Sex Equality: Rape Law* (New York: West Group).
Makarushka, Irena
    1995   'Women Spoken For: Images of Displaced Desire', in Martin and Oswalt (eds.) 1995: 142-51.
Man, Glenn
    1994   *Radical Visions: American Film Renaissance, 1967–1976* (Westport, CT: Greenwood Press).
Marcelline, Ashley
    1994   *Ashley Marcelline's Black Film and Video Guide* (Thornhill, ON: Black Cinema Network).
Marsden, G.M.
    1990   *Religion and American Culture* (New York: Harcourt Brace Jovanovich).
Marsh, Clive, and Gaye Ortiz
    1998   *Exploration in Theology and Film: Movies and Meaning* (Oxford: Basil Blackwell).
Martin, J.W., and Conrad E. Oswalt, Jr (eds.)
    1995   *Screening the Sacred: Religion, Myth, and Ideology in Popular American Film* (Boulder, CO: Westview Press).

Martin, Thomas M.
 1991   *Images and Imageless: A Study in Religious Consciousness and Film*
         (Lewisburg, PA: Bucknell University Press; London: Associated Uni-
         versity Presses).
Marty, M.E.
 1991   *Modern American Religion* (Chicago: University of Chicago Press).

Maxfield, James F.
 1996   *The Fatal Woman: Sources of Male Anxiety in American Film Noir,*
         1941–1991 (Madison, WI: Fairleigh Dickinson Press; London: Asso-
         ciated University Presses).
May, John R.
 1992   *Image and Likeness: Religious Visions in American Film Classics* (New
         York: Paulist Press).
May, John R., and Michael Bird (eds.)
 1982   *Religion in Film* (Knoxville: University of Tennesee Press).
Maynard, Richard A.
 1974   *The Black Man on Film: Racial Stereotyping* (Rochelle Park, NJ: Hayden
         Book Co.).
Mayne, Judith
 1990   *The Woman at the Keyhole: Feminism and Woman's Cinema* (Bloom-
         ington: Indiana University Press).
Mayo, Janet
 1984   *A History of Ecclesiastical Dress* (New York: Holmes & Meier).
McAlister, Elizabeth
 1995   'We Could Not, so Help us God, Do Otherwise', *Sojourners: Faith,*
         Politics, Culture 24: 60-65.
McCarthy Brown, Karen
 2001   *Mama Lola: A Vodou Priestess in Brooklyn* (Berkeley: University of
         California Press).
McClay, W.M., and Hugh Heclo
 2003   *Religion Returns to the Public Square: Faith and Policy in America* (Balti-
         more and London: The Johns Hopkins University Press).
McCreadie, Marsha
 1983   *Women on Film: The Critical Eye* (New York: Praeger).
McDannell, Colleen
 1995   *Material Christianity: Religion and Popular Culture in America* (New
         Haven: Yale University Press).
McKane, William
 1970   *Proverbs: A New Approach* (Philadelphia: Westminster Press).
McLemore, Elizabeth
 1995   'From Revelation to Dream: Allegory in David Lynch's *Blue Velvet*',
         in Martin and Oswalt (eds.) 1995: 134-41.
McNeil, Donald G., Jr
 2004   'Staving Off Starvation: When Real Food Isn't an Option', *New York*
         Times (23 May: 1).
Medved, Michael
 1992   *Hollywood vs. America: Popular Culture and the War on Traditional*
         Values (New York: HarperCollins).

Mellen, Joan
    1974   *Women and their Sexuality in the New Film* (New York: Horizon Press).
Miles, Margaret
    1996   *Seeing is Believing: Religion and Values in the Movies* (Boston: Beacon Press).
Miles, Rosalind
    2001   *Who Cooked the Last Supper? The Women's History of the World* (New York: Three Rivers Press).
Miller, Perry
    1939   *The New England Mind: The Seventeenth Century* (Cambridge, MA: Harvard University Press).
Mintz, Sidney W.
    1974   *Caribbean Transformations* (Baltimore: The Johns Hopkins University Press).
Modleski, Tania
    1988   *The Women Who Knew Too Much: Hitchcock and the Feminist* (New York: Methuen).
    1992   *Feminism Without Women: Culture and Criticism in a 'Postfeminist Age'* (London and New York: Routledge Press).
Moley, Raymond
    1938   *Are We Movie Made?* (New York: Macy-Masius).
Monaco, James
    1987   *Who's Who in American Film Now* (New York: New York Zoetrope).
Moore, R. Laurence
    1994   *Selling God: American Religion in the Marketplace of Culture* (New York: Oxford University Press).
Morgan, David
    1997   *Visual Piety: A History and Theory of Popular Religious Images* (Berkeley: University of California Press).
Morone, James A.
    2003   *Hellfire Nation: The Politics of Sin in American History* (New Haven: Yale University Press).
Morris, Kenneth Earl
    1996   *Jimmy Cater, American Moralist* (Athens: University of Georgia Press).
Morrison, Toni
    2003   *Love* (New York: Alfred A. Knopf).
Mulvey, Laura
    1989   *Visual and Other Pleasures* (Houndsmills: Macmillan).
Munro, Eleanor
    1982   *Originals: American Women Artists* (New York: Simon & Schuster/ Touchtone Books).
Myers, Kenneth A.
    1989   *All God's Children and Blue Suede Shoes: Christians and Popular Culture* (Wheaton, IL: Crossway Books).
Natoli, Joseph
    1994   *Hauntings: Popular Film and American Culture, 1990–1992* (Albany: State University of New York Press).

Navasky, Victor
    1980   *Naming Names* (New York: Viking Press).

Neal, Connie
    2001   *What's a Christian to do with Harry Potter?* (Colorado Springs: Water-book Press).

Nesteby, James R.
    1982   *Black Images in American Films, 1896–1954: The Interplay Between Civil Rights and Film Culture* (Washington, DC: University Press of America).

Niditch, Susan
    1982   'The "Sodomite" Theme in Judges 19–20: Family, Community, and Social Disintegration', *CBQ* 44: 365-78.
    1989   'Eroticism and Death in the Tale of Jael', in P.L. Day (ed.), *Gender and Difference in Ancient Israel* (Minneapolis: Fortress Press): 43-57.
    1993a   *War in the Hebrew Bible: A Study in the Ethics of Violence* (New York and Oxford: Oxford University Press).
    1993b   'War, Women, and Defilement in Numbers 31', in C.V. Camp and Carole R. Fontaine (eds.), *Women, War, and Metaphor: Language and Society in the Study of the Hebrew Bible* (Atlanta: Scholars Press): 39-58.

Noonan, Peggy
    2000   *The Case Against Hillary Clinton* (New York: Regan Books).

Nord, Thomas
    2003   'A Prophet-Making Venture: Bible Bobbleheads Celebrate Christianity', *Louisville Courier Journal*.

O'Connor, John E., and Martin A. Jackson (with a Foreword by Arthur M. Schlesinger, Jr)
    1988   *American History/American Film: Interpreting the Hollywood Image* (New York: Ungar).

Okin, Susan Moller
    1999   *Is Multiculturalism Bad for Women?* (Princeton, NJ: Princeton University Press).

Onyewuenyi, Innocent Chilaka
    1993   *The African Origin of Greek Philosophy: An Exercise in Afrocentrism* (Nigeria: University of Nigeria Press).

Orsi, Robert A.
    1985   *The Madonna on 115th Street: Faith and Community in Italian Harlem, 1880–1950* (New Haven: Yale University Press).
    1997   'Everyday Miracles: The Study of Lived Religion', in D. Hall (ed.), *Lived Religion in America* (Princeton, NJ: Princeton University Press): 3-21.
    1999   *Gods of the City: Religion and the American Urban Landscape* (Bloomington: Indiana University Press).

Oswalt, Conrad E., Jr
    1995   'Hollywood and Armageddon: Apocalyptic Themes in Recent Cinematic Presentation', in Martin and Oswalt (eds.) 1995: 55-63.

Owens, Craig
    1983   'The Discourse of Others: Feminists and Postmodernism', in H. Foster (ed.), *The Anti-Aesthetic: Essays on Postmodern Culture* (Port Townsend, WA: Bay Press): 57-82.

Pagels, Elaine
    1979   *The Gnostic Gospels* (New York: Random House).
    1987   *Adam, Eve and the Serpent* (New York: Random House).
    1995   *The Origin of Satan* (New York: Random House).
    2003   *Beyond Belief: The Secret Gospel of Thomas* (New York: Random House).

Paul, Willaim
    1994   *Laughing, Screaming: Modern Hollywood Horror and Comedy* (New York: Columbia University Press).

Penley, Constance
    1988   *Feminism and Film Theory* (New York: Routledge; London: British Film Institute).
    1989   *The Future of an Illusion* (Minneapolis: University of Minnesota Press).
    1991a   *Close Encounters: Film, Feminism, and Science Fiction* (Minneapolis: University of Minnesota Press).
    1991b   *Technoculture* (Minneapolis: University of Minnesota Press).
    1993   *Male Trouble* (Minneapolis: University of Minnesota Press).

Pettit, Arthur G.
    1980   *Images of the Mexican American in Fiction and Film; Edited with an Afterword by Dennis E. Showalter* (College Station, TX: A. & M. University Press).

Phillips, Kevin
    2004   *American Dynasty: Aristocracy, Fortune, and the Politics of Deceit in the House of Bush* (New York: Viking Press).

Phy, Allene Stuart
    1985   *The Bible and Popular Culture in America* (Philadelphia: Fortress Press).

Pietropaolo, Laura, and Ada Testaferri
    1995   *Feminism in the Cinema* (Bloomington: Indiana University Press).

Plaskow, Judith
    1990   *Standing Again at Sinai* (San Francisco: Harper & Row).

Plattner, Stuart
    1997   *High Art Down Home: An Economic Ethnography of a Local Art Market* (Chicago: Chicago University Press).

Pope, Marvin
    1977   *Song of Songs* (AB, 7C; New York: Doubleday).

Prebish, Charles S., *et al.*
    1993   *Religion and Sport: The Meeting of Sacred and Profane* (Westwood, CN: Greenwood Press).

Raboteau, Albert J.
    1999   *Canaan Land: A Religious History of African Americans* (New York: Oxford University Press).

Rad, Gerhard von
    1969   *Der Heilige Krieg im Alten Israel* (Göttingen: Vandenhoeck & Ruprecht, 5th edn).

Rampton, Sheldon, and John Stauber
 2003 *Weapons of Mass Deception: The Uses of Propaganda in Bush's War on Iraq* (New York: Jeremy P. Tarcher/Penguin Books).

Randall, Richard S.
 1968 *Censorship in the Movies: The Social and Political Control of a Mass Medium* (Madison: University of Wisconsin Press).

Rast, W.E.
 1977 'Cakes for the Queen of Heaven', in A.L. Merill and T.W. Overholt (eds.), *Scripture in History and Theology: Studies in Honor of J. Coert Rylaarsdam* (Pittsburgh, PA: Pickwick Press): 167-80.

Rausch, David A.
 1991 *Communities in Conflict: Evangelicals and Jews* (Philadelphia: Trinity Press International).

Real, Michael R.
 1977 *Mass-Mediated Culture* (Englewood Cliffs, NJ: Prentice–Hall).

Reid, Mark A.
 1993 *Redefining Black Film* (London and Berkeley: University of California Press).

Reinhartz, Adele
 2003 *Scripture on the Silver Screen* (Knoxville, TN: Westminster/John Knox Press).

Rey, Terry
 1999 *Our Lady of Class Struggle: The Cult of the Virgin Mary in Haiti* (Trenton, NJ and Asmara, Eritrea: Africa World Press).

Rich, Adrienne
 1979 *On Lies, Secrets, and Silence: Selected Prose 1966–1978* (New York: W.W. Norton).

Mary Roach
 2003 *Stiff: The Curious Lives of Human Cadavers* (New York: W.W. Norton).

Robinson, Jill
 1975 *Bed/Time/Story* (New York: Alfred A. Knopf).

Roediger, David R.
 1998 *Black on White: Black Writers on What it Means to be White* (New York: Schocken Books).

Rogin, Michael
 1996 *Blackface, White Noise: Jewish Immigrants in the Hollywood Melting Pot* (Berkeley: University of California Press).

Romano, Lois, and George Lardner, Jr
 1999 'Bush's Life-Changing Year', *Washington Post*: A1.

Rowe, John Carlos
 1998 *'Culture' and the Problem of the Disciplines* (New York: Colombia University Press).

Rowlett, Lori
 1996 *Joshua and the Rhetoric of Violence: A New Historicist Analysis* (JSOTSup, 226; Sheffield: Sheffield Academic Press).

Rowling, J.K.

1999   Harry Potter and the Prisoner of Azkaban (London: Bloomsbury).

Rushdie, Salmon

1997   'Europe's Shameful Trade in Silence', New York Times: 23.

Rushing, Janice Hocker

1983   'The Rhetoric of the American Western Myth', Communications Monographs 50: 14-32.

1995   'Evolution of the "New Frontier" in Alien and Aliens: Patriarchal Cooptation of the Feminine Archetype', in Martin and Oswalt (eds.) 1995: 94-117.

Said, Edward W.

1979   Orientalism (New York: Vintage Books).

1993   Culture and Imperialism (New York: Vintage Books).

Sanders, Cheryl J.

1995   Living the Intersection: Womanism and Afrocentrism in Theology (Minneapolis: Fortress Press).

Sanders, Theresa

2002   Celluloid Saints: Images of Sanctity in Film (Macon, GA: Mercer University Press).

Santner, Eric L.

1990   Stranded Objects: Mourning, Memory, and Film in Postwar Germany (Ithaca, NY: Cornell University Press).

Schaberg, Jane

1996   'Fast Forwarding to the Magdalene', Semeia 74: 33-46.

Schindler, Colin

1979   Hollywood Goes to War: Films and American Society, 1939–1952 (London: Routledge & Kegan Paul).

Schmidt, Leigh Eric

1995   Consumer Rites: The Buying and Selling of American Holidays (Princeton, NJ: Princeton University Press).

1997   'Practices of Exchange: From Market Culture to Gift Economy in the Interpretation of American Religion', in D. Hall (ed.), Lived Religion in American: Toward a History of Practice (Princeton, NJ: Princeton University Press): 69-91.

Schor, Juliet B.

1998   The Overspent American: Why We Want What We Don't Need (New York: HarperPerennial).

Schussler Fiorenza, Elisabeth

1994   Jesus: Miriam's Child, Sophia's Prophet: Critical Issues in Feminist Christology (New York: Continuum).

Schultze, Quentin J.

1991   Televangelism and American Culture: The Business of Popular Culture (Grand Rapids: Baker Book House).

Schumach, Murray

1964   The Face on the Cutting-Room Floor: The Story of Movie and Television Censorship (New York: Morrow).

Scorsese, Martin
    1989   *Scorsese on Scorsese* (ed. D.T. Christie; London: Faber & Faber).
Scott, Bernard Brandon
    1994   *Hollywood Dreams and Biblical Stories* (Minneapolis: Fortress Press).
Sella, Marshall
    2001   'Missing', *New York Times Magazine* (7 October).
Shah, Sonia
    1992   *Between Fear and Hope: A Decade of Peace Activism* (Baltimore, MD: Fortkamp Publishing Company).
Sheehy, Gail
    1999   *Hillary's Choice* (New York: Ballantine Books).
    2004   'Transforming Teresa', *Mother Jones* (July/August) (<http://www.motherjones.com/news/feature/2004/07/07_400.html>).
Sheppard, Gerald
    1980   *Wisdom as a Hermeneutical Construct* (Berlin: W. de Gruyter).
Siker, Jeffrey
    2003   'President Bush, Biblical Faith, and the Politics of Religion', *Religious Studies News*.
Silk, Catherine
    1990   *Racism and Anti-Racism in American Popular Culture: Portrayals of African-Americans in Fiction and Film* (Manchester: Manchester University Press).
Silko, Leslie Marmon
    1981   The Storyteller (New York: Arcade).
Silver, D.J.
    1982   *Images of Moses* (New York: Basic Books).
Silverman, Kaja
    1988   *The Acoustic Mirror: The Female Voice in Psychoanalysis and Cinema* (Bloomington: Indiana University Press).
    1992   *Male Subjectivity at the Margins* (New York: Routledge Press).
Skehan, Patrick W.
    1971   *Studies in Israelite Poetry and Wisdom* (Worcester: Heffernan Press).
Sklar, Robert
    1994   *Movie-Made America: A Cultural History of American Movies* (New York: Vintage Books, 2nd edn).
Smend, Rudolf, and Max Gray Rogers
    1970   *Yahweh War and Tribal Confederation: Reflections Upon Israel's Earliest History* (Nashville: Abingdon Press).
Smith, Dennis E.
    2003   *From Symposium to Eucharist: The Banquet in the Early Christian World* (Minneapolis: Fortress Press).
Smith, Jonathan Z.
    1982   *Imagining Religion: From Babylon to Jerusalem* (Chicago: University of Chicago Press).
Smith, Prudence
    1984   *Women and Film Bibliography* (London: British Film Institute).
Smoodin, E.
    1988   'Watching the Skies: Hollywood, the 1950s, and the Soviet Threat', *Journal of American Culture* 11: 35-40.

Snead, James
 1994 *White Screens Black Images* (New York: Routledge).
Snowden, Frank M.
 1970 *Blacks in Antiquity: Ethiopians in the Greco-Roman World* (Cambridge, MA: Belknap Press of Harvard University Press).
 1983 *Before Color Prejudice: The Ancient View of Blacks* (Cambridge, MA: Harvard University Press).
Stead, Peter
 1989 *Film and the Working Class: The Feature Film in British and American Society* (London and New York: Routledge).
Stevens, Matthew
 1992 *Jewish Film Directory: A Guide to More than 1200 Films of Jewish Interest from 32 Countries over 85 Years* (Westport, CT: Greenwood Press).
Stiglmayer, Alexandra
 1994 'The Rapes in Bosnia-Herzegovina', in *idem* (ed.), *Mass Rape: The War Against Women in Bosnia-Herzegovina* (Lincoln: University of Nebraska Press): 82-169.
Stoddard, Karen M.
 1983 *Saints and Shrews: Women and Aging in American Popular Film* (Westport, CT: Greenwood Press).
Stout, H.S.
 1986 *The New England Soul* (New York: Oxford University Press).
Strinati, Dominic
 2000 *An Introduction to Studying Popular Culture* (New York and London: Routledge).
Taves, Ann
 1999 *Fits, Trances, and Visions: Experiencing Religion and Explaining Experience from Wesley to James* (Princeton, NJ: Princeton University Press).
Thaman, Mary Patrice, Sr
 1977 *Manners and Morals of the 1920s: A Survey of the Religious Press* (Westport, CT: Greenwood Press, 2nd edn).
Thompson, Thomas L.
 1995 'A Neo-Albrightean School in History and Biblical Scholarship', *JBL* 114: 683-98.
Thorn, William, Phillip Runkel and Susan Mountin (eds.)
 2001 *Dorothy Day and the Catholic Worker Movement: Centenary Essays* (Milwaukee, WI: Marquette University Press).
Thumim, Janet
 1992 *Celluloid Sisters: Women and Popular Cinema* (Basingstoke and London: Macmillan).
Tocqueville, Alexis de
 2004 *Democracy in America* (trans. Arthur Goldhammer; The Library of America, 147; New York: Library of America).
Tompkins, Jane
 1992 *West of Everything: The Inner Life of Westerns* (New York: Oxford University Press).

Toorn, Karel van der
    1989   'Female Prostitution in Payment of Vows in Ancient Israel', *JBL* 108: 193-205.
Troyes, Chrétien de
    2000   *Yvain, le Chevalier au lion* (Paris: Gallimard).
Truett, Randle Bond
    1954   *The First Ladies in Fashion* (New York: Hastings House).
Turner, Victor
    1969   *The Ritual Process: Structure and Anti-Structure* (Ithaca, NY: Cornell University Press).
Tyrrell, R. Emmett, Jr, and Mark W. Davis
    2004   *Madame Hillary: The Dark Road to the White House* (Chicago: Regnery Publishing).
Usry, Glenn, and Craig S. Keener
    1996   *Black Man's Religion: Can Christianity be Afrocentric?* (Downers Grove, IL: Intervarsity Press).
Vincendeau, Ginnette
    1987   'Women's Cinema, Film Theory, and Feminism in France', *Screen* 28.
Vincendeau, Ginnette, and Berenice Reynaud
    1993   *20 ans de theories feministes sur le cinema: Grande-Bretagne et Etats-Unis* (France: Courbevoie).
Walcott, Derek
    1990   *Omeros* (New York: Farrar, Straus, & Giroux).
Wall, James
    1992   '2001: A Space Odyssey and the Search for a Center', in May (ed.), *Image and Likeness*: 39-47.
Walker, Janet
    1993   *Couching Resistance* (Minneapolis: University of Minnesota Press).
Walker, Nancy A. (ed.)
    1998   *Women's Magazines 1940–1960: Gender Roles and the Popular Press* (Boston: Bedford/St Martin's).
Washburn, Katherine, and John Thornton
    1996   *Dumbing Down: Essays on the Strip-Mining of American Culture* (New York: W.W. Norton).
Washington, Harold C.
    1994   'The Strange Woman of Proverbs 1–9 and Post-Exilic Judean Society', in T.C. Eskanazi and Kent H. Richards (eds.), *Second Temple Studies. II. Temple and Community in the Persian Period* (JSOTSup, 175; Sheffield: JSOT Press).
Weinfeld, Moshe
    1983   'Divine Intervention in War in Ancient Israel and in the Ancient Near East', in Hayim Tadmor and Moshe Weinfeld (eds.), *History, Historiography and Interpretation* (Jerusalem: Magnes Press): 121-47.
Weisenfeld, Judith
    1996   '"For Rent, 'Cabin in the Sky'": Race, Religion, and Representational Quagmires in American FIlm', *Biblical Glamour and Hollywood Glitz* 74: 147-66.

Wetta, Frank Joseph, and Stephen J. Curley
 1992 *Celluloid Wars: A Guide to Film and the American Experience of War* (New York: Greenwood Press).
Wilcox, Fred (ed.)
 2001 *Disciples and Dissidents: Prison Writings of the Prince of Peace Plowshares* (Athol, MA: Haley's).
Willemen, Paul
 1994 *Looks and Frictions: Essays in Cultural Studies and Film Theory* (Bloomington: Indiana University Press; London: British Film Institute).
Williams, Anna
 1998 'Conservative Media Activism: The Free Congress Foundation and National Empowerment Television', in Kintz and Lesage (eds.) 1998: 275-94.
Williams, D.S.
 1987 'Black Women's Literature and the Task of Feminist Theology', in C.H. Buchanan, C.W. Atkinson and M.R. Miles (eds.), *Immaculate and Powerful: The Female in Sacred Image and Social Reality* (London: Crucible): 33-110.
Williams, Peter W.
 1980 *Popular Religion in America: Symbolic Change and the Modernization Process in Historical Perspective* (Englewood Cliffs, NJ: Prentice–Hall).
Williams, Raymond
 1976 *Keywords: A Vocabulary of Culture and Society* (New York: Oxford University Press).
 1995 *The Sociology of Culture* (Chicago: University of Chicago Press).
Wilson, Nancy L.
 1995 *Our Tribe: Queer Folks, God, Jesus, the Bible* (New York and San Francisco: HarperSanFrancisco).
Wink, Walter
 1998 *The Powers That Be: Theology for a New Millennium* (New York: Doubleday).
Winthrop, John
 1931 *A Model of Christian Charity*, II (Boston: Boston Historical Society).
Wolf, Christa
 1984 *Casandra: A Novel and Four Essays* (trans. J. V. Heurck; New York: Farrar, Straus, & Giroux).
Wolff, Perry Sidney
 1962 *A Tour of the White House with Mrs. John F. Kennedy* (Garden City, NY: Doubleday).
Woll, Allen L.
 1980 *The Latin Image in American Film* (Los Angeles: UCLA Latin American Center Publications).
Woll, Allen L., and Randall M. Miller
 1987 *Ethnic and Racial Images in American Film and Television: Historical Essays and Bibliography* (New York: Garland).
Wood, Ralph C.
 2003 *The Gospel According to Tolkien: Visions of the Kingdom in Middle-Earth* (Louisville, KY: Westminster/John Knox Press).

Woodward, Bob
    2002   *Bush at War* (New York: Simon & Schuster).
Wright, Melanie J.
    2003   *Moses in America: The Cultural Uses of Biblical Narrative* (Oxford: Oxford University Press).
Wright, Stuart A.
    1995   *Armageddon in Waco: Critical Perspectives on the Branch Davidian Conflict* (Chicago: University of Chicago Press).
Wyke, M.
    1997   *Projecting the Past: Ancient Rome, Cinema and History* (London: Routledge).
Yee, Gale A.
    1989   '"I Have Perfumed My Bed with Myrrh": The Foreign Woman in Proverbs 1–9', *JSOT* 43: 53-68.
    1995   'The Socio-Literary Production of the "Foreign Woman" in Proverbs', in Brenner (ed.) 1995: 127-30.
Zakai, A.
    1992   *Exile and Kingdom: History and Apocalypse in the Puritan Migration to America* (Cambridge: Cambridge University Press).
Zarkovic, Radmila Manojlovic, with Fran Peavey (eds.)
    1996   *I Remember = Sjecam Se: Writings by Bosnian Women Refugees* (San Francisco: Aunt Lute Books).
Zeffirelli, Franco
    1984   *Franco Zeffirelli's Jesus: A Spiritual Diary* (San Francisco: Harper & Row).
Zornberg, Avivah Gottlieb
    2001   *The Particulars of Rapture: Reflections on Exodus* (New York: Doubleday).

INDEX

Printed in the United Kingdom
by Lightning Source UK Ltd.
115037UKS00001B/108